FLORIDA BASIC RECRUIT TRAINING PROGRAM:

CORRECTIONS

VOLUME 1

Florida Correctional Basic Recruit Training Program: Volume 1

ISBN 13: 978-1-71149-478-4

Disclaimer

FDLE makes a sincere effort to ensure accuracy and quality of its published materials; however, no warranty, expressed or implied, is provided. FDLE disclaims any responsibility or liability for any direct or indirect damages resulting from the use of the information in this course or products described in it.

Mention of any product does not constitute an endorsement by FDLE of that product. All referenced persons, places, or situations are intended to be fictional, unless otherwise stated. Any resemblance to real persons, places, or situations is coincidental.

The training in this course is provided to familiarize students with issues that may involve high liability and/or high stress. FDLE urges students to ensure that their practices are correct in accordance with their agencies' policies and procedures. Employing agencies are solely responsible for guiding their employees' actions in actual situations.

Effective Date

This textbook is effective for basic recruit training that begins on or after July 1, 2022 and no later than June 30, 2023.

Acknowledgments

This project is a collaboration between the Florida Department of Law Enforcement, Criminal Justice Standards and Training Commission Certified Training Schools, other state and local agencies, and volunteers. We extend our sincere appreciation to the agencies of the Florida Criminal Justice System that allowed their members to assist in the development of this training program.

Cover art by Robert Bates, FDLE
Published by XanEdu Publishing, Inc., 17177 Laurel Park Drive, Livonia, MI 48152

TABLE OF CONTENTS

Florida Basic Recruit Training Program: Corrections, Volume 1

FOREWORD

We are grateful for the many agencies and officers who contributed to making this textbook relevant to the job, practical, and concise.

The Florida Statutes define correctional officers and provide that the Criminal Justice Standards and Training Commission, through administrative rule, specify certain criteria for training and conduct for basic recruits and certified officers. Recruits and officers are expected to practice and maintain good moral character.

Florida statute further requires that cultural diversity be included in all officer Basic Recruit Training Programs. Particularly in Florida, correctional officers can expect to encounter populations very different from themselves. Training in how to effectively communicate, interact with, and respond to a range of populations is critical to your safety and that of others.

Your training will also outline the scope of your authority so that you will know how to exercise your job responsibly. Working in a correctional environment is challenging, and it can be stressful and dangerous. The instruction here aims to provide you with the basic skills needed to work effectively with inmates while exercising professionalism.

It is hoped that you will have a long and successful career as a correctional officer. This training program provides a clear picture of the job requirements and work environment. Your training academy is encouraged to coordinate a field trip so you may observe a correctional facility, preferably early on in your studies. You are encouraged to take full advantage of this training to learn and prepare for the day that you will be responsible for maintaining the care, control, and custody of inmates within Florida's prisons and jails.

INTRODUCTION TO CORRECTIONS

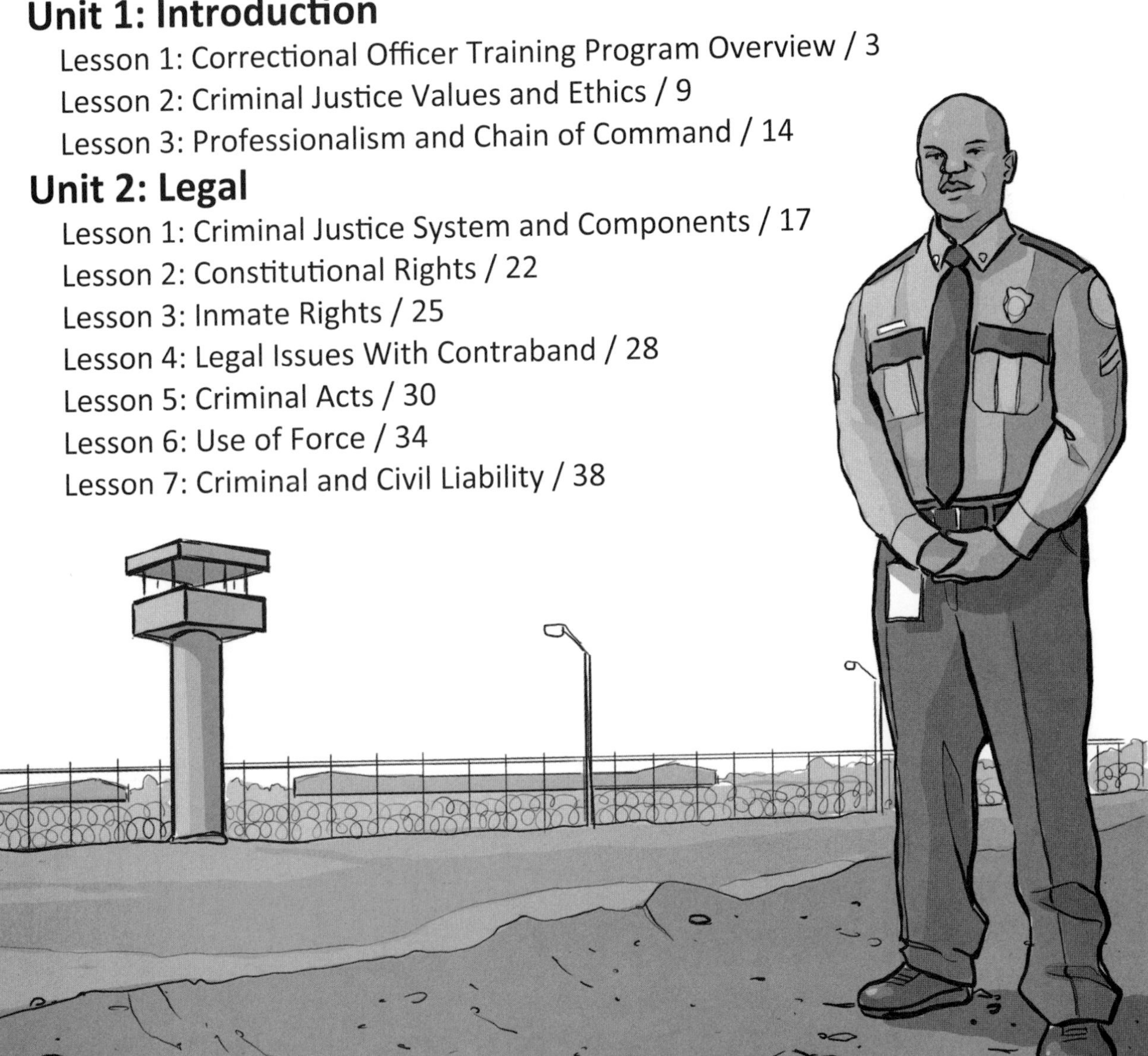

Unit 1 Introduction

Lesson 1
Correctional Officer Training Program Overview

Lesson Goal

This lesson tells you how to obtain your Florida correctional officer certification and how to avoid losing it.

Think About This

Every person who enters this training program has one goal in mind: to become a certified correctional officer in the state of Florida. This lesson explains how you achieve the goal of certification. It also explains the penalties you may face if you do not use your authority as a correctional officer in the right way.

Like a judge is to the court and police officers are to the streets, correctional officers are the most important members of the correctional system. Correctional officers are responsible for their own safety as well as that of inmates, fellow officers, staff, and the public. This training program introduces students to the most critical features of being a correctional officer in a Florida correctional institution.

This chapter provides an overview of the correctional officer training program and the requirements for becoming a certified officer. It also lays a legal foundation so that students may begin to function as correctional officers and understand their responsibilities in relation to inmate rights. Students will learn about basic criminal justice values, ethics, professionalism, and the command structure within a criminal justice agency.

Know the responsibilities of a correctional officer

A correctional officer's profession is governed by federal and state law, state rules, local regulations (for county officers and facilities), and agency and facility policies and procedures. You can find the law that defines a correctional officer in s. 943.10, Florida Statutes:

> ***Correctional officer*** *means any person who is appointed or employed full time by the state or any political subdivision thereof, or by any private entity which has contracted with the state or county, and whose primary responsibility is the supervision, protection, care, custody, and control, or investigation, of inmates within a correctional institution; however, the term "correctional officer" does not include any secretarial, clerical, or professionally trained personnel.*

Correctional officers are often mistakenly referred to as guards; this designation does a disservice to the profession. Correctional officers do far more than guard inmates. They interact with inmates on a daily basis, act as initial responders in emergency medical situations, perform basic law enforcement duties within the custodial environment, act as role models, and work toward the larger goal of inmate rehabilitation.

Correctional officers are considered professionals in their field, and much is expected of them as they provide care, custody, and control of inmates. Some of the personal characteristics supervisors look for in new officers include abilities to:

Know the personal characteristics supervisors look for in new officers

- work alone with little or no supervision
- perform tasks without getting distracted
- independently make decisions and stand by those decisions
- learn new techniques and procedures
- adapt to change without incurring undue stress
- be attentive to their environment
- be responsible for actions taken as well as the consequences of inaction
- interact appropriately with others

Officers who work for the Florida Department of Corrections and its entities are governed by the requirements and rules set out in the Florida Statutes and the ***Florida Administrative Code (F.A.C.)***, the body of law that oversees public regulatory agencies. By contrast, officers who work for county agencies and facilities are governed by the Florida Statutes and the ***Florida Model Jail Standards (FMJS)***, standards set by the Florida Sheriffs Association and with which all local jails must comply. It is important to understand this basic distinction; the type of agency an officer serves determines which regulatory codes govern their work and agency's policies and procedures.

Know the regulations that define your authority and job

CRIMINAL JUSTICE STANDARDS AND TRAINING COMMISSION

In addition to the Florida Statutes and F.A.C. or FMJS, certified correctional officers are overseen by the Criminal Justice Standards and Training Commission (CJSTC). The CJSTC (also referred to as the Commission in this textbook) was created to oversee the certification, employment, training, and conduct of Florida law enforcement, correctional, and correctional probation officers. The CJSTC meets quarterly and works "to ensure that the citizens of the state of Florida are served by the most qualified, well-trained, competent and ethical criminal justice officers in the nation."

PRIMARY RESPONSIBILITIES OF THE CJSTC

Section 943.12, F.S., explains the CJSTC's duties as follows:

Understand the statutory role of the CJSTC

- establish uniform minimum standards for the employment and training of full-time, part-time, and auxiliary law enforcement, correctional, and correctional probation officers

- establish and maintain officer training programs, curricula requirements, and certification of training schools and training school instructors
- certify officers who complete a Florida Basic Recruit Training Program or who are diversely qualified through experience and training and who meet minimum employment standards
- review and administer appropriate administrative sanctions in instances when an officer, instructor, or training school is found to be in violation of Florida Statutes and Commission standards
- set forth rules and procedures to administer the requirements of ss. 943.085-943.255, F.S.
- conduct studies of compensation, education, and training for correctional, correctional probation, and law enforcement disciplines
- maintain a central repository of records of all certified criminal justice officers
- develop, maintain, and administer the State Officer Certification Examination (SOCE) for criminal justice officers

The Criminal Justice Professionalism (CJP) Division within the Florida Department of Law Enforcement (FDLE) supports and assists the CJSTC in the execution, administration, implementation, and evaluation of the CJSTC's powers, duties, and functions. CJP manages the administrative functions involved in the certification and decertification of criminal justice officers in Florida. CJP writes and updates each of the basic and post-basic training courses that certified officers receive in Florida. CJP also maintains the automated training system for all officer records.

OFFICER CERTIFICATION

Correctional officers, like all criminal justice personnel, are held to the highest standard. The knowledge and skills that you learn during basic recruit training will prepare you for a rewarding and satisfying career. The CJSTC, the training academy, and the employing agency are devoted to ensuring that each recruit is fully trained and ready to assume the duties of a Florida correctional officer.

Know the requirements to become a certified officer in Florida

Section 943.13, F.S., sets the minimum requirements and standards that a person must meet before being employed or appointed as a full-time, part-time, or auxiliary correctional officer. An officer must:

- be at least 18
- be a U.S. citizen
- be a high school graduate or its equivalent
- not have been convicted of any felony or misdemeanor that involves perjury or a false statement, regardless of withholding of adjudication or suspended sentence
- not have received a dishonorable discharge from any of the Armed Forces of the United States
- not have pleaded guilty or ***nolo contendere*** (when a person does not accept or deny responsibility for the charges but agrees to accept punishment) or been found guilty of any felony or misdemeanor that involves perjury or a false statement after July 1, 1981
- have processed fingerprints on file with the employing agency

- have passed a physical examination by a licensed physician, physician assistant, or certified advanced registered nurse practitioner, based on specifications established by the Commission
- have a good moral character, as determined by a background investigation under procedures established by the Commission
- submit an affidavit-of-applicant form, adopted by the Commission, attesting to compliance with s. 943.13(1)-(7), F.S.
- satisfactorily complete a Commission-approved course of basic recruit training
- satisfactorily pass the SOCE

A recruit has four years from the starting date of the basic recruit training to complete the certification process. To become certified as a correctional officer, you must do all of the following:

- meet all the minimum requirements and standards
- complete the approved basic recruit training
- pass the SOCE
- become actively employed with a correctional facility in an auxiliary, part-time, or full-time officer position

Simply completing the basic recruit training and passing the certification exam does not mean that a person is a certified officer.

For example, if Rob Recruit begins basic recruit training on July 1, 2022, he must meet all the minimum requirements and standards, complete the approved basic recruit training, pass the SOCE, and become actively employed with a correctional facility as a certified officer by June 30, 2026. If Rob Recruit does not meet all these requirements by June 30, 2026, he will have to repeat the basic recruit training, and a new four-year period begins.

STATE OFFICER CERTIFICATION EXAMINATION

Upon completion of a basic recruit training program, you must pass the SOCE to be employed or appointed as a correctional officer. You must pass the SOCE within three attempts.

You can find more information on the SOCE on the FDLE website, including SOCE registration information and exam topics, at http://www.fdle.state.fl.us.

OFFICER COMPLIANCE

Before you are hired by a correctional facility, the hiring agency will conduct a thorough background investigation to determine your moral character. If you have entered the academy before employment, you are subject to the same moral character requirements as active certified officers and may be denied certification by the Commission if evidence indicates you do not meet these requirements.

DISCIPLINARY ACTION

In addition to certifying criminal justice officers, the CJSTC has the authority to impose discipline on your certification if you fail to maintain the required standards of conduct.

The CJSTC may take action against your certification if you do any of the following:

Know when the CJSTC will discipline an officer

- plead *nolo contendere*, plead guilty, or are found guilty of any felony
- plead *nolo contendere*, plead guilty, or are found guilty of a misdemeanor involving perjury or false statement
- fail to maintain good moral character as defined by the Florida Statutes and Florida Administrative Code (CJSTC Rule 11B-27.0011, F.A.C.)
- commit any act constituting a felony offense, regardless of criminal prosecution
- test positive for controlled substances by a urine or blood test, in accordance with the requirements for testing reliability and integrity set forth in Rule 11B-27.00225, F.A.C.
- are found guilty of excessive use of force under color of authority under Rule 11B-27.0011(4)(c)1, F.A.C.
- engage in sexual harassment involving physical contact or misuse of official position
- misuse your official position, as defined by s. 112.313, F.S.
- engage in sex while on duty
- have unprofessional relationships with an inmate, detainee, probationer, parolee, or community controlee; have written or oral communication that is intended to facilitate conduct that is prohibited by Commission rule; engage in any physical contact not required in the performance of official duties that is normally associated with the demonstration of affection or sexual misconduct as defined in s. 944.35, F.S.
- make false statements during the employment process
- commit conduct that subverts [undermines] or attempts to subvert the SOCE process in accordance with Rule 11B-30.009, F.A.C.
- commit conduct that subverts or attempts to subvert the CJSTC-approved training examination process or an employing agency's promotional examination process in accordance with, but not limited to, acts described in Rule 11B-27.0011(4)(c)9., F.A.C.

The CJSTC follows an established set of disciplinary guidelines when it imposes discipline on an officer's certification. These penalties could include written reprimand, probation, suspension, or revocation of certification.

Know the penalties the officer discipline process can impose

When the CJSTC revokes an officer's certification in accordance with s. 943.1395, F.S., the officer can no longer work as a certified correctional officer in the state of Florida. In cases of criminal violation, an officer can also be criminally prosecuted.

While these guidelines are specific to certified officers, the CJSTC and your training academy expect you to adhere to the same standards of conduct during basic recruit training. Violations may result in the denial of officer certification.

LESSON VOCABULARY

correctional officer

Florida Administrative Code (F.A.C.)

Florida Model Jail Standards (FMJS)

nolo contendere

REVIEW ITEMS

1. *List the responsibilities of a correctional officer.*
2. *What do supervisors look for in new staff?*
3. *What is the Florida Administrative Code?*
4. *What are the Florida Model Jail Standards?*
5. *What is the CJSTC?*
6. *What are the requirements to become a certified officer in Florida?*
7. *Explain the role of the CJSTC in officer discipline.*
8. *What types of penalties can be imposed on an officer through the officer discipline process?*

UNIT 1 INTRODUCTION

LESSON 2

CRIMINAL JUSTICE VALUES AND ETHICS

LESSON GOAL

You will be equipped to make ethical decisions in all personal and professional situations.

THINK ABOUT THIS

"Please, just let me go. I promise I won't do it again. C'mon, this is my first offense," Inmate Jones begs. Officer Roberts has just caught Inmate Jones stealing some books that belong to Inmate Michael. Officer Roberts returns the books, but instead of reporting the incident, Officer Roberts only verbally reprimands Inmate Jones. Later that night, Inmate Jones is caught trying to steal the books again. Only this time, he is caught by Inmate Michael, who severely beats Inmate Jones. Now, a formal investigation has to be conducted, a crime scene has to be processed, and Inmate Jones needs medical attention. Could Officer Roberts have done something different in this situation? Could his actions have prevented Inmate Jones' injuries or the issues this caused in the facility?

OFFICER ETHICS

Understand how values and ethics apply to a correctional officer's behavior

Values are principles, standards, or qualities considered worthwhile or desirable. They are core beliefs or desires that guide or motivate a person's attitude and actions. Values determine how people behave in certain situations; they reflect what people care about and what they think is important. These convictions may be based on many factors, including cultural background, personal experiences, organizational values, or personal beliefs. For correctional officers, honesty, truthfulness, and fairness are especially important values and should always be practiced both on and off duty.

Ethics is defined as the moral principles that govern a person or group. These principles are based on society's understanding of right and wrong. Values and ethics are interrelated; both are essential in the correctional officer's personal and professional life. As a correctional officer, you must always act within the boundaries of your authority and uphold the recognized standards of your profession's code of ethics.

Ethical behavior is principled, values-based decision-making that is practiced daily. Correctional officers should behave ethically on and off duty and avoid conflicts of interest. Examples of ethical behavior are obeying all laws, policies, and procedures; protecting the civil rights of all inmates; respecting confidential and privileged communication; and treating persons who may be different from you with courtesy and fairness.

Ethical violations can result in disciplinary action by your agency and the CJSTC, including termination of employment and decertification.

Know the American Correctional Association's Code of Ethics

THE AMERICAN CORRECTIONAL ASSOCIATION CODE OF ETHICS

Preamble: The American Correctional Association expects of its members unfailing honesty, respect for the dignity and individuality of human beings and a commitment to professional and compassionate service.

To this end, we subscribe to the following principles:

Members shall respect and protect the civil and legal rights of all individuals.

Members shall treat every professional situation with concern for the welfare of the individuals involved and with no intent to personal gain.

Members shall maintain relationships with colleagues to promote mutual respect within the profession and improve the quality of service.

Members shall make public criticism of their colleagues or their agencies only when warranted, verifiable and constructive.

Members shall respect the importance of all disciplines within the criminal justice system and work to improve cooperation with each segment.

Members shall honor the public's right to information and share information with the public to the extent permitted by law subject to individuals' right to privacy.

Members shall respect and protect the right of the public to be safeguarded from criminal activity.

Members shall refrain from using their positions to secure personal privileges or advantages.

Members shall refrain from allowing personal interest to impair objectivity in the performance of duty while acting in an official capacity.

Members shall refrain from entering into any formal or informal activity or agreement which presents a conflict of interest or is inconsistent with the conscientious performance of duties.

Members shall refrain from accepting any gifts, service, or favors that are or appear to be improper or imply an obligation inconsistent with the free and objective exercise of professional duties.

Members shall clearly differentiate between personal views/statements and views/statements/positions made on behalf of the agency or Association.

Members shall report to appropriate authorities any corrupt or unethical behaviors in which there is sufficient evidence to justify review.

Members shall refrain from discriminating against any individual because of race, gender, creed, national origin, religious affiliation, age, disability, or any other type of prohibited discrimination.

Members shall preserve the integrity of private information; they shall refrain from seeking information on individuals beyond that which is necessary to implement responsibilities and perform their duties; members shall refrain from revealing non-public information unless expressly authorized to do so.

Members shall make all appointments, promotions, and dismissals in accordance with established civil service rules, applicable contract agreements, and individual merit, rather than furtherance of personal interests.

Members shall respect, promote, and contribute to a workplace that is safe, healthy, and free of harassment in any form.

INFLUENCES ON ETHICAL PROBLEM-SOLVING

Know the factors that influence your ethics and decision-making

Many factors affect how people solve problems and whether they do so in an ethical manner. Some officers come from families that emphasize strong values, while others are taught that everything is acceptable as long as they are not caught. Some people grow up in violent neighborhoods, possibly exposed to unethical activities. The influence of family members and peers can greatly affect how officers solve problems. Values instilled during childhood can affect an officer's decisions in adulthood.

Officers' pasts are by no means the only things that influence their current problem-solving abilities. Home life is especially important—it can affect everything from officers' views of the world to their behaviors and decision-making. A good support system in place at home can give officers confidence in their opinions. Honest communications and working out differences at home enhance an officer's ability to communicate with others on the job.

Co-workers can influence the way officers respond to a problem by their attitudes alone, whether they are positive and upbeat or cynical and negative. The way officers view their roles and the roles of their co-workers can have a large impact on their actions.

Officers' time in the academy can also influence how they respond to situations both in and outside the criminal justice field. Instructors should display professionalism and act as mentors and role models, extending respect and courtesy to all members of the academy. Students should be respectful and take advantage of the fact that instructors are experts in their fields.

BEHAVIORS TO AVOID

When interacting with inmates and others, correctional officers should avoid demonstrating unprofessional behaviors.

Understand the consequences of stereotyping

Stereotyping is judging a group of people who are different from you based on your own or others' opinions or encounters. Labeling people, whether positively or negatively, may limit your ability to interact with inmates or work effectively with colleagues. Both positive and negative stereotypes hurt because they categorize people unfairly; therefore, they are not acceptable practices.

Understand why you should treat all people fairly and with dignity

Showing consideration for your co-workers as you work in a correctional facility lets others see that you handle your job professionally. You are expected to treat people fairly, with dignity and respect, regardless of their race, gender, creed, national origin, religious affiliation, age, or disability.

Know inappropriate and unprofessional behaviors that you must avoid in the performance of your duties

Bias or prejudice is a strong belief or feeling about a person, group, or subject, whether positive or negative, that is formed without reviewing all available facts or information. Prejudices may grow from learned behavior and attitudes. Officers who act with prejudice may exhibit inappropriate behavior toward people or groups who represent a race, color, ethnicity, religion, sexual orientation, national origin, mental or physical disability, advanced age, gender presentation, or other self-defining characteristic. This type of behavior may be destructive and can invite civil liability.

Discrimination is the negative behavior toward a person or group that is based on color, race, sex, age, religion, ethnic and national origin, disability, or marital status. Discrimination occurs because people choose to act on their prejudices. Each person has the right to live free from discrimination and prejudice.

An ***assumption*** is a notion, statement, or belief about a person, group, or event that may or may not be factual. People make assumptions when they consider something to be true or false without proof or demonstration. Assumptions are interpretations of what experience reveals and may not always be accurate.

The following are examples of often false assumptions:

Young inmates are disrespectful to elders and authority.

Older inmates pose less threat to officers.

Using stereotypes and assumptions to judge people limits officers' thought processes and can threaten safety. Stereotypes and assumptions may cause an officer to act on emotions rather than plan a response. Responsive behavior requires you to think, plan a response, and act appropriately using verbal and non-verbal skills.

ETHICAL DECISION-MAKING

Use the Ethical Decision-Making Tool to make ethical decisions while on or off duty

An Ethical Decision-Making Tool is an assessment tool that can assist you in making decisions in difficult ethical situations. It guides you through a series of questions that encourage you to think through what you plan to do. It analyzes alternative actions that can accomplish the goal.

1. Is my action legal?

   If no, stop! What action should I take?

   If yes, ask the next question.

2. Will the result of my action be good?

   If no, stop!

   If yes, ask the next question.

3. Will what I plan to do actually work?

   If no, stop!

   If yes, ask the next question.

4. Is there a less harmful alternative?

   If yes, stop and use the less harmful alternative!

   If no, ask the next question.

5. Does it undermine some equal or more important value?

   If yes, stop!

   If no, go ahead with the decision.

6. Does a good end ever justify a bad means?

   No!

7. Will I be able to justify my action if my decision is made public?

   If no, stop!

   If yes, go ahead with the decision.

Lesson Vocabulary

assumption

bias or prejudice

discrimination

ethical behavior

ethics

stereotyping

values

Review Items

1. *How do values and ethics relate to a correctional officer's behavior?*
2. *Describe factors that influence your ethics and decision-making.*
3. *What are some things that can go wrong when stereotyping others?*
4. *Why is it important to treat all people fairly and with dignity?*
5. *List some of the inappropriate and unprofessional behaviors that must be avoided in the performance of your duties.*
6. *What should you consider while making decisions?*

LESSON 3

PROFESSIONALISM AND CHAIN OF COMMAND

LESSON GOAL

You will be able to behave professionally and work effectively within a chain of command.

THINK ABOUT THIS

Place yourself in the shoes of an inmate for a moment. You are trying to find an officer who would be willing to sneak in a cell phone for you. You narrow down your search to two officers, Officer James and Officer Smith. Officer James is never late for a shift. His uniform is pressed and straight. He always looks well-rested and alert. He seems focused on his job and many other officers often come to him with questions. Officer Smith, on the other hand, usually arrives five to 10 minutes late. He has to be reminded to tuck in his shirt. He can be heard mumbling under his breath whenever he is given a direction by a supervising officer. He spends a lot of his shift talking to the inmates about the previous night's game or complaining about his girlfriend. Which of these two officers would you approach to sneak in a cell phone? Why?

Understand why professionalism is important to your role as an officer

Professionalism is behavior that demonstrates good character and is marked by pride in self and career. Examples of these characteristics include service, integrity, respect, quality, fairness, honesty, courage, compassion, moral and ethical leadership, trustworthiness, and common sense. Professionalism requires that you respect the people you serve and maintain a personal commitment to the continued development of your skills in the job.

Professionalism is also doing the right thing no matter who is looking or whose back is turned. This means applying appropriate values and ethics and knowing what to do in difficult situations.

Maintaining a professional attitude can protect you from inmate manipulation and ensure everyone's safety.

PROFESSIONAL BEHAVIOR

Know why you should be dependable and fulfill obligations

Model professional behavior and perform the job to the best of your ability. Always show respect for inmates, as well as staff, colleagues, and leadership. Take responsibility for your actions, admit and correct your mistakes, and maintain accountability. Be dependable, strive at all times to work efficiently and consistently, and fulfill your obligations. This includes reporting to your shift on time, wearing the proper uniform, being neat and clean, and consistently performing the best job possible. This behavior extends beyond the workplace to your personal life as well. For example, practice care and respect in your use of social media.

Your professionalism comes through your image and demeanor, how you communicate, and how well you do your job. Just because an action or behavior is **not** prohibited in agency policies does not mean it is smart or appropriate to do it. Gossiping about co-workers, discussing personal family problems, using inappropriate language, or attending to personal business at work are not professional behaviors.

Know why you must exhibit self-control in performing your duties

The work environment of a correctional officer can range from quiet to chaotic throughout the course of a shift. There will be times when you will have to make quick decisions in unexpected, stressful circumstances. Remain calm in these situations. Consider your actions, think through your professional response, and recall skills and information you received during training, and apply agency policies and procedures in your decisions. A sense of professionalism should instill self-control to resist abusing your authority. Remaining fair and level-headed when dealing with others can help avoid escalating a situation into unnecessary violence and endangering inmates and officers.

ORGANIZATIONAL STRUCTURE

Know chain of command as it is used in a criminal justice agency

Chain of command is the order of authority within an organization. It links the authority and responsibility of one level of an organization to another. Following a chain of command helps coordination, reduces confusion, and enhances the efficiency of the organization.

An ***organization*** is a group of two or more people who cooperate to accomplish one or more objectives. An organizational chart is a diagram that visually represents an agency and the connection between each position and its rank. Rank structure establishes boundaries between the different levels within the organization. In correctional agencies, this rank structure might be as follows:

- Sheriff or Warden
- Undersheriff or Assistant Warden
- Colonel or Chief of Security
- Major
- Captain
- Lieutenant
- Sergeant
- Corporal
- Deputy or Officer

Organizations use the chain of command to help with communication and make decisions. Questions that officers might have are typically answered at the lowest level possible of the chain of command. You should go to your immediate supervisor for information and assistance. In some emergency situations, your direct supervisor may not be available to answer an important question or meet an immediate need. This is when it may be necessary to bypass the chain of command. If this happens, contact your supervisor as soon as possible. For example, in a medical emergency, contact medical or the communications center immediately, and then notify your supervisor.

Understand how chain of command facilitates communication within the organization

As part of the chain of command and the organizational structure, an officer must be aware of the importance of following orders. Failure to follow lawful orders from supervisors in your chain of command is considered ***insubordination***, a very serious offense. However, an order known to be illegal must not be carried out, but an officer refusing to follow an order must be absolutely certain that it violates the law, or the officer will be subject to charges of insubordination.

Understand why chain of command within a criminal justice agency should be followed

Lesson Vocabulary

chain of command

insubordination

organization

professionalism

Review Items

1. *Why is professionalism important to a correctional officer?*
2. *Why is it important to be dependable and fulfill obligations?*
3. *Why should you exhibit self-control in performing the duties of a correctional officer?*
4. *What is chain of command? How is it used in a criminal justice agency?*
5. *What important organizational component does chain of command help facilitate?*
6. *Why is it important to follow chain of command?*

UNIT 2 LEGAL

LESSON 1
CRIMINAL JUSTICE SYSTEM AND COMPONENTS

LESSON GOAL

You will be able to work within the larger criminal justice system by understanding your important role.

THINK ABOUT THIS

Given what we have discussed so far, you may think that you will interact only with inmates and fellow correctional officers throughout your career. The truth is that you will also be interacting with members of law enforcement and the courts. You may work with law enforcement to transport an inmate, or be called to court to testify about a crime committed in your facility. For these reasons and others, it is important that you understand the criminal justice system as a whole, as well as how corrections and a correctional officer fit into that system.

STRUCTURE OF THE U.S. CRIMINAL JUSTICE SYSTEM

Know the role of the correctional officer as it relates to the criminal justice system

A correctional officer is part of a large, complex interrelated group known as the criminal justice system. Correctional officers play an important role in the criminal justice system and interact regularly with other components. An officer's ability to interact effectively within the organizational network directly affects the officer's job performance. The correctional officer is responsible for the care, custody, and control of inmates in a municipal or county jail, state correctional institution, or similar form of secure supervision.

Know the major components of the U.S. criminal justice system

Criminal justice refers to the structure, functions, and decision-making processes of those agencies that deal with the management and control of crime and criminal offenders. The three main components of the criminal justice system are law enforcement, the court system, and corrections.

Law enforcement, as its name implies, is responsible for enforcing and maintaining civil order. The court system is responsible for the interpretation of laws—both federal and state. Corrections is the part of the system responsible for enforcing penalties as defined by the court system and for the care, custody, and control of inmates and pretrial detainees.

LAW ENFORCEMENT AGENCIES

There are four levels of law enforcement agencies within the United States: local or municipal, county, state, and federal (U.S. government agencies).

Know the basic types of U.S. law enforcement agencies

Local or municipal law enforcement agencies enforce the ordinances of the municipality as well as state laws within the jurisdiction of the agency. Examples of local law enforcement agencies are city police departments and public safety departments.

The job of county law enforcement agencies is to enforce county ordinances and state laws within the county. Traditionally, they also handle unincorporated areas, the county jail, and civil processing. A sheriff's office is an example of a county law enforcement agency.

State law enforcement agencies are responsible for enforcing state laws within the state. Examples of state law enforcement agencies include FDLE, the Florida Highway Patrol, and the Florida Fish and Wildlife Conservation Commission.

Federal law enforcement agencies enforce federal laws across state lines and within the states. Examples of federal law enforcement agencies include the Federal Bureau of Investigation, the U.S. Marshals Service, and the U.S. Immigration and Customs Enforcement.

THE COURT SYSTEM

The judicial system directly affects the inmates a correctional officer supervises. The court system in the United States includes county, state, and federal courts. State judges in Florida are elected or appointed by the governor, while the president appoints federal judges. The federal courts are the highest courts in the United States and generally take precedence over the state courts.

There are courts of general jurisdiction and limited jurisdiction. ***Jurisdiction*** means the types of cases in which the court can make decisions. Federal courts hear only cases that are violations of federal laws, including constitutional violations. State courts hear cases involving violations of state law. Courts of limited jurisdiction decide only a limited set of case types.

FLORIDA STATE COURT SYSTEM

The state court system in Florida is made up of four levels:

Know the structure and duties of the U.S. and Florida court systems

Florida County Courts—The 67 county courts have limited jurisdiction and handle the following legal issues:

- minor criminal offenses (misdemeanors), which provide a maximum sentence of one year or less in the county jail
- county and municipal ordinance violations, including traffic infractions (some counties use hearing officers for these cases)
- civil cases involving amounts of $15,000 or less and small claims disputes (less than $5,000)
- issuance of search and arrest warrants within the county

Florida Circuit Courts—The 20 circuit courts handle the following legal issues:

- domestic relations cases, such as dissolution of marriage (divorce), guardianship, and juvenile delinquency
- major criminal offenses (felonies), which can result in imprisonment in a state correctional institution
- probate matters, such as the processing of wills and settling of the estates of deceased persons
- civil cases involving amounts greater than $15,000
- Baker Act and Marchman Act cases
- issuance of search and arrest warrants within the circuit
- appeals from county court judgments, except when a state statute or provision of the state constitution is held invalid

Florida District Courts of Appeal (DCA)—The five District Courts of Appeal decide appeals from circuit courts in most criminal and civil cases.

Florida Supreme Court—The Florida Supreme Court, which consists of seven justices who are appointed by the governor, is the highest court in the state. The Supreme Court hears cases such as final orders that impose death sentences and appeals from lower state courts.

U.S. FEDERAL COURT SYSTEM

U.S. District Courts—District courts are the federal trial courts presided over by U.S. district judges, who are assisted by magistrates. Magistrates are appointed by district judges and issue warrants, make pretrial motions, and preside over some civil cases, misdemeanor trials, petty cases, and preliminary hearings.

The scope of the federal judiciary system includes all federal codes (criminal, civil, and administrative) in all 50 states, U.S. territories, and the District of Columbia.

Courts of Appeal—Formerly known as the Circuit Courts of Appeals, these courts make decisions on appeals from lower federal courts that are subject to review in the U.S. Supreme Court.

Supreme Court of the United States—The U.S. Supreme Court is the highest court in the United States and the chief authority in the judicial branch, one of three branches of the U.S. federal government. The Court hears appeals from the decisions of lower federal courts and state supreme courts and resolves issues of constitutional and federal law. It stands as the ultimate authority in constitutional interpretation, and its decisions can be changed only by a constitutional amendment.

The Supreme Court's most important responsibility is to decide cases that raise questions of constitutional interpretation. The Court decides if a law or government action violates the Constitution. This power, known as judicial review, enables the Court to invalidate both federal and state laws when they conflict with its interpretation of the Constitution.

THE CORRECTIONAL SYSTEM

A general overview of the corrections system in Florida includes the following components:

Prisons (Federal and State)

Prisons are correctional institutions maintained by the federal and state governments for the confinement of convicted felons.

Understand the function of the correctional system

County Jails

County jails are used for in-processing and temporary detention of defendants awaiting trial or disposition on federal or state charges and of convicted offenders sentenced to short-term detention (a year or less). County jails may also hold convicted felons returned from prison for court appearances.

County and Municipal Holding Facilities

These provide a place for detainees to stay while booking procedures are completed or until transported to a county jail.

Treatment and Evaluation Centers

These are designed to meet the special needs of particular offenders. Treatment centers deal with alcohol / drug abusers or mentally ill offenders. In addition to general processing procedures, various testing (such as, medical, mental, educational aptitude) is performed at these facilities.

Probation, Parole, and Community Control

Probation, parole, and community control are parts of a community-based correctional system. Their purpose is to supervise the enforcement of specific restrictions on people who have received an alternative to incarceration.

- ***Probation*** is a court-ordered sentence that places a person under the supervision of a probation officer under specified court-ordered terms and conditions.
- ***Parole*** is the release of an inmate from a correctional institution before the inmate's court-imposed sentence ends.
- ***Community control*** (house arrest) is a form of closely monitored community supervision and is more restrictive than probation or parole.

Juvenile Assessment / Detention Center

Juvenile suspects are taken here for processing and possible pretrial detention.

THE FLORIDA DEPARTMENT OF CORRECTIONS

The Florida Department of Corrections is Florida's largest state agency. The Department administers state prisons and state probation in Florida.

Know the components of the correctional system in Florida

It employs correctional officers and correctional probation officers to provide security for and to supervise inmates and offenders.

The Department has two main divisions overseeing inmates and offenders: the Office of Institutions and the Office of Community Corrections.

Office of Institutions—This office manages facilities where inmates reside.

Office of Community Corrections—This office oversees supervision programs, including probation and community control.

Lesson Vocabulary

community control

criminal justice

jurisdiction

parole

probation

Review Items

1. *What role does a correctional officer have in the U.S. criminal justice system?*
2. *What are the three major components of the U.S. criminal justice system?*
3. *What are the four basic levels of U.S. law enforcement agencies?*
4. *List the three levels of courts in the U.S. court system.*
5. *List the four levels of courts in the Florida court system.*
6. *Explain the difference between jails and prisons.*
7. *What is the function of the correctional system?*
8. *Describe the components of the correctional system in Florida.*

LESSON 2
CONSTITUTIONAL RIGHTS

LESSON GOAL

You will be able to make decisions and act appropriately based on the guidance of the U.S. Constitution.

THINK ABOUT THIS

It is important to understand how the Constitution affects what you can and cannot do in the line of duty as a correctional officer. Consider the following example: Officer Adams attempts to make a random search of Inmate Charles' cell, but Inmate Charles yells at Officer Adams, "You can't search my cell! You have no proof I've got anything illegal in here! You can't search whenever you want!" Officer Adams counters, "The officers here can search your cell whenever it is deemed necessary. We do not need probable cause." Who is right in this situation?

BILL OF RIGHTS

Understand the role of the amendments to the U.S. Constitution and the Bill of Rights in relation to corrections

According to the U.S. Constitution, all people stand equal before the law and therefore share certain rights. Many of these rights, such as freedom of speech, protection against unreasonable searches and seizures, and prohibition of cruel and unusual punishment, are described in the first 10 amendments to the U.S. Constitution and together are known as the ***Bill of Rights***. Although many of these amendments focus on the courts and legislation, some, such as the First, Fourth, Fifth, Sixth, and Eighth Amendments, are of particular importance to correctional officers.

- The First Amendment protects freedom of speech, of the press, and of religion, and the right to peacefully assemble. In a correctional setting, the First Amendment is limited to access to religious practice and the press. An example of this limitation is that while inmates cannot assemble and protest, they can maintain the right to express their religious beliefs and communicate with the press.
- The Fourth Amendment prohibits unreasonable search and seizure. The purpose of this amendment is to protect people from governmental intrusion in areas where they have a reasonable expectation of privacy. For example, to search a home, a law enforcement officer needs a search warrant signed by a judge. However, in a correctional setting, there is a diminished expectation of privacy, and there is no general requirement for a search warrant.

- The Fifth Amendment is best known for prohibiting self-incrimination. It also requires grand jury indictment for capital crimes and prohibits double jeopardy and deprivation of life, liberty, or property without due process of law. Due process of law generally requires a notice and hearing.
- The Sixth Amendment guarantees the right to a speedy and public trial, to counsel, to an impartial jury, to be informed of the nature of the charges, and to confront witnesses. It is important to understand that the access to legal counsel in a correctional setting falls within the Sixth Amendment.
- The Eighth Amendment prohibits excessive bails and fines, and cruel and unusual punishment. This amendment plays a critical role in the care, custody, and control of inmates. Excessive use of force or withholding meals is prohibited under this amendment.

The Bill of Rights was originally intended to restrict actions of the federal government only. The Fourteenth Amendment expanded the application of the Bill of Rights to state and local governments as well.

SEARCH AND SEIZURE

Know what a search is and how it relates to corrections

The Fourth Amendment to the Constitution protects people from governmental intrusion. A ***search*** may be defined as governmental intrusion into a place where a person has a reasonable expectation of privacy. In a correctional setting, a search occurs to seek out and discover evidence and contraband in the possession of an inmate. ***Contraband*** is any unauthorized article or any authorized article in excessive quantities or altered from its intended purpose.

Know what probable cause is and how it relates to corrections

An officer working in a correctional facility does not require probable cause to search an inmate. ***Probable cause*** is a fair probability or reasonable grounds to believe that a crime was committed, based on the totality of the circumstances (all the factors known at the time).

Know what seizure is and how it relates to corrections

Seizure may be defined as the act of taking possession of contraband or evidence for a violation of rule or law. Inmates have less expectation of privacy in a correctional setting due to the compelling interest to maintain order in the correctional system.

> When a correctional officer finds evidence or contraband during a search in a correctional setting, the officer has the duty to seize it.

Know the types of searches used for visitors entering and exiting a correctional setting

Safety and security needs of a correctional facility include searching people entering the facility. Types of searches may include a pat search, canine, drug, body scan, and metal detector. Unlike inmates, visitors have the right to refuse a search; however, refusal may result in denial or termination of current or future visits.

APPLICATION OF *MIRANDA*

Understand how and when a *Miranda* warning is issued in a correctional setting

A ***Miranda warning*** provides the protections of the Fifth Amendment right against self-incrimination when a suspect in custody is interrogated in a criminal investigation. Though a correctional officer is not a law enforcement officer and therefore does not issue a *Miranda* warning, *Miranda* still applies to inmates in a correctional setting. If a crime occurs within a correctional facility, interrogation of the individual should be completed by either a law enforcement officer or prison inspector.

A correctional officer may encounter information regarding an ongoing criminal case that occurred outside the facility. This may occur in a jail setting during the intake process or when inmates are awaiting trial. You should not ask inmates about the circumstances under which they are charged. However, you have a duty to report information concerning criminal acts. If an inmate provides information regarding facts of a criminal case, you must document this information in accordance with your agency policies and procedures.

LESSON VOCABULARY

Bill of Rights

contraband

Miranda warning

probable cause

search

seizure

REVIEW ITEMS

1. *What is the role of the amendments to the U.S. Constitution in relation to corrections?*
2. *Describe how search applies to a correctional setting.*
3. *Do correctional officers need probable cause to search an inmate's cell?*
4. *How is seizure handled in a correctional setting?*
5. *What types of searches are used for visitors to a facility?*
6. *How does a Miranda warning apply to a correctional setting?*

UNIT 2 LEGAL

LESSON 3
INMATE RIGHTS

LESSON GOAL

You will be able to respect and protect inmates through your actions.

THINK ABOUT THIS

Many people believe that once a person has been sentenced to prison or jail, the person loses all rights. This is not the case; inmates do retain some rights. If these rights are violated, it could cause harm to the inmates and staff, as well as open up the facility and governing body to lawsuits. For these reasons, you should understand which rights inmates have and how you can help protect those rights, while continuing to ensure the safety and security of the facility.

RIGHTS RETAINED BY INMATES

Know which rights inmates retain within a facility

Inmates retain certain rights; however, in the correctional setting, inmates' rights are restricted because of the need for safety and security of the facility. Some of the retained rights include freedom from excessive punishments; access to courts; legal counsel, including help from other inmates in preparation of writs, petitions, and other legal papers; and access to an adequate law library. Inmates also have the right to freedom of expression, freedom from overcrowded conditions, freedom from unreasonable search and seizure, and freedom to worship and exercise religious beliefs. In addition, inmates have the right to exercise and fresh air; adequate medical treatment; correspondence through sending and receiving mail, including correspondence with the courts; and food that meets minimum nutritional standards.

HEALTH INSURANCE PORTABILITY AND ACCOUNTABILITY ACT (HIPAA)

Understand how the requirements of the Health Insurance Portability and Accountability Act operate in a correctional setting

The federal Health Insurance Portability and Accountability Act (HIPAA) sets privacy standards that make it a violation to knowingly disclose the protected health information of inmates and detainees. Correctional officers and staff who knowingly violate this HIPAA restriction may be fined, imprisoned, or administratively disciplined.

HIPAA requires that a correctional institution reasonably safeguard an inmate's health information to limit incidental uses or disclosures, unless there is a health, safety, or security need. See s. 456.057, F.S.

Inmate health information is confidential and may be shared only with people who have a need and right to know.

Also, you are prohibited from asking for inmate health information unless it is pertinent to your job or necessary to protect yourself or others or to assign work. For example, if an inmate has a contagious disease, such as tuberculosis, a transport officer needs to know so the officer can get the right personal protective equipment and take extra precautions. An inmate with diabetes may need a special meal and possibly a snack during work detail.

The health information that is disclosed to an officer will be limited to a particular incident or health and safety issue. You will not be given complete inmate health information; however, relevant information for precautionary measures will be available. For example, a correctional officer injured after a fight with an inmate can receive information regarding the inmate's bloodborne pathogens or transmittable disease status. The officer can be told if the inmate has HIV, hepatitis, or other communicable diseases. However, the officer will not know if the inmate has high blood pressure.

PRISON RAPE ELIMINATION ACT (PREA)

Congress enacted the ***Prison Rape Elimination Act (PREA)*** to address the problem of sexual abuse of people in the custody of U.S. federal, state, or local correctional agencies.

Know how PREA relates to your duties

There is a zero-tolerance standard for the incidence of rape in correctional facilities. The purpose of PREA is to make rape prevention and awareness in a correctional setting a top priority. It develops and implements national standards for the detection, prevention, reduction, and punishment of prison rape. PREA establishes policy or procedures for increasing the accountability of officials who fail to detect, prevent, reduce, and punish prison rape and protects the Eighth Amendment rights of federal, state, and local prisoners. The increase of available data and information on the incidence of prison rape as a result of PREA improves the management and administration of correctional facilities.

You should treat all allegations of prison rape seriously and take appropriate action when a complaint is made.

PRIVILEGED COMMUNICATION

Although there is no expectation of privacy in a correctional facility, some relationships are considered protected, such as between an inmate and an attorney. This is considered ***privileged communication***.

Inmates maintain the right to certain confidential or privileged communication. The attorney-client privilege is based on the inmate's Sixth Amendment right to counsel. Attorney-client phone conversations may not be recorded, visits do not have to conform to normal visiting hours, and visits may be within the sight of the officer but out of hearing.

Understand inmates' rights to privileged communication

Other types of communication generally considered privileged outside of a correctional facility may have a diminished expectation of privacy and may be recorded for safety and security concerns in a correctional setting.

Lesson Vocabulary

Prison Rape Elimination Act (PREA)

privileged communication

Review Items

1. *Explain which rights inmates retain and the limitations of those rights.*
2. *How do the requirements of HIPAA apply in a correctional setting?*
3. *How does PREA relate to your duties as a correctional officer?*
4. *What is an example of an inmate's right to privileged communication?*
5. *Do inmates have a right to privacy in a correctional facility?*

LESSON 4

LEGAL ISSUES WITH CONTRABAND

LESSON GOAL

You will be able to recognize contraband and react to it appropriately.

THINK ABOUT THIS

Contraband in a correctional facility is often hard to define. Is a bed sheet contraband? Is a fork contraband? Are clothes contraband? The short and confusing answer is, "It depends." As noted earlier, contraband is any unauthorized article or any authorized article in excessive quantities or altered from its intended purpose. Contraband may include anything, no matter how harmless it may appear. Contraband may be hidden in plain sight. In certain situations, bed sheets, forks, and clothes are perfectly fine for inmates to possess. In other situations, they are considered contraband. This lesson will explain how to tell the difference and what your legal responsibilities are in relation to contraband.

Understand why contraband is a problem

The presence of contraband in correctional facilities is an ongoing problem in prison systems worldwide. Contraband places everyone in danger, including prison staff, the public, and the inmates trying to stay out of trouble, do their time, and go home. Contraband has the potential to increase violence, leads to an increase of further crimes, and provides wealth and power for inmates. For example, inmates can use cell phones to help smuggle in drugs and weapons, organize attempts to escape, and order crimes to be committed inside or outside correctional facilities.

Know what items are regarded as contraband

Items identified as contraband in correctional facilities in ss. 944.47 and 951.22, F.S., include currency or coins, tobacco products, controlled substances, non-prescribed drugs of any kind or nature, articles of food or clothing that have been altered or are in excessive quantity, firearms or dangerous weapons, cell phones or portable communication devices, or any items used to aid or make an escape. The purpose of limiting items in a correctional facility is to maintain internal order, security, and discipline.

Know how the Florida Model Jail Standards address managing contraband

Section 951.22, F.S., along with the Florida Model Jail Standards (FMJS), provides authority to county facilities to establish policies and procedures relating to contraband. The FMJS provide for a facility's officer in charge to list articles or items that inmates are allowed to have. All other items they have are considered contraband. The inmate handbook generally includes information about acceptable items.

The ***introduction of contraband*** is a crime punishable by s. 944.47, F.S., that designates the introduction, taking, or sending of articles defined as contraband into a correctional facility as a felony. The attempted introduction of contraband is also punishable under this statute.

Understand how contraband is brought into or removed from a facility

Be aware that anyone may introduce contraband into a facility. This may include attorneys, visitors, contractors, and even staff. Other law enforcement agencies may also introduce contraband either intentionally or inadvertently into a facility, for example, during intake or while responding to the death of an inmate.

Dispose of contraband properly

Confiscated contraband may be destroyed, converted, or reused, according to ss. 932.704 and 932.7055, F.S. Depending on agency policies and procedures, contraband may be destroyed by flushing, incinerating, or compacting. Consumable items, such as food, drink, or any item that may be tampered with, should be destroyed. Certain items may be converted for inmate trust funds or charity as designated by the agency. Reusable items are only non-consumable items issued by the facility that may be returned to supply, for example, linens, clothing, books, pens, or mail supplies. The disposition of contraband must be documented.

Contraband may also be designated as evidence and require holding for use in a disciplinary hearing or criminal case.

Lesson Vocabulary

introduction of contraband

Review Items

1. *Explain why contraband is illegal in a correctional facility.*
2. *What are some common items in a correctional facility that are considered contraband?*
3. *How do the FMJS address managing contraband?*
4. *How does contraband typically get introduced into a facility?*
5. *Explain how to properly dispose of contraband.*
6. *Are bed sheets considered contraband? Why or why not?*

UNIT 2 LEGAL

LESSON 5

CRIMINAL ACTS

LESSON GOAL

You will be able to recognize and identify different crimes that may be committed in a correctional facility and the proper way to handle any evidence.

THINK ABOUT THIS

When you work in a jail, prison, or other correctional setting, you deal with people who have been accused or convicted of committing a crime. Some of these people go on to commit new crimes within the facility. Since you are likely to encounter these situations in your job, you need to know how facilities handle them. This lesson introduces basic terms related to criminal offenses and how to handle evidence from crimes committed within a correctional facility.

CATEGORIES AND CLASSES OF OFFENSES

Know the categories and classes of offenses

A ***criminal act*** is a violation of the law. In Florida, a crime is designated as either a felony or a misdemeanor, according to s. 775.08, F.S. A ***felony*** is any criminal offense punishable under Florida law by death or imprisonment in a state facility for more than one year. Felonies are classified into five degrees, based on the severity of the offense. A ***misdemeanor*** is any criminal offense punishable under Florida law by imprisonment for less than one year in a county correctional facility. It is possible for an inmate to spend an extended term of more than one year in a county facility if they receive consecutive sentences (two or more sentences in a row) for multiple charges.

All laws still apply in a correctional facility; therefore, while in prison or jail, an inmate who commits a crime may be charged with another crime. A correctional officer should be able to determine when a crime has been committed, and be able to distinguish a crime from a rule violation. Officers should protect themselves, inmates, staff, and visitors from harm and violations.

Know the common crimes committed by inmates in a correctional setting

Some common crimes committed in a correctional setting include petit theft, dealing in stolen property, assault, battery, sexual battery, battery on a facility employee, drug-related crimes, criminal mischief, arson, possession of contraband, introduction of contraband into a correctional facility, escape, lewd and lascivious behavior, bribery, security threat group (STG)-related crimes, gambling, vandalism, loan sharking, or homicide.

Note that the crime of assault or battery on a facility employee who is performing their duties reclassifies the offense to a more severe degree. This means that this offense carries a greater penalty. Battery against a correctional facility employee includes the suspect intentionally touching, striking, or attempting to touch or strike the victim by throwing, tossing, or expelling blood, saliva, chewed food, seminal fluid, urine, or feces at the victim, to harass, annoy, threaten, or alarm the victim.

Examples of common staff and visitor criminal acts include the introduction of contraband, sexual misconduct, and bribery.

Know the common crimes committed by staff and visitors in a correctional setting

ELEMENTS OF CRIMES

Understand the elements of crimes

Two basic elements—or components—are necessary to convict a person of a crime:

- proof that a crime has been committed, and
- proof the person being charged committed the crime.

Generally, to prove that a person committed a crime, the prosecution must show that the person committed an act specifically prohibited by law. The prosecution must also show that the person who committed the act at the time did so knowingly or intentionally. By purposely doing what the law declares to be a crime, the person demonstrates criminal intent, an important legal concept.

INSTRUMENTALITIES OF A CRIME

Instrumentalities of a crime may be anything used to commit a crime. Instrumentalities may take many forms, such as body fluids, a homemade weapon, a cell phone, a threatening letter, or a recorded phone call. Often these items become evidence.

FRUITS OF A CRIME

The ***fruits of a crime*** are anything gained or obtained by committing a crime. In a correctional setting, this may often be money and canteen or commissary items. It should be noted that the person who benefits from the crime is not always the subject or suspect who committed the crime. For example, an inmate steals to pay a debt to another inmate. The fruits of a crime can also become evidence.

EVIDENCE

Know the major types of evidence found in a correctional setting

Evidence is anything that proves or disproves a fact in a judicial case or disciplinary hearing. Five types of evidence are usually found in a correctional setting: direct, circumstantial or indirect, physical, testimonial, and documentary.

- **Direct evidence** directly proves a fact without inference or assumption. For example, an officer observes a stabbing; or DNA samples connect a suspect to a crime.

- **Circumstantial or indirect evidence** is based on an inference, not on personal knowledge through observation, and is presumed to be true. For example, the inmate was searched before a visit and was searched again after an attorney visit, and a cell phone was discovered. The officer did not overhear the meeting because of the privileged communication exception; however, the officer can infer that the attorney gave the inmate the cell phone.
- **Physical evidence** refers to material objects, such as weapons, drugs, or money.
- **Testimonial evidence** is verbal evidence obtained from a witness, victim, or suspect.
- **Documentary evidence** is printed or written evidence, such as a call log, written property receipt, letter, or recording.

CHAIN OF CUSTODY

The ***chain of custody*** is documentation of every person who handled evidence, as well as when, why, and what changes, if any, were made to it. Chain of custody documentation is also issued to prove that the evidence submitted in court or at a disciplinary hearing is the same evidence that was collected at the crime scene.

Know the components of the chain of custody in a correctional setting

The responding officer must take steps to preserve the chain of custody to protect the integrity of the evidence. Items must be documented even if what is collected does not immediately appear to be relevant to the incident. Documentation can be in writing or by video, photograph, or audio. Documentation must be clear and complete for understanding and testimony by another officer or person. The components of the chain of custody for documentation or preservation are:

- Who: people involved (inmate, visitor, staff); all people who touched the evidence from the time the situation was identified
- What: all materials used and secured
- When: date and time the incident occurred and any time the evidence was handled
- Where: location from which the evidence was collected, transferred to, or stored
- Why: reason the evidence or material was handled
- How: proper methods for preservation; how evidence is collected is crucial to verifying its integrity and thus its usability in trial or hearing

Lesson Vocabulary

chain of custody

criminal act

evidence

felony

fruits of a crime

instrumentalities of a crime

misdemeanor

Review Items

1. *List the categories and classes of offenses.*
2. *List three common crimes committed in a correctional setting.*
3. *List some common crimes committed by staff or visitors.*
4. *What are the elements of a crime?*
5. *Describe the major types of evidence found in a correctional setting.*
6. *Describe the components of the chain of custody in a correctional setting.*

LESSON 6
USE OF FORCE

LESSON GOAL

You will be able to decide when and how to use force appropriately and how to avoid using excessive force.

THINK ABOUT THIS

It is sometimes difficult to know when it is appropriate to use force. Consider the following example: Officer Dalton works for the state prison system. Inmate Foster is refusing to go into his cell at lights out. Officer Dalton repeatedly asks Inmate Foster to go into his cell. Eventually, Inmate Foster begins to personally insult Officer Dalton and his family. While Inmate Foster has not made any aggressive movements, his voice is steadily rising. If you were Officer Dalton, how would you handle this situation?

LAWS FOR USE OF FORCE

Understand reasonable force and how it is applied in a correctional setting

Chapters 776 and 944, F.S., govern all use of force by a correctional officer. Officers must refer to agency policies and procedures in use of force situations. To be considered justified, the use of force must be determined to be reasonable. ***Reasonable force*** is the type and amount of force that the officer reasonably believes necessary to overcome resistance. This is based on the totality of circumstances (all the factors known at the time) and the officer's perception at the time of the event on what force is reasonably required. Resistance may take two forms: resistance to a verbal command, and physical resistance. An example of resisting a spoken command is an inmate's refusing to leave a cell after being commanded by the officer. Physical resistance may take many forms, including spitting or striking.

In *Graham v. Connor*, 490 U.S. 386 (1989), the U.S. Supreme Court held that all law enforcement use of force cases are to be judged by an objective reasonableness standard based upon the Fourth Amendment. This means that the use of force is to be judged from the perspective of what a reasonable officer would do under the same circumstances without the benefit of hindsight. The Court clearly considered that officers are often required to make split-second and sometimes deadly decisions in circumstances that are "tense, uncertain, and rapidly evolving." The Court concluded that the objective reasonableness test is not a precise or clear rule but requires careful review of the facts and circumstances of each case, including the severity of the crime, whether the suspect posed an immediate threat to the safety of officers or others, and whether the suspect was actively resisting arrest or attempting to evade arrest by flight.

The objective reasonableness test requires the officer to answer two questions about the level of force used in any situation: 1) was the action reasonable and necessary, and 2) was the amount of force applied reasonable and necessary?

Know the questions you will need to answer in any use of force situation

U.S. Supreme Court case *Hudson v. McMillan* 503 U.S. 1 (1992) established that intent determines reasonableness in use of force situations in correctional settings. The Court recognized that correctional officers have to maintain order and discipline within a correctional setting; however, officers must act in good faith, not for punishment or revenge, to raise a legal defense. Officers acting in a sadistic or malicious manner do not meet the reasonableness standard.

Know the factors used in the objective reasonableness standard for use of force

OFFICER'S DUTY TO PROTECT SELF AND OTHERS

Correctional officers owe a duty of care to inmates, staff, visitors, and the general public. Officers may be required to act in defense of others in situations where the average person has no duty to intervene. Defense of self or others could include the use of reasonably necessary physical force up to and including deadly force. Section 944.35, F.S., holds the following:

Know when correctional officers can use force

An employee of the department [Department of Corrections] is authorized to apply physical force upon an inmate only when and to the extent that it reasonably appears necessary:

- To defend himself or herself or another against such other imminent [likely to occur] use of unlawful force;
- To prevent a person from escaping from a state correctional institution when the officer reasonably believes that person is lawfully detained in such institution;
- To prevent damage to property;
- To quell [suppress] a disturbance;
- To overcome physical resistance to a lawful command; or
- To administer medical treatment only by or under the supervision of a physician or his or her designee.

STATUTORY AUTHORITY FOR THE USE OF FORCE TO PREVENT ESCAPE

Florida law provides for correctional officers to use reasonable force, including deadly force, to prevent the escape of inmates. Section 776.07, F.S., states:

> *A correctional officer or other law enforcement officer is justified in the use of force, including deadly force, which he or she reasonably believes to be necessary to prevent the escape from a penal institution of a person whom the officer reasonably believes to be lawfully detained in such institution under sentence for an offense or awaiting trial or commitment for an offense.*

This topic is also addressed in s. 944.35, F.S., for state correctional officers, and s. 944.105, F.S., for private correctional officers.

This may include escape from a correctional facility, work squad, hospital, and other areas of extended supervision. An officer must have a reasonable belief that the inmate is escaping. Though you can use deadly force by statutory authority, this does not allow you to disregard agency policies.

The amount of force used by a correctional officer must always be reasonable and justifiable.

LIABILITIES AND PENALTIES FOR EXCESSIVE USE OF FORCE

When you are justified in using reasonable force, you will be protected from prosecution. However, if the amount of force used is judged to be excessive, you may face criminal, civil, and administrative penalties. Criminal, civil, and civil rights charges may be brought at both the state and federal levels, depending on the violation. The nature of injuries will determine the level of charge.

The liabilities and penalties that are attached to the officer and agency through the use of force include:

Know the liabilities and penalties for excessive use of force

Liabilities	Type of Penalties
criminal	job loss, incarceration
civil	job loss, payment of monetary damages
civil rights	job loss, incarceration, payment of monetary damages
administrative	written reprimand, probation, suspension, job loss, revocation of certification,

Excessive use of force can also result in negative community reaction and loss of trust in the profession.

LIABILITIES AND PENALTIES FOR FAILURE TO REPORT USE OF FORCE

You must document all use of force in a timely, clear manner, following agency policies and procedures and statute. Section 944.35, F.S., imposes penalties if an officer fails to document a use of force. If you use, witness, or have reason to believe force was used, you must report the incident. A reportable incident may be as simple as a hand placed on an inmate's arm. Even if force is completely justifiable, failure to document and report the incident may lead to officer discipline.

You may be held criminally liable, such as if an inmate dies due to failure to report to the medical center, or civilly liable if you fail to perform a legal duty by inaction. Any person who coerces or threatens another person to

Know the liabilities and penalties for failure to report use of force

alter testimony or a written report where force was used commits a felony. In addition, an officer may suffer administrative discipline from their agency or the CJSTC.

Lesson Vocabulary

reasonable force

Review Items

1. *How is reasonable force used in a correctional setting?*
2. *List the questions you will have to answer in any use of force situation.*
3. *What factors are used in the objective reasonableness standard for use of force?*
4. *In what situations can correctional officers use force?*
5. *List the liabilities and penalties for excessive use of force.*
6. *List the liabilities and penalties for failure to report use of force.*

LESSON 7

CRIMINAL AND CIVIL LIABILITY

LESSON GOAL

You will make decisions and act carefully to avoid liability and its serious results.

THINK ABOUT THIS

Correctional officers may be liable for damages or injuries if they improperly perform a job task or do not perform a job task that an officer reasonably should perform. While officers are open to these kinds of consequences, there are also immunities and defenses in place to protect officers who are acting correctly in the scope of their position. This lesson will discuss the liabilities and defenses that apply to a correctional officer.

LIABILITY AND NEGLIGENCE

Understand liabilities in a correctional setting

Criminal liability is when an officer is found guilty of committing a crime. ***Civil liability*** is responsibility for a wrongful act or the failure to do an act that an officer has a duty to perform that injures another person or damages property. ***Negligence*** is failure to use due or reasonable care, in a situation where an officer has a duty to act, that results in harm to another. For example, an officer is taking a personal phone call while supervising a meal. The officer doesn't see a fight break out, and an inmate is injured. Because the officer failed the duty to act with reasonable care, the officer and their agency could be held liable for damages caused by the incident. If the officer knew or should have known that an act or failure to act could cause serious bodily injury or death, the officer may be charged with a crime due to "gross" negligence.

Know the elements of negligence

The elements of negligence are:

- a duty to act with care,
- failure to perform that duty,
- proof that the failure caused damages, and
- actual damages resulted.

You have a duty to provide care, custody, and control of inmates while on the job to the best of your ability. Providing such care should be based on training, education, and experience.

Two main categories of damages that may be awarded in a civil suit are compensatory and punitive. Compensatory damages are designed to compensate a victim for their injuries, damages, and property loss. The victim is paid for the actual loss (such as lost wages, medical expenses, and property damage.). Punitive damages are awarded as a means to deter and punish the defendant for their negligence, recklessness, malice, or deceit and to discourage others from committing the same act. Punitive damages award the victim for pain and suffering or mental anguish. Defendants may be awarded for both compensatory and punitive damages.

Know the two main categories of damages that may be awarded in a civil lawsuit

CIVIL RIGHTS VIOLATIONS

A ***civil rights violation*** is an unlawful interference with the fundamental rights of another person, such as the right to due process and equal protection under the law. An example of a possible civil rights violation would be if officers refused to provide something to drink for a week to an inmate in solitary confinement. This may be seen as cruel and unusual punishment, and such an act intentionally deprives the person of a constitutional or other civil right. Federal law, 18 U.S.C. s. 242, prohibits an officer acting under color of law from violating an inmate's civil rights. When an officer acts or claims to act in performing official duties under any law, ordinance, or regulation, the officer is acting under ***color of law***.

An officer's use of force is often the basis for civil rights liability. For example, an inmate's death due to a beating by an officer can result in civil rights violations and a federal criminal investigation under this law.

In addition to criminal prosecution, an officer who violates an individual's civil rights may be sued in federal court under 42 U.S.C. s. 1983. Before imposing liability, the law requires proof that the officer acted under the authority of the employing agency and intentionally violated the inmate's civil rights.

Understand civil liability under federal laws

The penalties from being found civilly or criminally liable may include administrative discipline, suspension from work, loss of certification and employment, and incarceration.

Know the consequences if you are found civilly or criminally liable

An employing agency can be held liable for the wrongful acts of an employee. If a judge or jury decided that the officer committed a civil wrong or violated civil rights as part of their duties, the employing agency is likely to be liable for damages through direct or vicarious liability. Direct liability here refers to an employing agency's negligent hiring, assignment, training, or retention of a problem employee. Vicarious liability refers to an agency's being found liable even if it is not directly responsible for the injury. For example, an agency may be required to pay damages if an officer is found guilty of sexual harassment.

Understand that your agency may be liable for your acts as a correctional officer

IMMUNITIES

Federal and state laws protect officers acting within the scope of their employment against civil and criminal liability.

Know the legal protections available if you are faced with a potential civil or criminal liability

CHAPTER 111, F.S.

Chapter 111, F.S., protects officers charged with civil and criminal actions if those actions occurred within the scope and course of the officer's employment. ***Acting within the scope of employment*** refers to the range of reasonable and foreseeable activities that an officer does while carrying out the agency's business. If an officer acts outside the scope of employment, they may be held individually liable. An officer that intentionally violates agency policies and procedures may be regarded as acting outside the scope of employment. But if it is shown that the officer was acting within the scope of employment, the officer will not be held civilly or criminally responsible.

SOVEREIGN IMMUNITY

Know the effect of the sovereign immunity law, s. 768.28, F.S., in state civil actions

The ***sovereign immunity*** law, s. 768.28, F.S., provides one of the most important protections for state and county correctional agencies and their employees. It includes a list of circumstances and requirements that must be met before the agency or any of its employees can be sued in a state civil action. It also protects individual officers and agency employees from personal liability and from being named as a defendant in a state lawsuit. This means that unless an officer or employee fails to act or acts with willful or wanton disregard of someone's rights or property, the officer will not be held liable or named as the defendant.

QUALIFIED IMMUNITY

Understand the concept of qualified immunity

Qualified immunity protects the officer from personal liability. Agencies may pay for compensatory damages up to a certain amount. The defense of ***qualified immunity*** protects "government officials . . . from liability for civil damages insofar as their conduct does not violate clearly established statutory or constitutional rights of which a reasonable person would have known." See *Harlow v. Fitzgerald,* 457 U.S. 800, 818 (1982).

LEGAL DEFENSES

Know the legal defenses that protect you from civil and criminal liability

A number of established defenses are available for an officer to defend against civil or criminal liability.

ACTS DONE IN GOOD FAITH

To act in good faith, officers must be faithful to their duty and honestly intend to avoid taking undue advantage of others. Acts done in good faith are without malice, ill will, or the intent to unjustly harm anyone.

If you perform your duties correctly, you act in good faith; for example, accidentally giving the wrong snack bag to the wrong inmate. You followed agency policy and performed the appropriate distribution; however, the bag was assigned in such a way as to be confusing.

ACTS DONE IN A REASONABLE MANNER

Officers must act in a reasonable manner when responding to any incident. Reasonableness involves acting professionally within the law and agency policies and procedures. It can range from performing first aid to knowing what level of force is needed in a given situation. Reasonableness is judged objectively. For example, would a reasonable officer in the same situation have acted the same way?

ACTS JUSTIFIED UNDER THE LAW

Some seemingly offensive officer actions can be justified under the law. This occurs in situations in which case law or statutory law provides a defense for an officer's actions. For example, chapter 776, F.S., states that an officer may use deadly force in self-defense or defense of another from a threat of death or serious physical injury and to prevent escape; chapter 870, F.S., provides for the use of force in riots.

EMERGENCY DOCTRINE

When an emergency requires spontaneous action, an officer is not required to use the same degree of judgment and care as acting under non-emergency conditions. This is known as the emergency doctrine. An incident requiring an immediate life-or-death decision resulting in the violation of agency policy to protect others from harm or death falls under this doctrine; for example, a facility fire.

LIMITING LIABILITY

Correctional agencies enact policies and procedures to help guide officers in performing their duties. These policies are carefully developed to ensure they comply with legal and ethical guidelines. Agency policies and procedures are developed and published for the officer's benefit. By following such policies, you may avoid liability for acts committed while on duty.

Attending required and optional training lets you stay current on the law and up-to-date practices. Awareness of changes in legal and practice guidelines also helps you avoid liability.

LESSON VOCABULARY

acting within the scope of employment

civil liability

civil rights violation

color of law

criminal liability

negligence

qualified immunity

sovereign immunity

Review Items

1. *What are the liabilities that correctional officers need to be aware of in performing their duties?*
2. *List the elements of negligence.*
3. *Name the two main categories of damages that may be awarded in a civil case.*
4. *What are some of the consequences if a correctional officer is found civilly or criminally liable?*
5. *How can your agency be liable for your actions?*
6. *What are your protections from potential civil or criminal liabilities?*
7. *What is sovereign immunity, and how does it relate to corrections?*
8. *Explain qualified immunity.*
9. *What are your legal defenses from potential civil or criminal liabilities?*

COMMUNICATIONS

Unit 1 Interpersonal Communication

Lesson 1

Interpersonal Communication

Lesson Goal

You will be able to use communication skills with inmates and others.

Think About This

In a world filled with technology, many people communicate by texting or using social media. Communicating by text or social media can reduce face-to-face communication. As a correctional officer, you will be required to communicate face to face with inmates and others every day. This lesson will help you develop your interpersonal communication skills.

An important part of a correctional officer's job is to communicate with and manage a diverse correctional facility population. To achieve this, correctional officers use a variety of skills that include interpersonal verbal and non-verbal communication, situational awareness, verbal command, command presence, and courtesy. These skills not only demonstrate professionalism but also help create effective interpersonal relationships and reduce tension. For example, if an inmate is acting out, communicating properly with the inmate could de-escalate the situation.

Understand the concept of interpersonal communication

Interpersonal communication involves the exchange of ideas, messages, or information between two or more people through speaking, writing, or body language. Communication should be clear and prompt a response or change in behavior.

> Mastering the basic skills of effective communication is a necessity for navigating your daily job tasks.

Know the elements of effective communication

Plan your interactions by following these basic elements of communication:

- consider what you want to say and construct the message in your head
- convey the message via verbal, non-verbal, telecommunication, or written format to the person or group to whom it is intended

- allow time for the person or group to receive and understand the message
- gauge whether you have received an appropriate response or change in behavior from the person or group you addressed

As you gain experience and consistently practice effective interpersonal communication, you should continually improve your verbal and non-verbal skills.

NON-VERBAL COMMUNICATION

Non-verbal communication is a very important form of communication. When officers interact with inmates, visitors, and staff, they give and receive countless non-verbal signals. These behaviors may send strong messages and can include gestures, facial expressions, eye contact, and posture.

Know how to recognize the signals of non-verbal communication when interacting with others

You may sometimes notice that an inmate's verbal expressions don't align with their facial expression, posture, or other body language. For example, the following inmate's verbal and non-verbal responses illustrate inconsistencies:

> An inmate's verbal response to an officer: "I don't have a problem."
>
> The inmate's non-verbal behavior to the officer: Avoids eye contact, looks anxious, and paces up and down with clenched fists.

The inmate shows anger with non-verbal communication but not with their verbal communication.

Body language or non-verbal cues can help you analyze an inmate's responses. Watching for inconsistencies between non-verbal and verbal communication can help keep you safe.

Know how to analyze an inmate's non-verbal cues and provide an appropriate response

Some examples of non-verbal communication include the following:

- Sweating, rapid breathing, fidgeting, blinking, or rocking back and forth may indicate nervousness.
- Clenched fists, pacing briskly, clenched teeth, or a clear reluctance to communicate may indicate anger, rage, or irritation.
- Arms down by the side or comfortably placed in the lap may indicate friendliness or being at ease.
- Crossed arms and legs may indicate the person is closed off or resistant.
- Avoiding eye contact may indicate the person is shy, uneasy, shameful, fearful, deceptive, guilty, or experiencing strong emotion.
- Direct eye contact may indicate the person is being truthful or challenging.
- Frowning may indicate uneasiness or confusion, as well as displeasure.
- Smiling may indicate a failure to understand, as well as pleasure.
- Lack of obvious emotion may indicate shock, fear, poor understanding, not being focused, or not hearing.

> Interpreting an inmate's non-verbal behavior keeps an officer alert to signs of stress, deception, or aggression.

You should be mentally and physically prepared to take immediate action if a threatening physical situation occurs.

BARRIERS TO EFFECTIVE COMMUNICATION

Know the barriers to effective communication

Communication between an officer and inmates or others is effective and successful when actual and potential barriers are recognized and addressed. The following barriers may result in miscommunication:

- use of profane, derogatory, or disrespectful language
- stereotyping
- use of derogatory hand gestures or body movements
- stress and fatigue on the part of either person or group
- inability to communicate in the same language
- lack of cultural understanding
- failure to listen actively
- use of jargon
- tone of voice
- negative attitude
- environmental distractions, such as background noise

DIVERSITY OF POPULATION

Know how to interact with inmates in a diverse environment, applying officer safety

When you enter a jail or prison, you encounter an environment that includes many different people and personalities. Do not assume that you can communicate effectively with all inmates and staff using the same methods. For instance, some gestures may have different cultural or social meanings to different people or groups. Examples of this include lack of eye contact, shaking hands, bowing, hand gestures, and use of personal space.

Do not allow racial stereotypes to influence how you communicate with an inmate. Also, do not assume an inmate's racial identity based on physical appearance alone. The division of races is more subjective now than in the past, as the population of multiracial people is increasing.

Younger inmates may be more impressionable than older inmates. Be a role model and demonstrate professional behavior by being patient, firm, and fair, even if a young inmate pushes your limits and challenges your authority. Provide clear, consistent instructions and consequences.

Older inmates experience normal physical and psychological aging changes (loss of memory, impairment of judgment, sensitivity to touch, and decrease in mobility and in cognitive ability). They also have more medical issues (hearing, vision, and other physical and mental limitations) than younger inmates. An older person with mental decline may not be able to follow more than one- or two-step directions. They will probably need more time and help to do things. Keep this in mind when managing and interacting with older inmates.

When dealing with inmates of the opposite sex, take extra precautions to avoid an appearance of impropriety. For example, avoid spending too much time being overly friendly or becoming too familiar with inmates of the opposite sex. Take steps to keep conversations as neutral as possible. Even the perception of favoritism can damage your professional reputation.

Always strive to interact respectfully. As a professional representing your agency, avoid negative interactions with inmates and staff based on their diversities. By understanding diverse populations, you will be able to communicate with others more effectively.

COMMAND PRESENCE

Know how to communicate using command presence and verbal command

Just as an officer watches inmates for non-verbal messages and behavior, an officer should also use non-verbal techniques, such as positioning and posture, to communicate to inmates. When approaching an inmate, keep yourself at a safe distance, yet close enough to see and hear. Face the inmate directly and look them in the eye. This conveys that you are focused, attentive, and in charge. Stand upright, eliminate distracting behaviors, and lean slightly forward. Sometimes called ***command presence***, this body language projects confidence, poise, and a professional demeanor. Command presence also involves personal grooming and keeping a clean, neat uniform. The following example is a situation in which an officer uses command presence:

> Inmates Jones and Baldwin are arguing in the C-dorm.
>
> An officer walks in and looks sternly at the two inmates without saying a word. After seeing the officer, both inmates immediately stop arguing and separate.

Learn to use direct verbal commands to communicate desired actions or behavior to inmates. A ***verbal command*** is an authoritative statement used to direct, influence, or give orders to a person or group. You will often issue verbal commands to inmates to clearly indicate what is required. Be specific when you give directions.

Examples of verbal commands include the following:

> "Mop the floor."
>
> "Move back to your bunks."
>
> "Clean your cell before breakfast."

While using command presence sets a professional tone, do not abuse your authority or bully anyone. A show of force is not always the best response. Always treat inmates as you would anyone else. Just because inmates are confined does not mean they should be treated with disrespect.

COURTESY

Understand how courtesy impacts your behavior and interaction with inmates and others

Courtesy is being respectful when interacting with others and treating them in a dignified manner, regardless of their status, race, gender, appearance, or behavior. If you regularly address inmates with contempt or disregard, you're likely to develop hostile relationships. If you routinely express professionalism and respect for others, then respectful, professional relationships are more likely to develop. Maintaining a professional and courteous relationship is important, because this may help you avoid or de-escalate potentially violent situations.

ACTIVE LISTENING

Understand how active listening is used in effective communication

You should never allow personal judgment or bias to obscure your ability to listen. ***Active listening*** requires giving full attention to what is being said and taking time to understand the message without interrupting. Good listening skills require a great deal of practice and are essential for effective communication.

Know the elements of active listening

The elements of active listening include the following:

- maintaining eye contact, facing the speaker, and leaning slightly forward
- keeping an open mind and avoiding bias to hear all the facts
- identifying key words that should alert you, such as "kill," "suicide," "getting out," and "hang"
- identifying the intensity of speech in terms of voice volume, emotion, pitch, and tone
- paraphrasing back to someone what they said to ensure you properly understood the message
- asking questions for clarification or more information

Taking the time to listen carefully by rephrasing back to an inmate and clarifying their statements let them know that you heard their concerns. This can encourage them to talk more freely, allowing you to gather information.

Active listening can also be a way to help an inmate release frustrations. Become familiar with the behavioral patterns of the inmates you manage. Consider the speaker and try to determine if the statements the person expresses are typical of that person, or if something unusual may be going on. Being on your guard to subtle differences that could be indicators of potential conflict may help you anticipate ways to prevent or manage such situations. The ability to listen carefully is critical to your well-being.

Lesson Vocabulary

active listening

command presence

courtesy

interpersonal communication

verbal command

Review Items

1. *In your own words, define interpersonal communication.*
2. *List the basic elements of communication.*
3. *Recall five examples of non-verbal communication.*
4. *List the non-verbal behaviors that send a strong message when interacting with others.*
5. *Explain how barriers to communication can result in miscommunication.*
6. *Describe methods to use when interacting with a diverse population of inmates.*
7. *Identify three examples of when you would use command presence.*
8. *In your own words, define courtesy.*
9. *Explain the requirement of active listening.*
10. *List the elements of active listening.*

UNIT 2 RADIO COMMUNICATIONS

LESSON 1

RADIO PROCEDURES

LESSON GOAL

You will be able to use a radio to communicate effectively with other officers.

THINK ABOUT THIS

Officer Perkins used his radio to communicate with other officers concerning an emergency incident in the recreation area. Since Officer Reynolds was close to the incident, he was able to respond quickly. Can you imagine what could have happened if Officer Reynolds experienced difficulty with the radio transmission?

RADIO USE

Follow the guidelines for using a radio

Officers use radios to send and receive vital information. Some examples of radio use include calling for assistance, participating in general communication, identifying inmates and visitors, or notifying staff of an emergency situation.

Proper knowledge and use of the radio is essential for a correctional officer. Once you are issued a radio, it is your responsibility to ensure that it is operational. If you experience radio transmission difficulties, immediately use a land-line telephone to report the malfunction. You should know your agency's operating procedures, general orders, or policy on what to do if an assigned radio malfunctions.

The portable radio is the primary method of communication for correctional officers. The Federal Communications Commission (FCC) prohibits everyone using radios from:

- transmitting non-essential or excessive signals, messages, or communication
- using profane, indecent, or obscene language
- willfully damaging or permitting damage to radio apparatuses
- maliciously interfering with another unit's radio transmission
- making unidentified transmissions
- transmitting before the air is clear
- transmitting a call signal, letter, or numeral not assigned to the agency or unit

- adjusting, repairing, or altering a radio transmitter (except by agency-authorized radio technicians)
- using radio communications systems for illegal or personal business

When using the portable radio system, plan your message before transmission. The more you plan a message, the more coherent and professional the communication is. Adjust the volume level based on the situation and surroundings.

In stressful situations, an officer's voice may crack or become distorted or high-pitched, making the radio message difficult to understand. Officers must be proficient on the radio, speaking slowly and distinctly, using an evenly controlled tone of voice and avoiding the display of emotions.

Before transmitting, you should listen to make sure there is no other radio traffic. Depress and hold the transmit button for about one second before speaking. Make sure your mouth is 1 to 3 inches away from the microphone, and speak directly into it.

TYPES OF RADIO EQUIPMENT IN CORRECTIONS

Radio communications in corrections generally rely on three types of radios:

- the handheld or portable radio, which the officer carries
- the radio base station, normally located in the control room
- the mobile radio affixed in vehicles used for transporting inmates

PRIMARY COMPONENTS OF A PORTABLE RADIO

There are many brands, models, and types of radios. The basic corrections radio is generally fitted with switches or buttons to control power, volume, squelch, and channel selection. ***Squelch*** is a circuit that suppresses the output of a radio receiver if the signal strength falls below a certain level.

The portable radio unit may have an extended or built-in microphone. Agencies will train officers on the specific components and usage of a portable radio.

RADIO CODES

Understand the purpose and types of radio codes that you may be required to use

Transmitting radio messages in plain English is becoming the preferred method of communication in many correctional agencies. Plain English transmission is especially ideal during emergency situations, due to inter-agency involvement and coordination.

Some agencies, however, use correctional radio signals and codes. These save airtime and convey precise meanings. Types of radio codes include:

- signals—a system of communication using numbers that are preceded by the word "signal"
- phonetic-alphabet—a system of verbal communication using the letters of the English alphabet only

- 10 or numeric codes—a system of communication by which "10" precedes numbers that stand for specific activities
- numeric-alpha codes—a system of communication that combines numbers and letters of the alphabet, or the combination of some or all of the above to transmit messages

Refer to your agency policy concerning appropriate radio language and training.

RADIO BASE STATION

Understand the purpose of a radio base station

Even though radio base stations are not found in all correctional facilities, they are typically associated with correctional control room operations or the command center in case of an emergency. The radio base station operators send and receive messages to and from officers. These operators monitor radio frequencies for all operational units and also have the ability to override the portable radio system in an emergency. While receiving and sending messages, a radio base station operator will continue to coordinate the up-to-the-minute statuses of all units.

LESSON VOCABULARY

squelch

REVIEW ITEMS

1. *What are the FCC's guidelines?*
2. *List and describe the four types of radio codes.*
3. *Explain the purpose of a radio base station.*

UNIT 3 INTERVIEWING

LESSON 1

PREPARING FOR AND CONDUCTING AN INTERVIEW

LESSON GOAL

You will be able to interview inmates and visitors to obtain important information.

THINK ABOUT THIS

Have you ever been interviewed by someone? If so, do you remember what it was like? Were you nervous? Did you feel prepared? Consider these things when you conduct interviews. Be prepared before conducting an interview to allow for a smooth process. The interviewee may be nervous or unwilling to answer questions; however, you will learn questioning strategies to ensure an effective interview.

Know the goal of an interview

An ***interview*** is a conversation between a correctional officer and an interviewee (inmate, visitor) with the goal of obtaining factual information. An interview can use informal questions or more formal questions, such as in an interrogation.

After collecting such information, you are usually not required to take any action. If, however, it is determined in an interview that a crime has occurred, you must follow agency policies and procedures.

PURPOSE OF INTERVIEWING

Understand the purpose of an interview

Correctional officers need effective interviewing skills. These skills are used routinely in the officer's daily formal and informal interactions with others. An interview may be used for conducting investigations, obtaining facts for incident reports, and documenting routine activities, disciplinary actions, and use of force occurrences.

FACTORS THAT INFLUENCE THE SUCCESS OF AN INTERVIEW

Know when to conduct an interview

An officer responding to an incident should conduct questioning as soon as possible after securing the well-being of others and the officer's own safety. The daily operations of a correctional facility can affect or determine when questioning can happen. Always follow agency policies and procedures when questioning people after an incident.

OBTAINING INFORMATION

The location of the interview may be critical to obtain the necessary information. Before conducting an interview, remove the interviewee from the scene of the incident. Keep all people involved in the incident separate to discourage them from discussing or rehearsing their stories and to avoid potential intimidation.

If an interviewee has an autism spectrum disorder, follow agency policy when interviewing. An interviewee with an autism spectrum disorder has the right, upon request or the request of their parent or guardian, to have a mental health or other related professional present at all interviews. If this request is made, you must make a good faith effort to ensure that such a professional is present.

Ask non-threatening questions. If the interviewee feels threatened, they may be less likely to provide the necessary relevant information. You must also make sure that the interviewee understands what is being asked. Be alert and safety conscious and be careful to strictly abide by agency policies and procedures at all times.

EFFECTIVE QUESTIONING

Know the basic questioning techniques to use while conducting an interview

When interviewing, take care to obtain as much information as possible about the event.

Use questioning to obtain the facts of the event in the interviewee's own words. Types of questions to ask during an interview may include open-ended, closed-ended, leading, direct, and forced-choice questions. The table on the next page explains and provides examples of these techniques.

Using multiple questioning techniques in an interview may help you obtain additional information.

Convey professionalism, understanding, and genuine concern when asking questions. Avoid judging the interviewee's words, actions, or responses, and do not express doubt, anger, shock, disgust, or skepticism.

At the end of the interview, evaluate the obtained information for completeness. Ask the interviewee if they have anything more to say about the event. If the who, what, where, when, why, and how have been answered, then the interview has most likely been successful.

Questioning Techniques	Explanation	Example
open-ended questions	Encourage conversation and require the interviewee to think, reflect, and provide their opinions and feelings. Never suggest a conclusion or supply information to fill gaps. The interviewee is likely to answer open-ended questions with more detail.	"What happened next?"
closed-ended questions	Ask with a specific yes or no answer in mind.	"Have you read your rules and regulations?" Answer: "Yes" or "No"
leading questions	Avoid because they are framed in such a way as to produce a specific response from the person being questioned. The questioner uses language that suggests a particular answer.	"You removed the packet of candy from the canteen?"
direct questions	Combine closed-ended and leading questions.	"Did you take the inmate's shoes?"
forced-choice questions	Ask to obtain a precise answer to an important fit or preference question by defining the range in which answers can be given. This format requires the questioner to rank a series of possible responses, often in order of desirability, to provide the interviewee with specific insight into the questioner's expectations.	Example: "How many inmates were present when you hit Inmate Jones on the head?" 0–3 inmates 4–6 inmates 7–9 inmates 10+ inmates

OBTAINING A STATEMENT FROM THE INTERVIEWEE

Know how to obtain a statement

A ***statement*** is a permanent oral or written record of a person's account of an incident or occurrence, which may or may not be made under oath. Statements may be obtained as part of questioning for criminal or certain non-criminal incidents.

An officer may obtain a statement by having the interviewee write their account of the event. A written statement should be in the interviewee's own words and not dictated by the interviewer. If an interpreter is used, the interpreter should state exactly what the interviewee said. Instruct the interviewee to provide as much detail as possible in the statement. Review the statement to make sure it relates to the event.

SIGNS OF DECEPTION DURING QUESTIONING

Know how to recognize the common signs of deception during questioning

Be alert to common signs of deception during questioning. How the interviewee acts or reacts to a question may suggest deception. When used along with various interviewing techniques, verbal and non-verbal cues are essential in detecting deception.

Physical signs of deception may include increased perspiration, flushed or pale skin, dry mouth, and an increased pulse rate or observable change in breathing rate.

Behavioral signs of deception may include nervous movements, voice inflections, avoidance of eye contact, rehearsed answers, inconsistent responses, overeagerness to help, and repeated insistence that simple questions are not understood.

LESSON VOCABULARY

interview

statement

REVIEW ITEMS

1. *Describe the goal of an interview.*
2. *Describe the purpose of an interview.*
3. *Explain how you know when to conduct an interview.*
4. *List and explain the five effective questioning techniques.*
5. *List the important points to remember when obtaining a statement.*
6. *What are common signs of deception during an interview?*

UNIT 4 REPORT WRITING

LESSON 1

REPORT CONSIDERATIONS AND FOLLOWING-UP

LESSON GOAL

You will be able to recognize the type of report to create and the basic information to include.

THINK ABOUT THIS

Officer Lee witnessed a fight between two inmates in a cell. After the fight ended, Officer Lee prepared an incident report. He included his name, the names of the inmates involved, and the date and time that the fight happened. What other information should he include in the report?

REPORTS

Understand the importance of preparing reports

Report writing makes up a large share of the daily duties of a correctional officer. A ***report*** is a written account that communicates all available facts of an incident, situation, person, or event encountered by the correctional officer in a correctional setting. Reports are important because they record what an officer observes and knows; this information can be critical to the well-being of an inmate or officer. Reports are also used for legal cases, investigations, and discipline.

Even many years later, the information contained in a report can be used to prosecute an inmate or subject, shed light on an incident, or protect an officer from liability.

This means that providing careful, detailed, and timely reports is an essential part of a correctional officer's responsibilities.

Understand why you should prepare reports with care and truthfulness

Once a report is written, submitted, and approved, it becomes a permanent public record. It can be read by other officers, supervisors, attorneys, judges, victims, the media, and members of the public. It can end up on the desks of legislators or the governor, or quoted in newspaper articles. Because every report has the potential to be widely distributed, you must prepare your reports with care and truthfulness.

TYPES OF REPORTS

Each agency creates its own report forms to document its administrative and operational responsibilities. Some of the commonly used report forms and logs in a correctional facility include:

Know the common types of reports that you will prepare

Incident Report—used in many correctional facilities to report in detail any incidents involving inmates.

Corrective Consultation (CC) Form—used for minor disciplinary violations to report in detail the counseling and corrective actions taken.

Disciplinary Report (DR)—provides a detailed account of the facts surrounding an inmate's rule violation. This report sets in motion a series of events that make sure that the inmate receives due process.

Use of Force Report—completed any time force is used and is attached to an Incident or Disciplinary Report.

Counts Form—used to record inmate counts as required by the Florida Statutes.

Special Watch Form—used to record activities of inmates under any type of special watch, such as suicide watch, 15-minute watch, and direct observation.

Equipment Check Form—used to record the location of all equipment at each post.

ACTIVITIES THAT MAY NEED TO BE DOCUMENTED

Officers should have basic computer skills and apply agency policies and procedures regarding the use of computers when writing reports.

Know the types of activities to include in reports

Some activities that you may need to document include:

- identifying inmates, staff, and visitors
- searches (person—inmate, staff, visitor; cell; vehicle; and area)
- inmate counts (work groups and their locations)
- inmate movement
- all safety and security checks and breaches
- all crimes committed and disciplinary actions taken
- inmate visitation
- inmate counseling
- confiscation and disposal of contraband
- inventory of equipment and supplies issued to, and received from, inmates
- inventory of officer's equipment (flashlights, fire extinguishers, and so on)
- all investigations
- all emergencies, incidents, and unusual occurrences

In addition, at the start of each shift, agencies require correctional officers to start a log, which is a chronological timeline of activities performed during that shift.

WHAT SHOULD REPORTS CONTAIN?

The information you include in a report depends on the type of report you are preparing. In the event of an incident, the officer at the scene prepares the report. Certain incidents, such as use of force, may require additional documentation. Be familiar with and follow agency policies and procedures regarding the different types of forms to use for different reports. You should also know the required content and review requirements, and you should know how to store reports.

At a minimum, a report should answer who, what, where, when, how, and why, and state what follow-up action was taken:

Who:

- was involved (name, title and / or identification of persons / inmates)
- are the victims, the witnesses, the suspects
- reported it
- is the reporting officer

What:

- happened (report this chronologically)
- activity, rule violations, or crimes, if any, were committed
- action was taken
- items were lost, damaged, recovered, or stolen
- weapons or tools were used or recovered
- evidence was collected

Know the specific rule, activity, or law violation committed when writing reports

Where:

- did the incident occur (note the exact physical location)
- were all involved persons and officers at the time of incident

When:

- did the incident occur (use date and time, or approximate time)
- did the officer arrive at the scene of the incident

How:

- did the incident start

- did the incident progress
- was the incident reported

Through observation, an officer can often determine how something happened.

Why:

- did the incident happen

Attempt to verify reasons for the incident and the facts submitted in the interviewee's statement.

Follow-up action may include:

Know the follow-up actions you may be required to perform

- administration of first aid to the sick or injured
- arrangement of transportation for the sick or injured to a clinic, health center, or hospital
- notification to the supervisor or designated person of the incident, activity, or occurrence
- the method of collection and disposition of evidence
- a housing decision regarding inmates involved pending a hearing
- the escort or transportation of the inmates involved
- other follow-up activities

Lesson Vocabulary

report

Review Items

1. *In your own words, describe the importance of preparing reports.*
2. *Explain why you should prepare reports with care and integrity.*
3. *What are the common types of reports that you will prepare?*
4. *List some of the types of activities to include in reports.*
5. *Describe the elements that should be included in a narrative report.*
6. *List four follow-up actions that you may be required to perform.*

LESSON 2

PREPARING TO WRITE

LESSON GOAL

You will be able to gather, organize, and review facts before writing a report.

THINK ABOUT THIS

Recall from the previous lesson our discussion about the fight that Officer Lee witnessed. Officer Lee decided not to immediately write down any details from the incident, because he thought he had a good memory. When he had the opportunity to sit down and prepare his report, he could not remember all of the details that were necessary to include in the report. What should he have done differently?

Incidents in a correctional facility are primarily documented in a narrative format. This means written in paragraph form including the specific details and pertinent information. The officer collects information from victims, witnesses, possible suspects, and other sources. Relevant facts must be then organized to make sure a report reflects the recorded incident accurately.

BASIC STEPS TO PREPARE A REPORT

There are five basic steps to follow when writing a corrections report:

Follow the basic steps to prepare a report

1. Gather information.
2. Record facts.
3. Organize facts.
4. Write the report.
5. Evaluate the report.

NOTE-TAKING

Before you begin writing a report, gather the information relevant to the incident or event. This may require interviewing the people involved or collecting background details and facts that set the context for the incident.

Understand how note-taking is used when preparing a report

The second step to preparing a report is to record this information in the form of notes. ***Note-taking*** consists of writing down brief observations or, if it is an interview, quotes from people involved. Taking notes is a way to make sure that pertinent information is recorded, as it is difficult to rely on memory alone to recall all the details of an incident or event. Use note-taking to provide detailed documentation for writing a report, information for further investigation, and, in some cases, as evidence in court.

The following list of important rules will help you take the best notes:

- Use a notebook (not loose pieces of paper) to record notes.
- Write legibly and in ink.
- Identify notes by date.
- Record all relevant facts as soon as possible.
- Check spelling and numbers (inmate name, cell, or bunk number).
- Use only common abbreviations.

Types of critical, basic information that you should record in your notes include:

Know the types of critical information to record when taking notes

- Who—names of victims, witnesses, suspects
- What—details of the incident such as illnesses, injuries, and behavioral descriptions of persons involved
- Where—location of the incident
- When—date and time the incident occurred or timeline of events
- How—means by which the incident occurred
- Why—reasons or causes of the incident
- Action taken—steps taken to resolve the incident, such as disposition, confinement, medical treatment, or verbal reprimand

ORGANIZE AND REVIEW FACTS

The third step in writing a report is organizing all the information in your notes that you have gathered and recorded about the incident. Generally, there are two ways to organize facts for report writing that work together to present a complete account: chronologically and categorically.

Know how to organize facts

Arranging information ***chronologically*** is the grouping of recorded information by date and time of occurrence. This method of grouping information is especially useful when writing a narrative report, as readers can easily tell what happened and in what order.

Sorting information ***categorically*** is the grouping of recorded information into types of collection sources, such as informants, victims, witnesses, suspects, weapons, rule violations, evidence, and crime elements. This is especially helpful when an officer collects information from several sources.

Remember that the report reader needs to understand what happened when and who was involved. If you don't provide this information, your supervisor or reader will not have a complete picture of the incident, understand the purpose of the report, or grasp what you are trying to convey.

Once you have organized the information and selected the relevant forms and format, you are ready to write the report. Review the organized information regarding the incident to make sure that you have collected all the facts. If pertinent facts are missing—for example, an inmate's cell number, or time of incident—collect the additional information.

Understand the importance of reviewing facts before writing a report

Lesson Vocabulary

categorically

chronologically

note-taking

Review Items

1. *Recall the five basic steps to prepare a report.*
2. *Explain the purpose of note-taking.*
3. *Explain the critical information that should be included in your notes.*
4. *Explain the difference between organizing facts chronologically and sorting information categorically.*
5. *Why is it important to review facts before you write a report?*

UNIT 4 REPORT WRITING

LESSON 3

MECHANICS

LESSON GOAL

You will be able to use proper grammar and sentence structure to write a report.

THINK ABOUT THIS

Officer Lee wrote the incident report, and this was the first sentence in the report: "I had seen them Inmates fighting at approximately roun too o'clock." What's wrong with this sentence? How can this sentence be written free of mechanical errors?

The content of a report is often seen as the most important element of a report. However, grammar, punctuation, and spelling are equally important elements of a quality report. Mechanical errors will distract from the message, may change the meaning of a sentence, and reflect poorly on the writer's competence and professionalism. An effective, well-written report should be free of errors in sentence structure, grammar, and other writing mechanics.

STANDARD VS. NON-STANDARD ENGLISH

Understand the difference between standard and non-standard English

Standard English refers to language that is well established in the speech and writing of the educated and that is accepted wherever English is spoken and understood. Non-standard English is more casual or regional, may involve slang, and may not follow recognized grammatical rules or spelling. You should always prepare reports using Standard English.

PROPER GRAMMAR

Grammar involves the rules and guidelines that govern a language's usage and make it possible for users to have the same understandings of its sounds and symbols. Be conscious of grammatical rules when writing reports. Recognizing the parts of speech and using them properly makes for streamlined and effective reports.

Part of Speech	Description	Example
noun	name of a person, place, or thing—inmate, cellblock, handcuff, officer	**Officer Andrew** responded to the **disturbance** in the **dormitory**.
verb	describes action or state of being—ran, walked, ordered, appeared, seemed	The fire **started** in the laundry room.
pronoun	a substitute for a noun—I, me, she, her, he, him, it, you, they, them	The inmate said **she** was not coming out of **her** cell.
adjective	describes a noun or pronoun—large, dangerous, blue, burly	The officer tried talking to the **upset** inmate.
adverb	describes, identifies, or quantifies a verb, adjective, or another adverb—easily, warmly, quickly, mainly, freely, often	Backup officers arrived **quickly** to assist with the situation.
preposition	shows how something is related to another word or phrase and shows space, time, or logical relationship of an object to the rest of the sentence—above, near, at, by, after, with, from	The fire started **in** the garbage can **near** the door.
conjunction	word that joins other words, phrases, clauses or sentences—and, as, since, but, or, because, so, until, while	The officer did not go to work today, **because** he was needed in court.

PROPER SENTENCE STRUCTURE

A ***sentence*** is a group of words that contains a subject (a noun or pronoun), a verb (action), and usually an object (a noun or pronoun that is affected or receives action) and that expresses a complete thought. The subject and verb in each sentence must agree in number. A singular subject must have a singular verb, and a plural subject must have a plural verb.

> **Example:** "They are brothers" is correct since the subject, *they*, and the verb, *are*, are plural.
>
> "They is brothers" is incorrect because the singular verb, *is*, does not agree with the plural subject, *they*.

Use correct verb tense.

> **Example:** Since officers write reports in the past tense, they should write, "And then, I saw the subject," not "And then, I see the subject," or "And then, I seen the subject."

Understand the importance of applying proper sentence structure when writing a report

Understanding the parts that make up a simple sentence will help you write proper sentences. The subject of a sentence tells what or who performs an action; the verb states the action, existence, or state of being of the subject. The object indicates what or who is affected or receives the action of the verb.

John	hit	Monica.
subject	*verb*	*object*

A ***sentence fragment*** is a group of words that lacks a subject or verb or fails to express a complete thought.

Avoid fragments such as "Witnessed a fight on the rec yard." Because the sentence has no subject, it is unclear who witnessed the fight.

"The knife on the floor next to the body" should be "The knife was lying on the floor next to the body," or "I saw the knife lying on the floor next to the body."

Incorrect grammar and sentence structure can damage your credibility by affecting the accuracy and readability of your report.

CORRECT SPELLING AND CAPITALIZATION

Use proper spelling and capitalization rules when writing a report

Spell words correctly in your reports. If you are using a computer to write a report, be sure to use the spellcheck feature. Remember, though, that spellcheck does not always know whether you have used the correct word, only if you have misspelled the word.

Example: "The thief took there money" may not be flagged by spellcheck.

Have another person proofread your report to help ensure that you use the correct words. If you are unsure of the spelling of a word, consider using a different word.

Example: Instead of "penitentiary," an officer might use "prison." Instead of "contusion," the officer could use "bruise."

You can also use a dictionary to check your spelling when writing a report by hand. The following table lists the correct spelling of some commonly misspelled words.

Commonly Misspelled Words				
absence	approximately	delinquent	negligence	sheriff
accessory	argument	deposition	occasionally	statute
accident	barbiturate	disciplinary	occurred	surveillance
accomplice	colonel	en route	omitted	suspicious
acquittal	committed	grievance	possession	trial
aggravate	conscious	incoherent	receive	unconscious
alleged	conspicuous	license	seize	unnecessary
amphetamine	contraband	lieutenant	separate	vicious
apprehend	convenience	maintenance	sergeant	which

Whichever method you choose to check your spelling, use it consistently during the entire evaluation process of the report.

Some agencies recommend or require the use of all capital letters in reports. When not using all capitals, the following capitalization rules apply:

1. Capitalize the names of people, cities, states, and streets.

   "I spoke with the victim, Greg Alexander, at his house on 999 Monroe Street n Tallahassee, Florida."

2. Capitalize the names of specific organizations and buildings.

   "The neighborhood meeting will be held at the city hall." (non-specific)

   "The Oakbrook Neighborhood Association meeting will be held at the Tallahassee City Hall." (specific)

3. Capitalize days, months, and holidays.

   "Independence Day is on Saturday, July 4th."

4. Capitalize geographic locations, but not directions.

   "She is from the South." (specific region or location)

   "I drove south on Monroe Street." (direction)

5. Capitalize titles of professionals only when names are used.

   "I spoke to the inmate to explain the situation." (inmate not named)

   "I spoke to Inmate Smith to explain the situation." (inmate named)

6. Capitalize brand names.

   "Mr. Jones says that his Smith & Wesson revolver was stolen."

HOMOPHONES

Homophones are words that are easily confused in use and spelling. They sound the same but have different spellings and meanings. Examples include:

accept	except		
two	too	to	
they're	their	there	
right	write	rite	wright
site	sight	cite	
its	it's		
seen	scene		
knot	not	naught	
night	knight	nite	
ad	add		
aisle	I'll	isle	

buy	by	bye	
know	no		
raised	razed		
rain	reign	rein	
seas	sees	seize	
principle	principal		
personal	personnel		
where	wear	were	ware
weather	whether		
ordinance	ordnance		

PROPER PUNCTUATION

Use proper punctuation when writing a report

Improper punctuation can result in confusing or even misleading reports.

The comma is probably the most misused punctuation mark. Commas are not inserted whenever the writer desires a pause. There are specific rules covering the use of commas:

1. Use a comma to separate two complete sentences joined by a coordinating conjunction. There are seven coordinating conjunctions: for, and, nor, but, or, yet, so—sometimes remembered as "fanboys."

    I met with the victim, and she gave me a statement. (Correct)

    I met with the victim, she gave me a statement. (Incorrect)

   If the two complete sentences are not joined by a coordinating conjunction, use a semicolon or period to separate them.

    I met with the victim, she gave me a statement. (Incorrect)

    I met with the victim; she gave me a statement. (Correct)

    I met with the victim. She gave me a statement. (Correct)

2. Use a comma after an introductory clause (a group of words with a subject and verb).

    When the alarm sounded, the officer ran to his post.

3. Use a comma to separate items in a series of three or more items.

    The victim said his digital camera, television, DVD player, radio, and computer were stolen.

4. Use a comma to separate non-restrictive (unimportant) phrases in a sentence. A phrase is a group of words that forms a grammatical unit, though not necessarily a complete sentence; it is considered non-restrictive when it can be omitted without disturbing the correctness of the grammar.

    The fingerprints, which I found on the window, belong to the victim.

5. Use a comma between two or more adjectives when they separately describe the same noun.

The inmate used a small, metal object to cut his own arm.

Do not place a comma between two or more adjectives if the phrase does not make sense when you reverse the order of the adjectives or when you add "and" between the adjectives.

He threw the white toaster oven at me. (You wouldn't say: "He threw the toaster white oven at me" or "he threw the white and toaster oven at me.")

6. Use a comma to introduce a quote.

    When I confronted her, she said, "I'm going to burn this place down."

7. Use commas when writing dates in the month-day-year sequence and when writing addresses.

    The first robbery occurred on January 12, 2019, at 345 Monroe Street, Tallahassee, Florida.

The apostrophe is another misused punctuation mark. An apostrophe is used to show possession or to create a contraction. Possession means that certain objects or qualities belong to a person or thing.

An officer's size and skill are factors to consider in making a decision to use force.

A contraction is the result of combining two words. Contractions should not be used in reports except when documenting a direct quote.

Inmate Smith does not want Officer Jones to search his cell. "You **don't** need to check my cell," Smith yelled.

Sometimes, a person's exact words may be used in an incident report. If using a direct quote, you must place quotation marks around the person's words. An example of a direct quote is:

Inmate Smith said, "Go ahead and search."

Quotation marks are not used when paraphrasing or summarizing a person's statement.

Inmate Smith told me to search his cell.

Lesson Vocabulary

homophones

sentence

sentence fragment

Review Items

1. *Explain the difference between writing in standard and non-standard English.*
2. *Give an example of a sentence with proper sentence structure.*
3. *Give an example of a sentence with proper spelling and capitalization rules.*
4. *Explain why it is important to use proper punctuation when writing a report.*

UNIT 4 REPORT WRITING

LESSON 4
ELEMENTS OF EFFECTIVE REPORTS

LESSON GOAL

You will be able to write an accurate and complete report that others can understand and use.

THINK ABOUT THIS

Do you remember the process for writing essays in high school? Writing a report is very similar, because it includes an introduction, body, and conclusion. Make sure that your report is detailed and professional. This lesson provides tips to help you write an effective report.

Writing an effective report is an important part of any officer's duties. People read reports without ever seeing or knowing the officers who wrote them. Readers evaluate not only the officers but also their agencies by the quality of the reports they read. Officers should write reports that reflect professionalism.

FORMAT AND CONTENT OF A REPORT

Know how to write a report with relevant content using proper format

The fourth step in preparing a report is writing the content. Write your report in the proper format and include all the important content associated with the incident. ***Format*** is the way information is organized and presented, while ***content*** refers here to the significant facts of the incident. Generally, a report format is arranged in three parts: introduction or opening, body, and closing.

The **introduction** section usually includes information such as:

- the date and time
- the location of the incident
- the case number
- the officer's assignment or location

The **body** section is the detailed (typically chronological) account of the incident. In this section, include the actions you took upon arriving at the scene, such as first aid, call for medical, interviews, elements of any rule violations or crimes committed, actions taken to obtain evidence, and call for backup if necessary.

The **closing** section explains action taken or how the incident was resolved; how the information and evidence were handled, including the need for further investigation; and any recommendations for disciplinary action.

UNPROFESSIONAL WRITING TO AVOID

Understand why you should avoid unprofessional writing

The content of a report is important, as it is expected to convey the significant details of an incident. However, correct grammar, punctuation, sentence structure, and spelling are equally important elements. A poorly written report containing numerous errors destroys the message and reflects badly on the writer.

Prepare reports in standard English, and make them easy to read and understand. Unless you are directly quoting someone, your reports should be free of non-standard English, jargon, slang, abbreviations, and textspeak.

Jargon is language used by a particular trade or profession that are not commonly understood by the general public; the technical vocabulary of a particular profession that has meaning specific to people who work in that field. It is also a term for specialized language that may include acronyms used by a profession or other group, often meaningless to outsiders. Officers may share common expertise and communicate quickly using jargon, but you should not use it in your reports.

Slang is an informal vocabulary composed of invented words or expressions that are often used by a specific group, region, trade, or profession.

Slang and jargon hinder clear communication, because these words may mean different things to different people. Also, slang and jargon are not professional in tone. Someone reading a corrections report should be able to follow the events and comprehend exactly what happened without having been at the scene or having to interpret slang.

Having a good vocabulary will help you avoid jargon and slang. As you encounter unfamiliar words and phrases, take the time to find their meanings and proper usage.

An improved vocabulary will help you accurately describe things that need to be documented in a report.

Some jargon and slang used by officers includes:

Jargon	Explanation
shakedown	cell/pat-down/strip-search
PC	Protective Custody
Jit	juvenile
DC	Disciplinary Confinement
3 hots and a cot	3 meals and a bed
CERT	Correctional Emergency Response Team
DR	Disciplinary Report
52-blocks	types of inmate fighting styles
I-So/Hole	isolation confinement

Some slang used in correctional settings includes:

Slang	Explanation
rabbit	an escape risk inmate
fish/new Jack	new inmate or correctional officer
The Hole or Box	disciplinary confinement cell
chow	meal
shank	homemade weapon
buck	homemade alcohol
rip	tobacco
411	information
kite	illegal note passed from inmate to inmate

The following is an example of use of jargon and slang, which is inappropriate in report writing:

Incorrect: "Yesterday after evening chow, Officer Jones while assigned as B-dorm supervisor, heard Inmate Coker state that he had the 411 on the fish who received a DR for the buck and a shank. He said that he sent out a kite from the box for some rip."

Correct: "Yesterday after evening meal, Officer Jones, B-dorm supervisor, heard Inmate Coker state that he had information on the new inmate who received a disciplinary report for homemade alcohol and a weapon. He said that he sent out a note from Disciplinary Confinement for some tobacco."

Textspeak is language used in text messages and digital communications, typically using abbreviations, acronyms, or initials, and usually not following standard grammar, spelling, or punctuation. Do not use textspeak in reports. While textspeak may be convenient for taking notes, using it in final reports gives the impression that you are lazy and unprofessional, or that what you are writing is not important. Remember that the reports you prepare become part of public record.

TIPS FOR EFFECTIVE REPORT WRITING

Use the elements of an effective report when writing

An effective report is factual, concise, accurate, clear, and grammatically and structurally correct. The report should be legible, timely, and complete and should comply with agency policies and procedures.

FACTUAL

- Never include in a report personal opinions from the writer, other officers, or witnesses.

  Incorrect: "I know Inmate Jones stole the book, because he has a history of taking other people's belongings."

  Correct: "I saw Inmate Jones take the book from the table."

- Do not include your personal inferences or presumptions of the officer.

Incorrect: "Inmate Jones said he did not steal the book, even though he was the only one in the area."

Correct: "Inmate Jones said he did not steal the book."

- Clearly identify the details of witnesses' accounts of the incident.

  Incorrect: It seems Inmate Smith was trying to suggest that Inmate Jones had hidden a shank under his bed.

  Correct: Inmate Smith said that he had seen Inmate Jones put a shank under Inmate Jones' bed.

- Avoid irrelevant information (stick to the facts).

  Incorrect: "Officer Dodson set the book on the table. He turned his back and was discussing last night's football game with Inmate Smith when Inmate Jones walked over to the table. It was about that time, maybe about a minute later, when Officer Dodson turned around in time to see Inmate Jones take the book."

  Correct: "Officer Dodson saw Inmate Jones take the book off the table."

- Avoid humor and dramatic flourishes or words with emotional overtones.

  Incorrect: "Officer Dodson and Inmate Smith were having a discussion about last night's football game when Inmate Jones slithered over to the table, real sneakylike, and snatched up the book just like the sucker belonged to him."

  Correct: "Inmate Jones took the book from the table while Officer Dodson and Inmate Smith were talking."

CONCISE

- Avoid wordiness.

  Incorrect: "Officer Williams and Officer Perez were walking down the hall going to get a Coke on their way to take their morning break when they came around a corner and saw two inmates huddled together, and it looked to them like they were trying to hide something. They were standing outside the utility closet where lots of contraband can be hidden. They decided they had better pat them down just to make sure they didn't have anything on them that they weren't supposed to have."

  Correct: "Officer Williams and Officer Perez searched two inmates, who were standing outside the utility closet in the hallway."

- Be brief, but do not leave out important information.

  Correct: "Officer Jones and Officer Barnes saw two inmates talking in low tones. The inmates stopped talking suddenly as they approached. The officers searched the inmates for contraband."

ACCURATE

Before submitting a report, make sure it is accurate.

Check a report for accuracy

- Ensure that it contains only what happened based solely on information, statements, and physical evidence collected.
- Verify that all facts and names are recorded and spelled correctly and that numbers written in the report match those in the notes.

CLEAR

- Choose words that have only one interpretation.

  Correct: "Officer Sanders warned Inmate Garcia not to go into cell 104. Approximately 10 minutes later, Officer Sanders saw Garcia go into cell 104."

- Present events in logical order.

  Correct: "Officer Roberts saw Inmate Williams take Inmate Brophy's book. He saw a piece of paper fall from the book, and then asked Inmate Williams to hand the items to him."

GRAMMATICALLY AND STRUCTURALLY CORRECT IN STANDARD ENGLISH

- Paint a picture of what happened in short, simple, and correct language, free of repetition, jargon, and slang.

LEGIBLE

- Make sure that the report is readable if written by hand.

TIMELY

- Write without delay after an incident. This enables management to deal decisively with issues arising from the incident, event, or occurrence. A prompt report also helps the officer remember relevant facts.

COMPLETE

Make sure that the report is complete.

- Check that all pertinent information has been included. All the facts, whether favorable or unfavorable to any of the people involved, should be part of the report.
- Answer the basic questions of who, what, when, where, why, and how, and make sure the action taken is fully recorded.

Lesson Vocabulary

content

format

jargon

slang

textspeak

Review Items

1. *Describe the three parts a properly formatted report should contain.*
2. *List three examples of unprofessional writing.*
3. *What are the elements of an effective report?*
4. *Explain how you can make sure that a report is accurate.*

LESSON 5

EVALUATING THE REPORT

LESSON GOAL

You will be able to evaluate and edit your reports before submitting them.

THINK ABOUT THIS

Officer Petersen misspelled an inmate's name as she was writing an incident report. She wrote "Inmate Spites was involved in the fight," instead of Inmate Spights. What could have happened as a result of the inmate's name being misspelled?

EVALUATING THE REPORT

Use editing and proofreading to evaluate a report

The final step in preparing a report is evaluating it to ensure accuracy and correct errors. This involves editing and proofreading. ***Editing*** is the process of ensuring that all pertinent facts have been included in a report in an organized and accurate manner. ***Proofreading*** is the checking of a report to ensure that all words are spelled correctly, punctuation is used accurately, appropriate words are capitalized, and proper grammar is used. If possible, ask another officer to read the report to see if it makes sense.

The following methods will help you catch mistakes that you might otherwise overlook:

- Begin by taking a break—allowing some time to pass between writing and evaluating helps you return to the report with fresh eyes and makes finding errors easier.
- Read aloud—reading a written narrative aloud encourages you to read every word. An alternative is asking someone else to read the report aloud, as another person often hears more errors than you can see.
- Read with a cover—sliding a blank sheet of paper down the page while reading the report will help you review the report in a detailed, line-by-line manner.
- Know personal weaknesses—find out what your typical writing problems are and look for those specific errors.
- Check paired punctuation—ensure that you have used both sides of paired punctuation (quotation marks or parentheses). It is a common error to forget the closing punctuation.

Below is an example of a poorly written narrative report with improper grammar, punctuation, capitalization, and spelling. An improved version of the example with proper grammar, punctuation, capitalization, and spelling is also provided.

> *[On May 16 2012 at approximately 1220 hours. I was on a routin patrol inside D Dorm when inmate Dennis Shaw, handled me a book and said "you'll find that quotation we were talking about on page 24". Since I had not discussed any quotation with Shaw, I decide to take the book to the officer and take a look at page 24. When I opened the book a folded piece of paper feel out. On the paper were the following words. "My roommate has some marijuana hidden inside a hole in his pillow." I show the note to Corp Larson, the Dorm Supavisor, and since the dorm was skeduled to go to the rec yard that afternoon, we desided to wait until then to conduct a search. At approx. 1:30 p.m., the inmates were excorted too the recreation yard, an it was about that time Corporal Larson and I searched cell D-234, the cell assigned to Dennis Shaw; and his roommate, inmate Schneider, Jonathan. I examined Schneider's pillow and I find a hole as described by Shaw. Inside the hole I find approx. two handfuls of a green leafy substance. I place the substance in a clear plastic bag and called a dual sworn officer, Corrections Deputy George Abrams, to test it it tested positive for maryjuana. Inmate Schneider was was brought in from the recreation yard and was question by Abrams. Schneider states, "That stupid roommate of mine set me up. He wants me out of their because I won't have anything to do with his drug business." Schneider was placed in Admin Confinement pending a investegation. Corporal Larson and I conducted a through search of the rest of the Dorm, however, no additional contruband is found.]*

Below is the narrative report with improved grammar, punctuation, capitalization, and spelling.

> *[On May 16, 2012, at approximately 1220 hours, I was on a routine patrol inside D Dorm when Inmate Shaw, Dennis, handed me a book and said, "You'll find that quotation we were talking about on page 24." Since I had not discussed any quotation with Shaw, I decided to take the book to the office and take a look at page 24. When I opened the book, a folded piece of paper fell out. On the paper were the following words: "My roommate has some marijuana hidden inside a hole in his pillow." I showed the note to Corporal Larson, the Dorm Supervisor, and since the dorm was scheduled to go to the recreation yard that afternoon, we decided to wait until then to conduct a search. At approximately 1330 hours, the inmates were escorted to the recreation yard, at which time Corporal Larson and I searched cell D-234, the cell assigned to Inmate Shaw and his roommate, Inmate Schneider, Jonathan. I examined Schneider's pillow and found a hole as described by Shaw. Inside the hole, I found approximately two handfuls of a green leafy substance. I placed the substance in a clear plastic bag and called a dual sworn officer, Corrections Deputy George Abrams, to test it; it tested positive for marijuana. Inmate Schneider was brought in from the recreation yard and was questioned by Abrams. Schneider stated, "That stupid roommate of mine set me up. He wants me out of there, because I won't have anything to do with his drug business." I placed Schneider in Administrative Confinement pending an investigation. Corporal Larson and I conducted a thorough search of the rest of D Dorm; however, we did not find any additional contraband.]*

FINALIZING THE REPORT

As part of the evaluating and finalizing process, verify that the report is complete and understandable by taking the following actions:

Finalize a report

- Ensure that all details, including who, what, where, when, how, why, and action taken, are fully answered. Include rule violations, if any.
- Ask this question, "If I was not involved or did not witness this incident or event, would I have a clear picture of what happened after reading this report?" If the answer is yes, then you wrote a good report.
- Ensure that you identified and corrected all errors.
- Sign, date, and distribute the report according to agency policies and procedures.

The more you practice writing and evaluating reports, the more professional your reports will be.

LESSON VOCABULARY

editing

proofreading

REVIEW ITEMS

1. *In your own words, describe the methods for evaluating a report.*
2. *Explain the difference between editing and proofreading.*
3. *What should you do to finalize a report?*

OFFICER SAFETY

LESSON 1

SAFETY AND SECURITY

LESSON GOAL

You will demonstrate situational awareness at all times while on duty to minimize threats to yourself and your facility.

THINK ABOUT THIS

You face many dangers working in a correctional facility. You must, therefore, continually stay alert. Use your senses to study your work environment for threats to you, to others, or to the facility. This lesson will help you understand safety concerns at work, know your work environment, and apply situational awareness in your daily assignments.

As a correctional officer, you represent one of the most important resources available to any correctional agency. You will be the front line for your facility and will be responsible for supervision of inmate activities, enforcement of rules and regulations, and maintaining order in the facility. Your responsibilities will carry a lot of weight as you protect not only yourself, but the safety of other facility staff, inmates, and the public.

This chapter provides an overview of safety and security including identification, manipulation and deception, contraband, and searches. You must be engaged, remain mentally alert, and be proactive.

SAFETY HAZARDS AND SECURITY CONCERNS

Understand the personal safety and security concerns for a correctional officer

Recall the concept of command presence from Chapter 2. Safety and security begin with a professional attitude. You should come to work well-rested and physically ready to perform your duties. Coming to work prepared creates a safe and professional work environment. Avoid missing work if at all possible. When you miss a shift, someone else will have to cover it. This means fewer officers will be available to watch inmates and respond to an emergency.

Another aspect of an officer's preparation is being in good physical shape. The duties of a correctional officer are often physically demanding. Maintain good physical health by eating a balanced diet and exercising daily. Lack of stamina, agility, and mobility can hinder your ability to protect yourself, as well as staff and visitors. For example, you may have to sprint long distances or climb flights of stairs and still be able to control a combative inmate successfully or assist in other emergency situations.

Always project a confident, competent, and capable demeanor. This sends a message to inmates that you can handle any situation. Practice good communication and listening skills to avoid conflict as much as possible. Treat each inmate with respect. For example, if an inmate or visitor approaches you with a request, remember that they are people and have needs. Handle each situation fairly, firmly, and consistently, while remaining professional.

Inmates may challenge your authority by committing minor infractions. Address violations professionally and according to policy. Failure to do so may result in inmates' behavior escalating into more serious problems, both for you and the other inmates.

Complacency is your worst enemy.

Complacency is a comfortable or relaxed state of mind, which lulls you into a false sense of safety and security. When complacent, you may not be aware of what is happening or what could happen in any given situation. Failure to be alert can jeopardize the safety of the officer, inmate, visitors, and general public, and the facility's security.

Stress can affect your focus and attention to detail, which can negatively influence decision-making. All officers will experience some level of job-related stress such as fear, intimidation, and anxiety. For example, being the only officer assigned to a dormitory that houses 80 inmates is a stressful situation. You can minimize stress with proper training, knowledge of policies and procedures, and familiarity with various inmate behaviors. Knowledge of policies and procedures will help keep staff, visitors, and inmates safe.

Four categories of stress an officer may experience are:

Know the categories of stress that can influence your safety

- environmental—weather, noise levels, lighting conditions, crowded areas
- personal—family issues, health, lack of sleep, poor eating habits, financial situation, academic demands
- work-related—shift work, supervisors, co-workers, contact with the general public, court appearances, performance standards
- self-induced—personal attitudes toward work, perception of others, work or academic goals

Personal stress can be particularly distracting. A number of factors outside work can affect an officer's focus. Make an effort to leave your personal life at home when you begin a shift. This will help you stay focused on the safety of the public, staff, and inmates and on maintaining a secure facility.

SITUATIONAL AWARENESS

Situational awareness is a state of mental responsiveness. It is the ability to pay attention to what is going on around you.

Situational awareness in a correctional setting occurs in three stages:

Know the stages of situational awareness

1. **Being alert**—be aware of what is going on around you at all times. Pay attention to sights and sounds to help maintain a high level of alertness. For example, when walking through a dormitory area, be aware of people behind you as you take in your surroundings. Mentally visualize where a threat may appear and the options you have for responding to any potential threat.

2. **Identifying a potential threat**—concentrate on possible threats while remaining aware of your surroundings. This stage can occur several times during a shift. For example, while you are assigned to the recreation yard, a group of inmates suddenly and quickly approaches you for unknown reasons. You should observe body language, verbal tone, or any other threatening demeanor of the group.
3. **Responding to a threat**—focus your attention on potential threats while maintaining intense concentration and avoiding tunnel vision, which is when your attention and field of view narrow because of stress. In response to an actual threat, you should be mentally ahead of the threat and take appropriate action.

Questions you may ask yourself to evaluate a situation include:

- What does the inmate's body stance, posture, or positioning show?
- What does the inmate's facial expression show?
- Is the inmate physically reaching for something or someone?
- Is there a communication barrier?
- What do the tone, volume, and pitch of the inmate's voice show?
- What response is appropriate for the situation?
- Could other inmates become involved?
- Is assistance available? Do I need backup from other personnel?
- How long will it take for backup to arrive?
- Is the area defensible?

Demonstrate the four basic skills you can use in evaluating a situation

You should consider the use of positioning, posture, observing, and listening when evaluating a situation for threats.

Positioning is placing yourself in a tactically advantageous location to observe an area. Positioning allows you to size up a situation while remaining in a safe place. Positioning includes:

Keeping a safe distance—Distance yourself far enough away to be safe but close enough to observe what is happening. What is considered a safe distance in a correctional setting will vary depending on the size of the location, and the behavior and number of inmates. Assess the situation to determine a safe distance.

Being familiar with your environment—Know the layout of the facility and plan the best possible positioning and escape route before entering an area. Areas that are large or house large numbers of inmates may require you to move around throughout your shift. Avoid establishing a set pattern. If inmates can predict what position you will take, they may be able to gain a tactical advantage.

Watching groups and individuals—Place yourself in a position where you can see and hear what is going on around you. Being in a good position allows you to pay attention to what is being said and lets inmates know you are paying attention to them. Always face inmates when speaking with them, because it allows you to use your peripheral vision to monitor activities. When you watch them closely, inmates are less likely to commit rule violations or cause minor problems. By closely observing inmates, you can pick up on important non-verbal cues and body language. Constantly scan the area for potential threats even when watching inmates.

Posture is holding your body in a manner that shows strength, confidence, interest, and control. Posture includes using command presence to project an image of confidence in your skills and abilities. If you appear to lack confidence, inmates will attempt to manipulate or deceive you.

Practice ***controlled behavior***, demonstrating confidence and control by avoiding such distracting behaviors as foot tapping, nail biting, and fidgeting.

Observing is another skill of situational awareness. ***Observing*** is being aware of any occurrence or activity, such as irregular mood changes, emotional outbursts, acting out, threatening behavior, or changes in inmate energy levels, that may signify safety and security problems.

Examples of things you may observe include:

- an inmate uniform worn incorrectly—misplaced identification, shoe untied, belt hanging to the right or left, one pant leg rolled up
- physical condition of inmate—limping, bruises, bloody nose
- physical structures during inspection or search—broken window, graffiti on wall

Active listening is a learned skill that you should use to quickly determine the context, threat, and relevance of events unfolding around you. Be sure to pay attention to volume, pitch, tone, and inflection. Listen for key and inflammatory words that could indicate trouble. Never allow personal judgment and prejudice toward an inmate to obscure your listening abilities.

By applying situational awareness, you will always be alert for potential threats, and rapidly respond to incidents before they escalate beyond control. For example, two inmates begin an argument, and the officer intervenes before a physical altercation begins, thus preserving safety.

Demonstrate effective situational awareness skills

Lesson Vocabulary

controlled behavior

observing

positioning

posture

situational awareness

Review Items

1. *Describe safety hazards and security concerns that you might have as an officer.*
2. *What are the categories of stress that can influence your safety?*

3. *List the stages of situational awareness.*
4. *In your own words, describe the four basic skills used in evaluating a situation.*
5. *What does effective situational awareness mean to you?*

LESSON 2
IDENTIFICATION

LESSON GOAL

You will be able to recognize valid personal identification and altered, false, or counterfeit identification.

THINK ABOUT THIS

All people—inmates, visitors, and staff—entering or leaving a correctional facility must be identified and verified properly. Efficient identification checks provide an accurate account of everyone within the facility. They also help keep you, others, and the facility safe and secure from unauthorized and dangerous individuals. Do not compromise safety through improper identification of people.

Identity verification is a secure and reliable form of recognizing individuals based on sound standards. Identity verification can also be resistant to fraud or counterfeiting and can be rapidly checked electronically.

Access inside a facility is not limited to staff and inmates. Based on the facility's entrance and identification requirements, visitors may be granted access. Visitors may include family, friends, attorneys, vendors, and volunteers. If a visitor is granted access without proper identification, a security breach has occurred.

Agency records may be used to identify inmates, staff, visitors, or vendors. The verification process may include using automated or manual resources. Officers can verify a person's identification by comparing photographs in facility records with the individual.

Verify the identity of an inmate, staff, or visitor using information from photo identification or facility records

VALID IDENTIFICATION

There are two main categories of valid identification: automated and manual. Personal knowledge or recognition of a person is not acceptable as an official method of identification.

Know the common methods of identification

AUTOMATED

- facial recognition software—recognizes distinct facial features and links to a database, which may contain all information listed below under Types of Valid Personal Identification.
- automated visitor registration (AVR) hand scanner—recognizes distinct fingerprint features and links to a database, which may contain identifying information for visitors and vendors. This system links authorized visitors to specific inmates they are allowed to visit.

- automated barcode scanner—reads barcodes located on the wristband, armband, or identification card and verifies information
- Rapid Identification System—fingerprint recognition system
- Automated Biometric Identification Solution (ABIS) (formerly known as AFIS)

MANUAL

- inmate face sheet—printed from the agency database
- inmate gate pass—authorizes supervised inmates to exit the secure perimeter
- inmate files—contains all known information about the inmate
- agency identification card—issued to staff and visitors
- armband / wristband—issued to inmates at intake or reception center
- government-issued identification cards

TYPES OF VALID PERSONAL IDENTIFICATION

Some of the common information contained in the automated and manual identification systems includes a photograph, identification number, height, weight, date of birth, Social Security number, address, race, gender, age, charge, aliases, identifying marks, receipt / release date, facility location, barcode, and magnetic strip.

Know types of valid personal identification

Valid forms of identification can include:

- state driver's license
- state identification card
- criminal justice agency or correctional facility identification card or records
- U.S. military identification card
- U.S. passport
- facility-issued inmate wristband
- birth certificate (for minors younger than 12)
- student identification cards

Understand features of personal identification documents

For an identification card to be acceptable in a correctional facility, the card should contain several common features, which may include:

- photograph
- identification number
- signature
- personal information
  - name

- address
- date of birth

- physical features
  - gender
  - height
  - weight
  - hair color
  - eye color
  - scars, marks, tattoos
- security features
  - hologram—a hidden image that is visible when viewed at certain angles or with appropriate lighting, such as on a driver's license
  - watermark—a recognizable image or pattern in paper that appears lighter or darker when held up to the light
  - raised or embossed seal
  - magnetic stripe or bar code—a dark stripe on the back of the identification card that contains all information on the card
  - expiration date—the date the identification is no longer valid

Understand the differences between valid and altered or counterfeit identification

Valid identification is unexpired and unaltered and may contain security features. Counterfeit identification appears to be valid but may be missing some or all of the essential security features and information. A visitor may attempt to enter a facility using counterfeit or altered identification. Most facilities accept only original documents to avoid counterfeit attempts. If, something looks suspicious during the identification process, question the person. Ask for information on the card that the person should know, such as their date of birth or address. Examine the identification, looking for obvious alterations or inconsistencies, such as missing vital information, missing security features, raised lettering or photo relamination, use of different fonts, or variations in background.

Compare physical appearance of an inmate, staff, or visitor to their photo identification

Document the identity of an inmate, staff, or visitor

To ensure a positive identification, compare the person's physical appearance to their identification. Features to compare include skin color, eye color, hair, facial structure, and any other distinctive features like scars, birthmarks, or tattoos. However, you can use these identifiers only if they have been previously documented. Once you confirm identification, document the verification of the inmate, staff member, or visitor on the appropriate form or electronic record.

Review Items

1. *List the common methods of identification.*
2. *What are the types of valid personal identification?*
3. *Describe features of personal identification documents.*
4. *What are some of the differences between valid and counterfeit identification?*
5. *Why is it important to verify the identity of everyone in the correctional facility?*
6. *What is done once the identity of an inmate, staff, or visitor has been confirmed?*

Lesson 3

Manipulation and Deception

Lesson Goal

You will be able to recognize manipulation and deception and avoid their influence.

Think About This

"How is your son feeling today? I know he was sick yesterday," Inmate Thomas asks Officer Lofton. Is this a problem in a correctional setting? It seems harmless enough, and the inmate seems thoughtful and concerned about Officer Lofton and his family. However, is that really the case? Many inmates and visitors are experts in manipulation and deception. There will be severe consequences, such as loss of certification, demotion, dismissal, or prosecution, if you fall for inmate manipulation and deception. You must be ethical and professional when dealing with inmates to avoid personal consequences and threats to safety and security.

Understand the difference between manipulation and deception

Inmate ***manipulation*** occurs when an inmate attempts to get something they want by influencing the officer or staff member to do something the officer or staff member would not ordinarily do. Manipulation can be an isolated incident or an ongoing series of events. Manipulation may result in more severe consequences for the officer, staff, or inmate.

Deception is lying to, misleading, tricking, or fooling another person. Deception may happen on the spur of the moment or may be a habitual behavior. Manipulation and deception are difficult to distinguish, but the ultimate goal of both is personal gain or avoidance of disciplinary action.

Assume an inmate asks an officer one of the following:

"Did you watch the game last night?"

"Would you like a candy bar?"

"Do you have a cigarette?"

"You smell good. What cologne or perfume are you wearing?"

While these questions might seem harmless, they could be the beginning of manipulation or deception by an inmate. You should know how to recognize and handle such questions. When manipulation or deception occurs, you are being controlled. This jeopardizes the safety and security of staff, visitors, and inmates.

If you give in to inmate manipulation and deception, you may face disciplinary action, termination, and even criminal charges.

Methods inmates use to manipulate and deceive correctional staff can range from subtle to extreme, such as:

Know the methods inmates use to manipulate and deceive

- attempting to create bonds with staff members—an inmate going above and beyond expected job duties in an attempt to get a favor or special consideration
- circumventing or disobeying rules—testing the boundaries of the supervising officer
- using special circumstances or situations—using a disability or illness to gain preferential or special treatment
- distracting staff—creating a diversion to distract your attention
- attempting to engage staff in casual non-job related conversation—requesting personal information regarding staff, such as asking where you are from, what school you attended, your age or marital status, the number of children you have, or your favorite sports team
- spreading rumors about staff or attempting to turn one staff member against another—discussing information about staff members with you; "I heard Sgt. Doe talking about you yesterday and he said that you were lazy."
- over familiarizing with staff—knowing enough about you to notice a change in your routine
- attempting any illegal activity—bribing, blackmailing, or offering sex

Inmate manipulation and deception can also come in the form of an organized team. Inmates may coordinate and execute a plan to manipulate or deceive you or a staff member. The participants of the team may consist of, but are not limited to, observers, contacts, runners, turners, and point men. The following are the roles of each participant:

Observers

- observe correctional officers who use inmate jargon, ignore minor rule infractions, play favorites, enforce rules for some and not others, or are easily distracted

Contacts

- supply information about the correctional officer's work habits, likes, and dislikes

Runners

- usually the only paid members of the team because they must expose themselves to the correctional officer by asking for small items like candy, cigarettes, or pencils

Turners

- befriend the correctional officer and use the friendship to ultimately coerce the officer into engaging in rule infractions
- are least suspected by the correctional officer

Point men

- stand guard when the officer is in the process of granting illegal favors, violating institutional rules, or being compromised or harmed

Whether targeted by an individual or a team, you will be subjected to inmate manipulation and deception. You must also recognize when other staff is being targeted by these tactics. By staying alert and focused, you can stop manipulation and deception.

To avoid inmate manipulation or deception, refrain from being overly friendly or giving out personal information. Engaging in personal conversations and talking about other staff pose a serious safety and security risk. Avoid doing any personal favors for inmates such as bringing items in or removing items from the facility, or offering inmates items like food and drink. Another situation to avoid is giving one inmate authority over another inmate. This creates a power structure that can be exploited and generate a hostile environment. Under no circumstances should you or a staff member engage in sexual conversations or activities with inmates.

Behaviors you should display to avoid inmate manipulation include:

Know behaviors officers should display to minimize inmate manipulation and deception

- be part of the correctional team
- follow rules and procedures
- monitor remarks, gestures, and actions
- communicate with supervisors and fellow workers when you suspect a problem
- know your job and perform it properly
- document incidents
- learn to say "no" and mean it
- address inmates by "inmate" or their last name
- restrict your relationship with inmates to activities and discussions that are part of your official duties
- be suspicious
- be truthful
- be professional
- be cautious

Be aware of signs of manipulation and deception used by visitors. Visitors may bring gifts or offer favors to staff or use intimidation in an attempt to

Know methods visitors use to manipulate and deceive

get staff to violate facility rules. For example, a visitor may threaten to harm staff members or their family, or to report the staff member to a supervisor.

Lesson Vocabulary

deception

manipulation

Review Items

1. *In your own words, describe the difference between manipulation and deception as used by inmates.*
2. *What are the methods inmates might use to manipulate and deceive an officer or staff member?*
3. *List three behaviors officers should display to minimize inmate manipulation and deception.*
4. *List methods visitors might use to manipulate and deceive an officer or staff member.*

LESSON 4
CONTRABAND

LESSON GOAL

You will be able to detect contraband and follow the appropriate processing and disposal procedures.

THINK ABOUT THIS

As discussed in Chapter 1, contraband is dangerous within a correctional facility. Inmates often use contraband items to harm other inmates, officers, or themselves; contraband may also be used to attempt an escape, create a disturbance, damage property, and even spread infectious diseases. The control and proper disposal of contraband are extremely important to both your position as an officer and to the safety and security of your facility.

Know the correctional officer's duty to control contraband

Correctional officers are tasked with preventing, controlling, and disposing contraband through regular and irregular searches. As defined in Chapter 1, contraband is any unauthorized item or any authorized article in excessive quantities or altered from its original state. This includes an inmate giving authorized items to another inmate. Drugs, firearms, and knives are all obvious safety and security concerns. However, the presence of cell phones, unauthorized food, clothing, or any contraband item poses a breach in security that endangers staff, visitors, and inmates. If seemingly minor contraband finds its way into the facility, there is a great likelihood that more serious contraband may be introduced in the same way.

Know the categories of contraband

Contraband can be categorized as either nuisance or hard/hazardous. ***Nuisance contraband*** is any authorized item found in excessive amounts or altered from its original state that usually does not pose an immediate threat to the safety or security of the staff, inmates, and facility. Nuisance contraband includes excessive clothing, linen, laundry items, canteen and hygiene items, photos, reading materials, over-the-counter medication, and letters. Be aware, however, that some nuisance contraband can be used to create hard/hazardous contraband.

Hard/hazardous contraband is any item that poses a serious threat to the safety and security of the staff, inmates, and facility. Firearms, homemade knives (shanks), other weapons, drugs, alcoholic beverages, toxic materials, prescription medication, inhalants, cell phones, and electronic devices that store or receive data are examples of hard/hazardous contraband.

Know common inmate weapons

Inmates can be very creative and have ample time to think of ways to make weapons. Any item can be used as a weapon. Shanks are the most common inmate weapon and can be made from almost anything. Many common items can be turned into weapons.

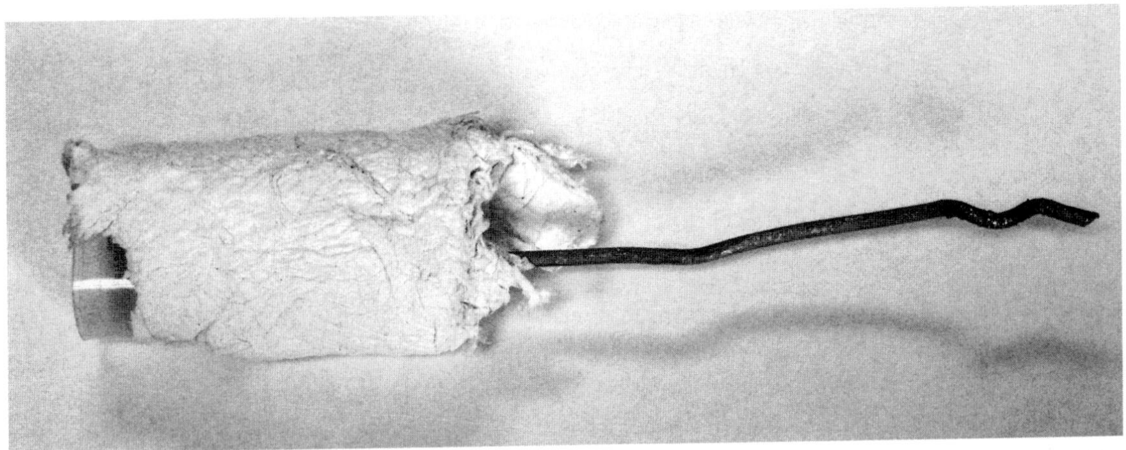

A homemade shank

Figure 3-1

Sports equipment, food service equipment, office supplies, liquid substances (bleach, urine), toothbrushes, disposable razors, heavy objects placed in a sock, and writing utensils can all be used as weapons.

Know common methods of introducing contraband into correctional facilities

Contraband may enter correctional facilities by various means. Inmates, visitors, vendors, and even staff can conceal contraband in their clothing, on their person, or in other items. Other methods of introduction are through body cavities, mail, canteen or commissary items, and deliveries. For example, an inmate may personally know one of the food delivery drivers and ask the driver to bring in contraband. The contraband is then introduced into the facility within the food items. Or the inmate might ask the driver to take contraband out of the facility and deliver it to someone on the outside.

DETECTION OF CONTRABAND

Understand methods of detecting contraband

Detecting and recognizing contraband are important means of controlling and minimizing its introduction and presence in a facility. Some search methods used to detect contraband are:

- visual search—visually scanning for contraband items
- pat down—physically frisking a subject in a predetermined pattern to locate weapons or other types of contraband
- clothed search—physically patting and squeezing the clothing of a person in a systematic pattern, following the quadrant search approach; used in a secure environment
- custodial search—physically patting and squeezing the clothing of a person in a systematic pattern; used when a subject is taken into custody in an unsecured environment
- cell / area search—visually and physically inspecting an area in a systematic manner
- metal detection—using electronic devices to detect a metal object on or within a person or concealed within an item

- strip-search—visually searching an unclothed person and physically searching their clothing
- vehicle search—visually and physically inspecting a vehicle to locate contraband
- body cavity search—visually and physically inspecting body openings; such searches are to be conducted by medical staff only

COLLECTING CONTRABAND

Know the process of collecting, processing, and disposing of contraband

When contraband is located and identified, the items must be removed or secured immediately. General practices should be followed when collecting contraband. Always use universal precautions and personal protective equipment (gloves, mask) when searching for and collecting contraband. Never taste or smell any material found in a facility or handle suspected contraband more than is absolutely necessary. Contraband could contain body fluids, communicable diseases, toxic chemicals, or filth. Confiscate the contraband and store or dispose of it according to agency policies and procedures.

The way the item is removed depends on whether the contraband is nuisance or hard/hazardous. All contraband must be identified, confiscated, and documented. Confiscating excessive supplies (such as extra clothing or sheets) is handled differently than confiscating a weapon.

Contraband may be kept as evidence if it is part of an investigation, was used in the commission of a crime, or is required for disciplinary proceedings. The manner in which you process contraband could determine the outcome of an investigation; mishandling these items may compromise the value they have as evidence. It is also important to document the chain of custody, which you will recall from Chapter 1 is the witnessed written record of all individuals who have handled the evidence since its collection. Common types of contraband stored as evidence may include weapons, illegal drugs, or items used in a serious incident or to commit a crime. Officers should take special care to follow the protocols of the Prison Rape Elimination Act (PREA), such as securing clothing of the victim and suspect, and DNA collection.

Chain of custody and inventory forms help ensure a complete and comprehensive contraband collection process. It may be necessary to issue a receipt to the appropriate individuals for confiscated unauthorized personal items. Contraband is commonly stored in paper or plastic bags, boxes, or storage bins in a secured, locked area inaccessible to inmates. Label the container with the inmate's name and identification number, and document where it will be stored.

DOCUMENTATION

Photograph contraband

When hard/hazardous contraband is found, it may be necessary to photograph it before confiscation, storage, or disposal. Failure to photograph and properly document contraband could negatively impact the legal process and hinder disciplinary actions. Initiate the chain of custody for narcotics, weapons, and other dangerous items. These items should always be photographed for possible presentation in criminal proceedings.

Document confiscation and disposal of contraband

When documenting the confiscation and disposal of contraband, follow agency policies and procedures. Documentation may include an inventory of the contraband and an incident report. Include as many details as possible, such as where the contraband was found, descriptions of what was found, quantity, and method of disposal.

DISPOSITION

The final disposition of contraband includes either immediate disposal or storage for future inmate disciplinary action, case reference, or training purposes. Document the final disposition of the collected contraband. In some instances, final disposition may involve outside investigators. For example, when a visitor attempts to introduce contraband into or remove contraband from a facility, local law enforcement may handle disposition.

Understand the final disposition of contraband

DISPOSAL

You must get authorization before disposing of contraband. If you find nuisance contraband in common areas and cannot link it to an inmate, confiscate and process it according to agency policies and procedures. These items may be disposed of in receptacles, trash bins, or incinerators not accessible to inmates.

Know the appropriate receptacles for contraband disposal

Forward personal property considered contraband to the inmate property storage area. According to agency policies and procedures, these items may be released or mailed to the inmate's family. Hard / hazardous contraband must be stored as evidence in a secure location. For example, with most agencies, a tattoo gun may be photographed and stored. Never receive or take for personal use any contraband.

Know contraband disposal methods

Items that require special disposal include:

Know contraband items that need special disposal

- money—Although some facilities allow inmates to have money up to a specified amount, many do not allow it at all. You should count confiscated money in the presence of the inmate. Staff should sign and give a receipt to the inmate. The money may be deposited into the Inmate Welfare Fund or the inmate's personal account. Money is not thrown away.
- medication—You must confiscate any unauthorized medication or authorized medication in excessive amounts. The facility's medical staff or the issuing authority should determine the appropriate method of disposal.
- illegal drugs—The discovery of illegal drugs in a correctional facility may lead to criminal charges. Illegal drugs should be held as evidence by the investigating agency.
- weapons—Possessing a weapon may result in criminal charges. This requires holding the weapon as evidence.
- biohazardous materials—Materials such as a tattoo gun needle or soiled bedsheet may contain blood or body fluids. Place these items in the appropriate biohazard containers or bags and follow agency policies and procedures to dispose of them.

Lesson Vocabulary

hard/hazardous contraband

nuisance contraband

Review Items

1. *Describe the correctional officer's duty to control contraband.*
2. *What are the two categories of contraband?*
3. *Describe some common inmate weapons.*
4. *List common methods of introducing contraband into correctional facilities.*
5. *What are the methods of detecting contraband?*
6. *In your own words, explain how to collect, process, and dispose of contraband.*
7. *Describe the final disposition of contraband.*
8. *What are the appropriate receptacles for contraband disposal?*
9. *What are the contraband disposal methods?*
10. *List contraband items that need special disposal.*

LESSON 5
SEARCHES

LESSON GOAL

You will be able to conduct a thorough and proper search of both persons and facility areas.

THINK ABOUT THIS

Do not underestimate what inmates can do with so much free time at their disposal. They can create or introduce contraband and hide it in the most obscure places. Conducting searches is critical in discovering contraband and maintaining safety and security. People tend to conceal contraband wherever they think officers are least likely to look. A door that is usually locked is left ajar, dirt is disturbed in the yard, or an inmate has bulging pockets; these are some indicators that a search should be initiated.

Searches prevent the spread of contraband, weapons, and other dangerous items in a facility. A search can detect the manufacture of weapons and escape devices, or escape attempts. For example, during a fence inspection, you notice a washed-out area under the fence line. This early detection could prevent an escape or possible injury.

During a search you may also discover damaged facility property and health hazards. To avoid exposure to biohazardous materials, always use universal precautions and personal protective equipment when conducting a search. Gloves can range from latex or non-latex to puncture- or cut-resistant gloves, which provide varying levels of protection while conducting area and person searches.

A typical day room in a correctional facility *Figure 3-2*

Know techniques for examining visitor property

When entering a facility, everyone and their property, including vehicles and keys, are subject to search. When examining property, open and search all bags, briefcases, books, and papers for contraband. Be sure to inspect all clothing items. Check containers for hidden compartments that may conceal unauthorized items. You may conduct pat-down searches of visitors. Some agencies may have other resources, such as scanning devices, to complement the search process.

A typical cell

Figure 3-3

Searches should be conducted in all facility areas, including day rooms, cells, dormitories, recreation yards, kitchens, and parking lots. Structures and furnishings also need to be searched, including bars, locks, windows, doors, bunks, and chairs. You must search outside transport destinations, including work-release sites, courtrooms, or medical offices.

Know types of areas to be searched

Use your judgment to determine when to conduct a pat down of inmates to look for weapons and other contraband. This may include searching inmates as they enter and exit the housing area. These types of searches are intended to prevent the movement and introduction of contraband within the facility. Chapter 5 contains information on searching an inmate and inmate property at intake or reception, and in Defensive Tactics you will learn the steps to conduct a pat down.

Conduct pat down of inmates

Prior to the area search, subjects should also be searched and closely monitored. Always ask the subject if they have anything that would harm anyone during the course of the search, giving them the chance to reveal anything that may be concealed. This provides safety for the officer and prevents interference.

Remove all people from a location being searched. While visually scanning the area, make a mental plan of how to conduct the search and select a starting point. Search in a thorough and systematic manner. Search one area or item completely before going to the next. If you find contraband, secure it and continue until you complete the search. Return property or furnishings to their original condition and position. Never put your hands in places where you cannot also see what you are inspecting. Avoid rubbing or sliding your hands over objects or clothing; a pat or pat-and-squeeze method is recommended instead.

Conduct a systematic search of an area

You may use one or more of the following search patterns for outside or large areas and may use modified versions for smaller areas:

spiral search pattern—usually used by one person. The searcher begins at a central point and moves in increasingly larger circles to the outermost boundary of the search area.

strip/line search pattern—usually used in a predetermined area by several people. The search area is divided into lanes that are searched by one or more people in both directions until the entire area has been examined.

grid search pattern—a variation of the strip/line search pattern. It overlaps a series of lanes in a cross pattern.

zone/quadrant search pattern—used for an area that is large. Divide the area into four sections and search using one of the patterns above.

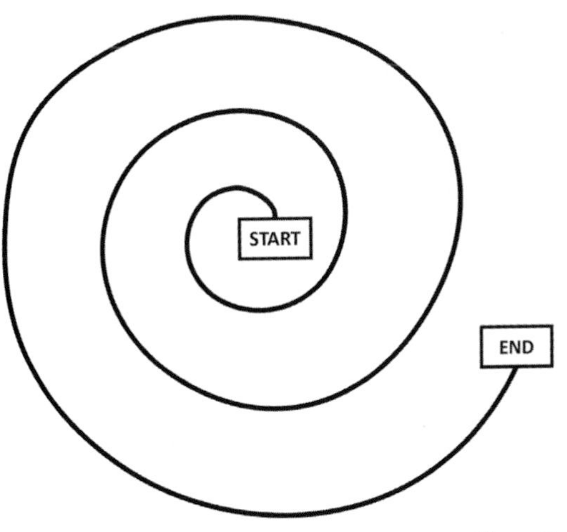

Spiral search pattern *Figure 3-4*

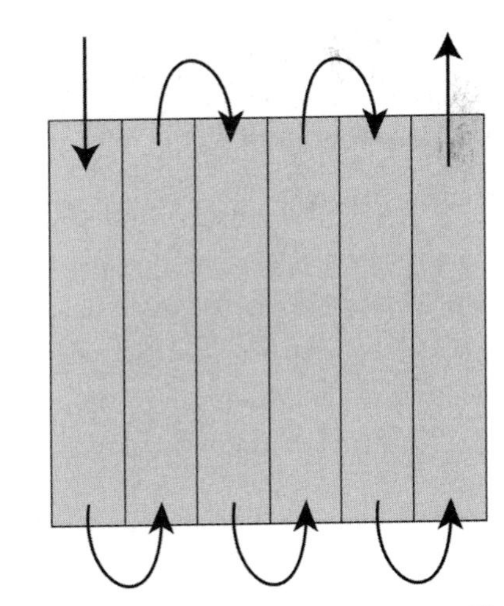

Strip line search pattern *Figure 3-5*

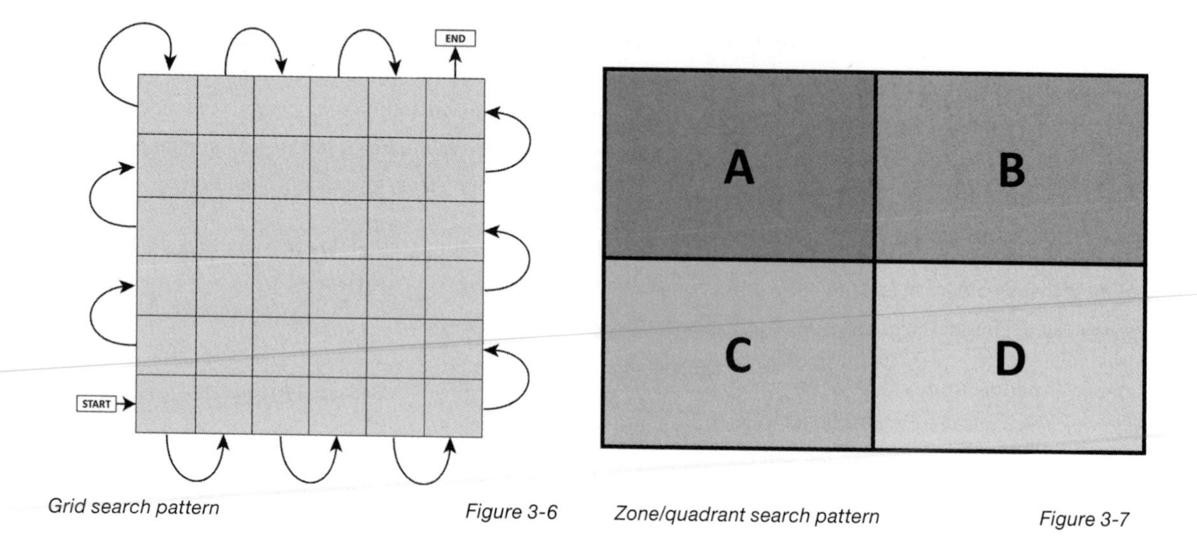

Grid search pattern *Figure 3-6*

Zone/quadrant search pattern *Figure 3-7*

Know the common equipment used in searches

While the techniques for conducting a search are important, it is also necessary to have the proper equipment. Equipment used during a person search includes gloves, metal detectors, ion and X-ray scanners, body imaging, or a canine. Equipment for an area search includes flashlights, screwdrivers, mirrors, probing devices, collection bags or containers, and forms to record any contraband found.

Various types of search equipment include:

- flashlights—used to illuminate dim or unlit areas
- screwdrivers—used to remove panels or covers
- mirrors—used for viewing areas not easily seen, such as under or behind bunks, sinks, toilets, and other areas; mirrors can also be used to search above and beneath vehicles
- probing devices—any item used to search holes, cracks, or hollow areas; one such method is using a wire to check grills, door tracks, faucets, and drains
- bags or containers—used to collect contraband
- notepads or other forms—used to record contraband found
- metal detectors (handheld or walk-through)—devices, often found at entrance and exit points of the facility, used to detect metallic objects or materials. When searching a bunk, the officer can scan the mattress instead of physically handling it. Using this method will protect the officer from possible injury and prevent the destruction of property.
- X-ray scanners—used to detect contraband in articles like shoes and clothes
- canines and their handlers—specially trained to detect certain types of contraband such as drugs, other chemicals, and cell phones

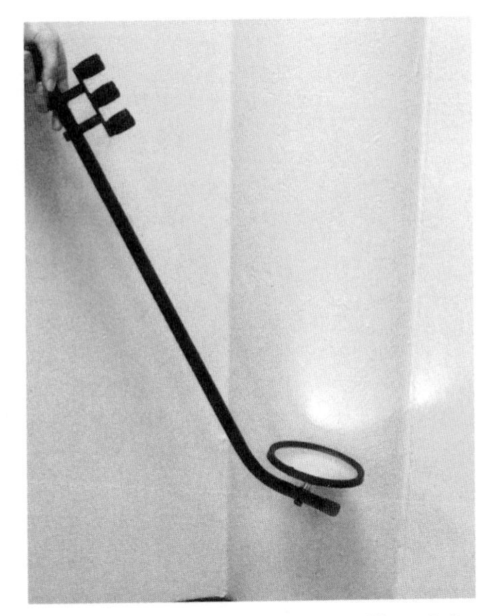

A mirror used in searches *Figure 3-8*

Using a mirror to search a transport vehicle before unloading an inmate *Figures 3-9 and 3-10*

Document details of an area search

Once you complete the search, document the search details using logs, electronic databases, checklists, or any other identified method. Details may include the subjects' names, locations, items confiscated, and the officers who conducted the search.

Conduct a vehicle search

All vehicles on facility property are subject to search, including visitors and staff vehicles. Inmate transport vehicles are of particular concern. You must thoroughly search vehicles before and after transport. Conduct these searches systematically. Make sure you search all compartments and areas, including above and below the vehicle, the interior, the exterior, the engine, the glove box, the consoles, and the toolbox.

A handheld metal detector used in searches *Figure 3-11*

Lesson Vocabulary

grid search pattern

spiral search pattern

strip/line search pattern

zone/quadrant search pattern

Review Items

1. *Describe techniques for examining visitor property.*
2. *What are the areas that need to be searched in a correctional facility?*
3. *Describe how to conduct a pat down of inmates.*
4. *Describe how to conduct a systematic search of an area.*
5. *What are the common pieces of equipment used in searches?*
6. *Describe what details should be documented after an area search.*
7. *What are some areas of a vehicle that should be searched?*

Facility and Equipment

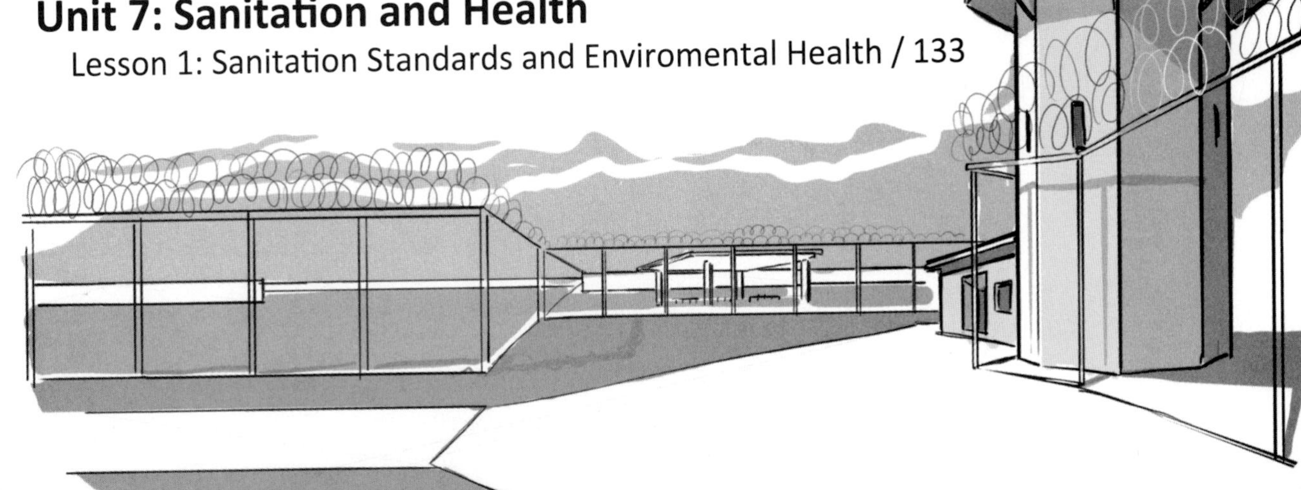

UNIT 1 EQUIPMENT MANAGEMENT

LESSON 1
ISSUING, RECEIVING, AND DOCUMENTING EQUIPMENT

LESSON GOAL

You will be able to manage the equipment necessary to keep a correctional facility operating smoothly and safely.

THINK ABOUT THIS

Making sure that the facility operates safely and effectively 24 hours a day and 365 days a year depends on equipment being in good repair and having a sufficient amount of supplies. Facility operations also depend on the responsibility of the officers to respond to and correct any problems related to facility operations. Your job duties include managing the facility equipment.

Correctional officers are responsible for equipment and materials used to keep correctional facilities clean, safe, and secure. You need a basic knowledge of standard equipment used, including weapons, hazardous materials, and sensitive supplies. You should also know about common problems found when managing equipment; this will help you ensure the safe and efficient operation of equipment and provide a safe environment for inmates, staff, and visitors.

INSPECTING EQUIPMENT

Know the common equipment assigned to specific areas and activities in a facility

A correctional officer is responsible for identifying and properly accounting for inventory and issuing and storing equipment. In addition, you must know how to safely and efficiently operate various types of equipment. Your equipment is your lifeline, so it is important to know how to use it and to check that it is functional.

Equipment is assigned for use in specific areas, such as inmate living quarters, food service areas, building maintenance, health care services, and security. Though some equipment may be assigned to specially trained staff, you will be trained by your agency to identify, manage, and inventory all common equipment used at your facility. Common equipment and accessories that can be issued to officers include:

- security equipment, such as radios, restraints, weapons, and chemical agents
- housing equipment, such as search mirrors, restraints, and personal protective equipment (used while entering housing units to conduct searches to address disturbances and other situations)

Inspecting your equipment ensures that it will be available and ready for use when needed. Inspection is important for safety reasons; it also helps management train staff on the appropriate ways to maintain equipment. If not inspected periodically, equipment may be neglected. Neglect can result in damage, such as when poor vehicle maintenance causes mechanical problems. Likewise, poorly maintained or improperly inspected items, such as electronic control devices, can cause malfunctions, and even result in injury or death.

Inspect common equipment used in a facility

To inspect an item means making sure that the item works, that it has the correct serial number or property identification number, and that it has not passed an expiration date, if it has one. Automatic external defibrillators (AEDs), fire extinguishers, batteries, and handcuffs in each pod must be inspected to determine that they are in working condition.

Inspect your own equipment regularly to make sure it is sound, safe, and working properly. Also, inspect equipment before issuing it or receiving it back into inventory. Advise the inventory officer of any substandard equipment, so that it is removed from inventory.

Use caution when inspecting items during issue and receipt. Mishandling equipment can result in injury to an officer or inmate, or breaking the equipment. Mishandling can include incorrectly identifying equipment, not using equipment for its intended purpose, or using equipment without proper training.

ISSUING EQUIPMENT

Issue and receive common equipment used in a facility

Each agency has its own identification system to make sure that the person receiving or returning the equipment is authorized to handle the item. If one of your duties is to issue or receive equipment in the correctional facility, you will need to verify the recipient's identity, and document the activity for which the recipient will use the equipment. Check ID cards or a digital database to verify the person's identity.

To make sure that the correct equipment is issued and received, compare the item to be issued against information found in a database or log, such as appearance or serial numbers. Inspect all equipment before issuing it. Document the time, date, item, item number, and the names of the issuing and receiving officers. Your agency may require you to record signatures or identification numbers. You may also need to document the condition of equipment when items are received back into inventory, but you should always document their receipt.

INVENTORYING EQUIPMENT

Inventory common equipment used in a facility

Inventorying is the process of compiling a complete list of tools or equipment on hand. Common equipment and accessories that should be inventoried include:

- building equipment—including maintenance tools and materials used to complete common upkeep and repairs

- sanitation equipment—used for inmate living areas, such as brooms, mops, cleaning carts, and cleaning supplies
- health care equipment and accessories—including medical supplies, dental tools, and restraints
- food service equipment—including serving utensils, trays, dishes, and cookware

Counting equipment is an important part of inventory procedures. To count equipment efficiently, organize the equipment so it is easy to see. Have an orderly method or plan to physically count items by hand, such as laying items out in order, or grouping similar items together before the count. Keep track of items that cannot be grouped together, such as heavy equipment or sensitive supplies. You may keep a mental or written list as you count, to keep track of your progress before you record the official count.

Compare the number of items previously listed in the inventory against the actual number of items you count. Some agencies use shadow boards to store items; an outline of each item is traced onto a board where the item is hung. When the item is not returned to the board, it is easy to see what is missing.

It is important to correctly identify what is in the inventory. Inventory control techniques for identification include:

- etching the inventory control number on the tool
- comparing the tool markings with recorded facility markings
- color-coding items by classification, for example, restricted or non-restricted
- using inventory lists with descriptions and numbers together
- using prepared spaces on a shadow board for storage

Your agency will train you in the proper procedures for inventory control and documentation; the agency may use logs, inventory sheets, or an electronic database. Maintaining accurate logs during inventory is important for identifying the location of equipment. Reviewing logs is commonly done before, during, and after shifts to verify what equipment has been issued. Logs allow you to identify when an item is missing or when an item has been issued, replaced, or repaired. Each agency's policies for inventory control will determine how responsibilities are assigned, whether by shift, area, job assignment, or equipment type.

Catalog and preserve the documentation used in inventory and storage processes. Retain forms or logs so that they are available for later review and for public record. A master inventory log or a daily inventory sheet may document items in the inventory that are issued or returned.

STORING EQUIPMENT

Store common equipment used in a facility

Correctional officers are responsible for properly storing all equipment in their care and control.

Types of equipment that inmates can use in escapes or assaults include tools, chemical agents, electronic control devices, restraint devices, or other non-lethal weapons.

If you are not paying attention, items can be stolen and used to aid in an escape or assault.

Always store equipment in secure, designated areas with access limited to authorized persons. Secured storage areas may be considered temporary or permanent. Some of the secured storage areas typically found in a correctional facility can include an armory, a mini-arsenal, a caustic chemicals locker, a master tool room, a tool cage, an exterior building, or any designated room within the facility.

Store equipment in its proper area immediately after inventory to preserve the integrity of the inventory, to ensure that equipment is ready for reissue, and to ensure security. Where you store an item is based on the type of equipment and agency resources.

MANAGING HAZARDOUS EQUIPMENT

Know the types of hazardous equipment used in a facility

You may need to use hazardous equipment or tools. Inmates may also use hazardous tools under staff supervision when completing work assignments. Consider tools that are automated, sharp, heavy, or awkward to manipulate especially dangerous. You are responsible for tool and equipment control for safety reasons; inmates can use these tools to commit a crime, such as to assault another person, to damage the facility, or to aid in an escape.

Examples of hazardous equipment in a correctional setting include:

- basic construction tools—hammer, screwdriver, pliers, shovel, ladder, hoses
- power tools—electric drill, jigsaw, chainsaw
- cutting tools—band saw, handsaw, hacksaw
- building and grounds maintenance equipment—painting supplies, lawn mower, pipe wrench
- culinary instruments—knife, cleaver, cooking fork, spit, skewer
- medical/dental instruments with sharp points or cutting edges

Stay vigilant regarding hazardous equipment, such as knives or peppery food items. Failing to safeguard these items from inmates can kill you.

Review Items

1. *List the type of equipment you might find in the following areas or activities in a facility:*
    a) *inmate living areas*
    b) *food service areas*
    c) *health care service areas*
    d) *building maintenance*
    e) *security equipment*
2. *What is some of the hazardous equipment used in a facility?*

3. *What is the process for inspecting equipment used in a facility?*
4. *What is the process for issuing and receiving equipment in a facility?*
5. *Describe various ways to count equipment while inventorying equipment in a facility.*

LESSON 2

WEAPONS IN A CORRECTIONAL FACILITY

LESSON GOAL

You will be able to issue and receive weapons, lethal and non-lethal, when faced with an emergency situation.

THINK ABOUT THIS

Imagine a situation in which an inmate gets access to weapons within the facility. Facilities avoid this type of scenario by establishing a rigid process for issuing and receiving weapons and ammunition. Be sure that you have a full understanding of this process and follow it each and every time. The last thing you need is to be responsible for any type of injury or death to another officer, a visitor, or an inmate because you did not follow your facility's process for managing weapons and ammunition.

WEAPONS AND AMMUNITION

Issue and receive weapons and ammunition in a facility

Correctional agencies may choose to issue certain firearms and ammunition depending upon the correctional officer's training and qualifications. Some agencies do not issue duty weapons and ammunition to their correctional staff. Some weapons, such as firearms, are considered lethal (deadly force); some weapons are considered non-lethal. The purpose of a non-lethal weapon is to incapacitate a person. Non-lethal weapons include electronic control devices, impact weapons, and chemical agents such as oleoresin capsicum (OC) spray.

Staff do not carry firearms while on duty inside a correctional facility. In an emergency, though, command staff may issue firearms. If an agency issues firearms and ammunition to staff, you will be required to secure these in designated storage areas or secured lockers when entering the facility. If you have a firearm secured at the facility, you must retrieve it when you leave.

When issuing weapons and ammunition, an officer must verify the recipient's identity. Each agency will have its own identification system, such as ID cards, weapons cards, or digital database checks. The officer issuing weapons and ammunition will need to process documents authorizing the transaction. This documentation will contain details of the firearm or weapon (serial number, physical characteristics) and information on the receiving officer. Your agency may require signatures for each transaction. The issuing officer will document the time, the date, the make, the model and serial number, the total rounds of ammunition, and the name of the receiving officer. The officer in charge of equipment should perform a safety check when issuing or receiving any firearm.

Inspecting firearms and other weapons involves checking the physical parts of the weapon for operational soundness, completing a safety check, and making sure the ammunition is the proper type and is in good condition. After an officer has verified that a person has been authorized to receive a weapon, they will perform a safety check. Both people must use caution during this process, because mishandling the weapon can result in injury or death. Once they have completed the safety check, the receiving officer can have the weapon and ammunition. The person receiving the items must properly record the transaction.

Review Items

1. *How does an officer issue and receive weapons and ammunition in a facility?*
2. *What are the types of weapons that are issued in a corrections facility?*
3. *What is the purpose of a non-lethal weapon?*
4. *What is the process for managing a weapon permanently assigned to an officer?*
5. *What are the general steps for verifying that an officer is authorized to receive a weapon?*

UNIT 2 HAZARDOUS MATERIALS AND SENSITIVE SUPPLIES

LESSON 1

HAZARDOUS MATERIALS AND SENSITIVE SUPPLIES

LESSON GOAL

You will be able to use a Safety Data Sheet (SDS) to manage hazardous and sensitive facility supplies.

THINK ABOUT THIS

Keeping a sufficient amount of supplies on hand is an important part of facility operations. Running out of an essential supply can keep the facility from running smoothly. Your job duties include managing special supplies and hazardous materials within the facility. How the facility stores, moves, and controls supplies should ensure a safe and secure environment for officers, visitors, and inmates. Being familiar with standard supply management supports the efficient and safe operation of a facility.

HAZARDOUS MATERIALS

Know the important role of the Safety Data Sheet (SDS)

Hazardous materials are substances (solids, liquids, or gases) that, when released, may be capable of causing harm to people, the environment, and property.

Safely managing dangerous, hazardous materials and sensitive supplies in a correctional facility requires an understanding of the proper care, storage, and control of these items to promote a safe working environment for staff and inmates.

Hazardous materials include the following:

- acids
- bleach
- insecticides
- glue
- gasoline

A ***Safety Data Sheet (SDS)*** is required for any hazardous material shipped to and from a correctional facility. An SDS includes the manufacturer's name, the product name, and the procedures for spills and leaks. An SDS also includes the following information:

I. Identification—includes product identifier; manufacturer or distributor name, address, phone number; emergency phone number; recommended use; restrictions on use.

II. Hazard(s) identification—includes all hazards regarding the chemical; required label elements.

III. Composition/information on ingredients—includes information on chemical ingredients; trade secret claims.

IV. First-aid measures—includes important symptoms/effects, acute, delayed; required treatment.

V. Fire-fighting measures—lists suitable extinguishing techniques, equipment; chemical hazards from fire.

VI. Accidental release measures—lists emergency procedures; protective equipment; proper methods of containment and cleanup.

VII. Handling and storage—lists precautions for safe handling and storage, including incompatibilities.

VIII. Exposure controls/personal protection—lists exposure limit used or recommended by the Occupational Safety and Health Administration (OSHA) or the chemical manufacturer, importer, or employer; also includes appropriate engineering controls and personal protective equipment (PPE).

IX. Physical and chemical properties—lists the chemical's characteristics.

X. Stability and reactivity—lists chemical stability and possibility of hazardous reactions.

XI. Toxicological information—includes routes of exposure; related symptoms, acute and chronic effects; numerical measures of toxicity.

XII. Ecological information (non-mandatory)—includes data from toxicity tests performed on aquatic and/or terrestrial organisms; effects of chemical degradation to the environment; other adverse effects.

XIII. Disposal considerations (non-mandatory)—includes information on appropriate disposal and disposal containers; sewage disposal; special precautions for landfills.

XIV. Transport information (non-mandatory)—includes UN number and proper shipping name; transport hazard classes; guidance on transport in bulk.

XV. Regulatory information (non-mandatory)—includes national and/or regional regulatory information of the chemical or mixtures.

XVI. Other information—includes information on when the SDS was prepared or when the last known revision was made.

An SDS is required wherever a potentially hazardous material is stored or used. The SDS will help you be aware of all hazardous materials in your assigned area and what they are used for. An SDS is essential for identifying and understanding information regarding a hazardous material and must be made available to staff and inmates. OSHA standards require that all SDS documents are available to anyone who is exposed to a potentially hazardous substance.

You must be able to read and understand the manufacturers' guidelines and the SDS to properly handle hazardous materials. You are responsible for consulting the SDS.

Properly managing hazardous materials includes inventory control and monitoring the location and issue of these supplies. You must know how to control the inventory and have a general knowledge of the use of these items, as well as an understanding of how hazardous materials and supplies can become a danger when misused.

Control hazardous materials in a correctional facility

To control hazardous materials:

- Issue items only to authorized staff.
- Record staff name, date, amount, description of material issued, date of material's return, and condition of material when returned.
- Supervise inmates using hazardous materials closely.
- Perform frequent inventories.
- Keep items in secured storage areas.
- Store items in original containers.
- Store gasoline in approved safety cans.

SENSITIVE SUPPLIES

Sensitive supplies refer to supplies used throughout the facility for health, sanitation, or housing maintenance. It is especially important to record the identity of any person receiving sensitive supplies.

Store and move sensitive facility supplies

Sensitive supplies include medical equipment, medicine, industrial strength cleaners, or other substances used for different purposes in the facility. Some of those purposes are facility maintenance, vehicle maintenance, pest control, laundry services, and firearms cleaning. Examples of sensitive supplies include, but are not limited to, paints, fuel, oil, cleaning solvents, wax, window cleaner, gun oils, solvents, thinners, and bleach. These supplies can pose a hazard or be easily misused. They may or may not be considered hazardous materials.

Sensitive supplies also include supplies for food service, such as cooking oils, vanilla, yeast, and nutmeg. These sensitive supplies must be controlled at all times. Inmates can produce illegal substances, such as alcohol, with yeast, sugar, and fruit. Pepper can be used to incapacitate a person.

It is important to use supplies only for their intended purpose. Follow any listed instructions and precautions. Improper handling of sensitive supplies can result in items becoming contaminated or dangerous, which may result in injury or death. Sensitive supplies may become explosive if they come in contact with other chemical substances or if they are exposed to temperature changes or movement.

To properly maintain and care for sensitive supplies, you must:

- Issue and transport supplies according to the SDS.
- Use appropriate safety gear or protection, for example, gloves, masks, eye protection.

- Handle supplies only after receiving proper training.
- Never mix cleaning supplies.
- Be careful and thoughtful while moving supplies.
- Ensure a well-ventilated area when necessary.
- Close containers.
- Properly dispose of used cleaning supplies and cloths.
- Appropriately supervise use of all supplies.

To safely handle sensitive supplies:

- Store them in proper containers, such as boxes (wooden, paper, plastic), drums (metal, plastic), cylinders (metal, plastic), and bags (multi-walled paper, multi-walled plastic).
- Follow inventory processes.
- Keep supplies clean and securely closed.
- Remove any substandard items.

Facilities often receive sensitive supplies in concentrated form. These supplies need to be diluted before use. Be aware of possible allergic reactions when supplies are handled or mixed. Each agency will vary on how it monitors the use of sensitive supplies and identifies and manages requests and purchases by using logs, charts, and electronic databases.

LESSON VOCABULARY

hazardous materials

Safety Data Sheet (SDS)

REVIEW ITEMS

1. *What are examples of hazardous materials found in a correctional facility?*
2. *What is the role of the Safety Data Sheet (SDS)?*
3. *List the information found on an SDS.*
4. *How do you store and move hazardous materials?*
5. *What are some examples of sensitive supplies used in a correctional facility?*
6. *What are some of the food items that can be used to produce illegal substances?*
7. *How do you store and move sensitive supplies?*

UNIT 3 ENTERING, EXITING, AND MOVING WITHIN FACILITIES

LESSON 1

SECURITY EQUIPMENT AND MOVING WITHIN SECURED AREAS

LESSON GOAL

You will be able to operate security equipment and use entry and exit equipment to keep a facility safe and secure.

THINK ABOUT THIS

Since security is critical in correctional facilities, it makes sense that getting into, through, and out of a facility would not be a simple task. While working in a facility, almost all of the gates and doors you will encounter will be locked. Typically, you will find yourself pressing a button on an electronically locked door or gate to signal an unseen officer in the control room, who will allow you access by viewing different camera monitors and operating a switchboard. While this may slow down an officer's progress through a facility, using security equipment, such as locks and cameras, is crucial for controlling traffic entering, moving within, and exiting a facility.

SECURITY EQUIPMENT

Understand your responsibility as a correctional officer to keep the facility safe and secure

Preserving security is critical in a correctional facility, and it begins with knowing the equipment that is needed to protect it. ***Security equipment*** refers to any item or technology used to enhance or maintain protection, and to ensure safety. Security equipment can be electronic, such as a security camera, or gates or barriers. Types of security equipment in a correctional facility include equipment for personal security, such as a body alarm system, or equipment used to preserve normal facility operations, such as radios, perimeter alert systems, perimeter lights, cameras, or microwave motion detectors. Security equipment may confine a person or allow an officer to watch the activities of inmates. The purpose of security equipment is to alert staff to any unauthorized activity and to discourage unauthorized movement.

Officers need to know the proper procedures to handle security equipment and the approved methods to manage it. Become thoroughly familiar with the different types of security equipment at the correctional facility and the process for issuing and authorizing its use.

A ***perimeter*** is a secure area that surrounds a facility and is a critical element of security. Perimeters may be large walls, single or double fences, or any other barriers that prevent unauthorized exit or entry.

Other types of institutional security equipment include the following:

Know the different types of facility security equipment

- gates—entrances that open in sequence, one after the other to confine a person in the space in between
- doors
- locks
- surveillance devices that enable you to view others' activities from a distance
- internal alarm systems designed to alert staff when an unauthorized activity occurs
- contraband or metal detection systems
- razor wire

Doors that allow one section of passage to be closed before opening another section. *Figure 4-1*

Available security equipment and the application of security measures will differ according to each agency's resources. Security measures and the application of security technology also depend upon your job duties, which may require certain devices, such as electronic shields, restraint devices, chemical agents, detection systems, or radios. Agencies may apply security measures differently in confinement units, entrances, exits, or special areas.

ENTRY AND EXIT EQUIPMENT

Follow the guidelines for operating entry and exit equipment in a facility

Agencies can vary in the equipment, systems, and operational procedures they use for entering or exiting the correctional facility, or restricting movement throughout the facility. Movement into or out of a facility, or within secure areas, can be controlled at every entrance and exit through a variety of gates and doors. One special structure for controlling movement is a sally port. A ***sally port*** is a system of two openings (doors or gates) designed to open only one at a time. This is used to control the movement of either vehicles or pedestrians by creating a secure area between the two openings. Sally ports can be operated manually or by remote control.

The following steps outline the operation of a sally port system:

- Identify persons or vehicles to be admitted or released.
- Verify authorization for admittance or release.
- Report the activity/presence of persons or vehicles, if required.
- Open the first gate or door of the sally port.
- Once persons or vehicles have cleared that gate's or door's threshold, close the gate or door.
- Search persons and vehicles when both gates or doors are closed, if required.
- Open the second gate or door after the first gate or door has closed completely. Never have both open at the same time, unless emergency situations dictate otherwise.
- Close the second gate or door after persons or vehicles have cleared the threshold.
- Report the movement of persons or vehicles.
- Record the movement of persons or vehicles through the gates or door in a log.

A sally port gate within an enclosed garage

Figure 4-2

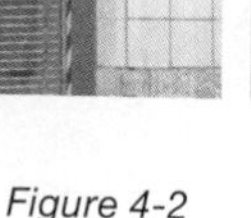

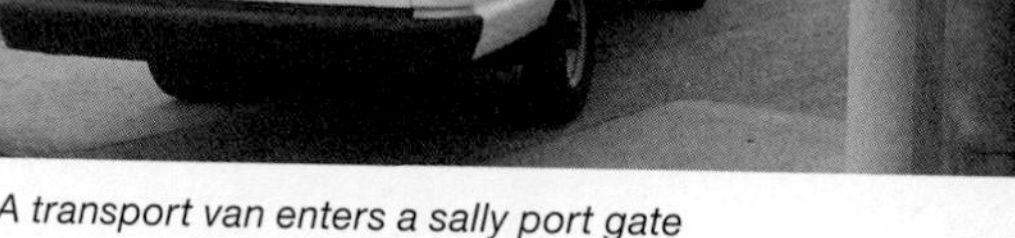

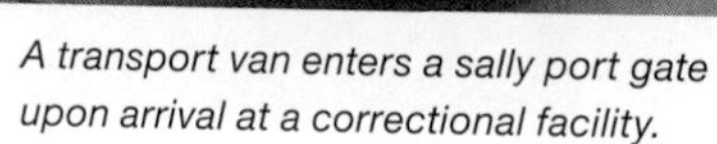

A transport van enters a sally port gate upon arrival at a correctional facility.

Figure 4-3

For security and safety reasons, be alert during the operation of doors and gates. Doors or gates are opened either manually or electronically. Locking systems on doors and gates can also be manual or electronic. Manual locking devices consist of doors, gates, or windows that are operated by keys, locks, chains, levers, or cranks. Electronic locking

An exterior sally port gate large enough for vehicles to pass through *Figure 4-4*

devices consist of doors, gates, or windows operated by a system of electronic switches, panels, buttons, and key cards. Remote-control panel systems for gates and cell doors may differ in their function and operation. To operate these panels, you may need to push a button, flip a switch, turn a knob, or touch a screen. Injuries and escapes are major concerns during gate and door operations of sally port systems. Keep all items (vehicles, equipment, and extremities) clear of the gate's moving parts during operation. You should know the location of the manual or operational safety overrides on the gate in case of an emergency.

To prevent escapes, you must make sure that doors are closed correctly and are not manipulated or tampered with. If the locking mechanism is not functioning properly, report it immediately so that it can be fixed as soon as possible.

Notify appropriate personnel of the entry or exit of individuals by completing logs and by making phone and radio calls. Use a person's identification to confirm whether they are authorized to enter or exit an area. Information collected will usually include items such as the driver's license; state identification information; tag number, make, model, and color of vehicle; or other official documentation.

Lesson Vocabulary

perimeter

sally port

security equipment

Review Items

1. *What are an officer's responsibilities to keep the facility safe and secure?*
2. *What are the different types of facility security equipment?*
3. *What are the steps for operating entry and exit equipment such as a sally port in a facility?*
4. *Describe how to verify a person's authorization to enter or exit a secure area.*

UNIT 4 INSPECTIONS

LESSON 1

INSPECTION CRITERIA AND METHODS

LESSON GOAL

You will be able to follow the proper procedures for inspecting the equipment and structure of a correctional facility.

THINK ABOUT THIS

Equipment or facility inspections can occur before or after a specific activity, such as visitation, recreation, or inmate transports. Inspections can happen on a regular or irregular schedule. To ensure the smooth operation of the facility, you need to know how to perform thorough and systematic inspections. Failure to do so can lead to the introduction of contraband, threats to officer safety, and inmate escape.

INSPECTIONS

Inspect facility equipment

Depending on the type of inspection being conducted, you may follow a list, schedule, or check-off sheet. The type of equipment needed depends upon the purpose and location of the inspection. Inspections must be thorough, systematic, timely, and safe. Criteria may include confirming the presence and functionality of equipment assigned, and following a schedule for inspections. Inspections are generally done on a regular schedule, and conducted before or after certain activities, such as visitation, recreation, or inmate transports.

Common items are used for inspection, such as flashlights, mirrors, gloves, and probes (a probe can be as simple as a pencil). Common items used to record inspections include logs, writing pads, inventory lists, and report forms.

To complete a basic inspection:

- Begin the inspection at a specific location.
- Inspect in an orderly sequence.
- Make sure the equipment operates properly.
- Record any deficiencies found during the inspection.
- Make any possible on-the-spot corrections.
- Leave the area the way it was found, never in disorder.

Inspections must be done systematically. Identify starting and ending points, and then organize the inspection in a step-by-step process. Inspection techniques may also include taking notes and closing doors when finished.

To inspect a facility for structural or property damage:

- Schedule the inspection.
- Consult the agency's inspection guidelines for each type of inspection.
- Be familiar with the structure.
- Review safety procedures for the operation of equipment to be used for the inspection.
- As determined by the type of inspection, search inmates, remove inmates from the area to be inspected, and place inmates under supervision until the conclusion of the inspection.
- Check the area for cleanliness, structural integrity, and safety.
- Review documentation as available and appropriate to complete the inspection and ensure its accuracy.

Conduct a facility structural inspection

Inspect for structural deficiencies by making sure that the structure has not been tampered with, and to confirm proper functioning of its components. Structural deficiencies generally refer to issues that affect normal operation or functionality of buildings and their security. You should routinely examine your surroundings to make sure equipment such as gates, doors, and locks are operational.

Some structural deficiencies require special equipment or training to conduct an inspection. These instances may require special inspection methods. For example, inspecting windows on the second floor of a building at night may require a ladder and a flashlight. Another example would be inspecting firefighting equipment or testing gas lines, both of which may require special training.

Review Items

1. *What are the guidelines for inspecting facility equipment?*
2. *What are the guidelines for conducting a facility structural inspection?*
3. *What are some of the common items used to conduct an inspection?*

UNIT 5 SECURITY

LESSON 1

SECURITY STANDARDS AND INSPECTIONS

LESSON GOAL

You will be able to conduct facility security checks and inspections to maintain the correctional facility's security standards.

THINK ABOUT THIS

One of your job duties includes providing security for the facility by enforcing security standards. These are the checks and balances that preserve the operational effectiveness of the facility. They ensure the care, custody, and control of inmates and the supervision of visitors within the facility. Security standards ensure the health, safety, and well-being of all persons in the facility.

SECURITY STANDARDS

Understand the important role of security standards for the safety of inmates, officers, and visitors in a facility

Correctional officers are responsible for the security of the entire facility as well as their assigned work area. To ensure safety and security, conduct general security inspections throughout the day. Inspection methods and schedules are followed based upon the work assignment or assigned work area. Security inspections may involve checking the integrity of the perimeter, fencing, windows, doors, lighting elements, and furniture to make sure they are sound and operational (such as no loose nuts or bolts or broken furniture pieces), and the proper functioning of locks, keys, and microwave motion detectors. Apply situational awareness by observing activity and the surroundings for any potential problems, and be prepared to address any security concerns immediately. Use four of the five senses (seeing, hearing, smelling, and touching) when performing security inspections.

Conduct facility security inspections

Security levels must be maintained to support the normal operations of the facility and response during emergencies. Security measures require maintaining appropriate levels of supervision, securing and managing the environment, following basic facility rules, and enforcing proper behavior and conduct of inmates. Security inspections are done to verify "known" elements involved in security, whereas a security check is performed to check for "unknowns" or the unexpected.

Conducting security inspections serves to verify operational norms, or "knowns," and may include the following:

- testing security casings, locks, and keys of all openings
- checking for broken windows, cut screens, cracked skylights, defective hinges, loose or scarred bars, loose floor tiles, or holes in walls

- checking compounds, warehouses, perimeter buildings, storage areas, work areas, service areas (such as libraries or gyms), and fences for structural damage
- checking audible alarms and microwave motion detectors for proper function
- checking window bars, gates, fences, and emergency exits for free operation
- testing communications and audiovisual monitoring devices for proper function
- examining fire extinguishers and fire hoses for proper function
- checking lights and other electrical systems
- checking plumbing, heating, and ventilation systems

Conduct frequent security inspections of high-use areas, such as cell rooms, dorms, and day rooms. Frequently inspect medical areas or hospital rooms as well. Inmates who are temporarily housed in these locations will require extra supervision due to escape attempts at these types of facilities. Another example is a mental health clinic where inmates receive treatment. The mental health facility may not require or allow mechanical restraints. The lack of restraints can pose an increased security risk when new routines and requirements are introduced, and security is reduced. You must perform inspections upon an inmate's arrival to any clinic or hospital room, while they are there, and after they leave.

You may be able to resolve an equipment problem found during an inspection if available resources allow. Broken locks, bent or broken keys, malfunctioning hardware on doors and gates, inoperable camera or video surveillance equipment, and broken control panels are all examples of problems that you might find during an inspection. When you find a problem item that poses a danger, you must notify your supervisor immediately and follow the supervisor's directions to resolve the concern. When a problem is identified and addressed, you should do a follow-up inspection. In other cases, more formal action may be needed, in which trained personnel are called in to resolve the issue.

Conduct facility security checks

How often you perform a security check will be based upon the security standards in place or the agency's policies, or in response to special conditions, such as a pending escape. Security checks are varied in schedule so that inmates do not expect them. Checks are done more frequently if the facility is in a lockdown status or in a high-security situation. You may initiate a security check based on an observation. Inform staff of the intention to do a security check. Check all structures in the facility, such as doors, closets, windows, and locks. Open cell doors to make sure they work. Security checks may include monitoring video, either live camera feeds or recorded tapes.

Review Items

1. *What is the role of security standards for the safety of inmates, officers, and visitors in a facility?*
2. *When and how should you conduct facility security inspections?*
3. *When should you conduct facility security checks?*

LESSON 2
PERIMETER SECURITY

LESSON GOAL

You will be able to maintain security standards for the correctional facility perimeter.

THINK ABOUT THIS

A secure perimeter keeps inmates inside the facility, away from the community. It also keeps the community from illegally entering or introducing contraband into the facility. Any change in a facility's perimeter security is a direct reflection on how well you perform perimeter patrols and maintain security standards.

PERIMETER SECURITY

Maintain a secure facility perimeter

Correctional officers are responsible for maintaining security levels of the perimeter for operational readiness. They must also be prepared to respond to perimeter security deficiencies. Perimeters are often monitored or patrolled on both a regular and an irregular basis, either on foot or with vehicles. The perimeter may also be monitored through video surveillance, armed observation towers, stationary posts or stationary vehicles (where correctional staff remain in the area for observation), or in roving vehicles patrolling a facility.

Razor wire tops a fence on the perimeter of a correctional facility.

Figure 4-5

You may identify discrepancies (deficiencies, or differences between proper procedures of the facility and what's actually done) through your inspections or during your regular patrols. Security discrepancies of a perimeter can involve barrier failure, inoperable communications systems, or weather-related events that negatively impact the integrity or visibility of the perimeter and the facility. Security discrepancies can also occur because of staff negligence or when a correctional officer is not paying attention to details. A security breach can include: unauthorized inmate activity either near the perimeter or in a usually unoccupied area, inmates with changed clothing attempting to approach a perimeter, items hanging in windows, broken windows, civilians or vehicles approaching the perimeter from the outside, or inmates approaching perimeters while people are outside.

While patrolling the perimeter, regularly check in with the appropriate staff. This communications check should include your location and the perimeter status. You are responsible for following established protocols, such as notifying a supervisor when you complete a perimeter check. Let staff know about any security concerns by using the radio or telephone, and keeping written or digital logs.

Document perimeter patrols and include the following:

- the condition of gates and fences, windows, lights, cameras
- any unfamiliar and unsecured vehicles in the parking lot

There is a heightened level of security and awareness when responding to an identified security breach. Steps to resolve a security breach could include immediately locking down the facility, performing a thorough security check, and formally counting the inmates. Additional staff may be assigned to the perimeter to accommodate security needs while the breach is addressed. Other agencies may be requested to supplement staff as necessary. Depending on the severity of the breach, specially trained response teams may be called in to assist.

Review Items

1. *What are the different ways a facility can secure a perimeter?*
2. *How should you maintain a secure facility perimeter?*
3. *What should you include when documenting perimeter patrols?*

UNIT 6 FACILITY SAFETY CONCERNS

LESSON 1

IDENTIFYING AND RESOLVING SAFETY CONCERNS

LESSON GOAL

You will be able to correct facility safety deficiencies based on organizational safety standards for emergency preparedness and response.

THINK ABOUT THIS

Safety is one of the most important elements of your job. Maintaining a safe work environment will help ensure that you go home at the end of the day. It will keep visitors to your facility safe, as well as the inmates you supervise. Following your facility safety standards is not only an important part of your job duties, but a responsibility that you should take seriously for your own safety.

SAFETY STANDARDS

Know the organizations that may govern a facility's safety standards

The safety standards each agency observes will depend on accreditation guidelines from organizations that oversee those standards. These organizations include the Occupational Safety and Health Administration (OSHA), the Florida Corrections Accreditation Commission (FCAC), the American Correctional Association (ACA), the Florida Model Jail Standards (FMJS), the National Detention Standards (NDS), Florida Administrative Code (F.A.C.) Division: 33 Department of Corrections, and Chapter 64E-11, F.A.C. (Department of Health, Division of Environmental Health, Food Hygiene).

Know the facility safety standards for emergency preparedness and response

Correctional officers are responsible for maintaining a safe environment for staff, visitors, and inmates. You can prepare for emergencies by: communicating instructions to inmates to help maintain good behavior during an emergency; applying knowledge of basic facility rules, regulations, and standards for operation; and following your facility's emergency or contingency plans.

Maintaining a safe work environment will help ensure that you go home at the end of the day.

Your chain of command will brief you on the safety standards for emergency preparedness for your facility. You will learn more about preparing for facility emergencies in Chapter 8.

Know the possible hazards that can cause facility safety deficiencies

Be aware of hazards that influence safety. All areas of the facility are safety concerns; these include grounds, dining halls, recreation areas, housing areas, work crews, medical areas, visitation areas, the control center, officer stations, sally ports, and the chapel. Some safety standards and guidelines are uniform throughout each agency, and other standards may depend on the accrediting association of which the agency is a member.

Safety standards reflect the mission of the facility, and can address equipment management, such as chemical labeling and equipment storage procedures. Operational safety standards for facilities include guidelines for inmate classification, lighting, space, temperature, air control, dietary concerns, and the ratio of inmates to staff.

Potential hazards that could cause unsafe conditions include:

- exits covered and not accessible, or exit lights not operable or visible
- cluttered walkways
- water fountains leaking or overflowing
- inadequate number of fire extinguishers
- inmates smoking
- frayed electrical cords
- inadequate electrical grounding
- loose items on floors
- improper use of tools and equipment
- failure to wear safety equipment
- spills on floor surfaces
- unattended cooking pots; scattered cooking utensils
- grease buildups in hood systems and around cooking surfaces
- disorderly conduct in dining areas
- improperly maintained fire extinguishing equipment

CORRECTING SAFETY DEFICIENCIES

Understand your responsibilities for correcting facility safety deficiencies

Resolve safety concerns immediately. These concerns include dealing with inmate housing and maintaining proper visual and audio surveillance. Apply reasonable judgment when enforcing policies and addressing concerns.

Factors that influence safety can involve deficiencies in equipment or the facility's structure. Equipment such as fire alarms, emergency lights, fire extinguishers, Self-Contained Breathing Apparatus (SCBA), automatic external defibrillators (AEDs), handrails, and improperly stored equipment pose a safety concern when they are deficient. An inspection may require that you touch or visually inspect an item, compare components with manuals, compare the item's normal functioning to its current status, look for the expiration date, and determine that the item is functional. Other factors that can influence safety in the facility include structural deficiencies related to poor conditions, or facility layout or design that poses a potential for disruptions of normal facility operations.

When you find a dangerous item, you must notify your supervisor immediately and follow the supervisor's directions to resolve the safety concern. After a deficiency is identified and addressed, a follow-up inspection will be conducted. In other cases, more formal action may be needed, where trained personnel will be called in to resolve the deficiency.

Review Items

1. *What organizations govern your facility's safety standards?*
2. *How can you prepare for an emergency response in a facility??*
3. *What are possible hazards that can cause facility safety deficiencies?*
4. *What are your responsibilities for correcting facility safety deficiencies?*

UNIT 7 SANITATION AND HEALTH

LESSON 1
SANITATION STANDARDS AND ENVIRONMENTAL HEALTH

LESSON GOAL

You will be aware of common health hazards found in a correctional facility based on the guidelines of a sanitation plan and environmental health program.

THINK ABOUT THIS

The sanitation standards your facility complies with depend on accreditation guidelines from organizations that govern those standards. Your facility's sanitation plan should provide guidelines for applying sanitary measures to ensure cleanliness and protect the health of officers, visitors, and inmates. Your knowledge of facility sanitation standards and the ability to follow those guidelines will ensure that the environment you work in, and inmates live in, is healthy, clean, and disease free.

SANITATION STANDARDS

Know the elements of a facility sanitation plan

Sanitation standards are guided by s. 944.31, F.S., which refers to requirements for facilities to provide clean, orderly, and safe surroundings for inmates and staff. How sanitation needs are addressed is determined by each agency's resources and is guided by professional standards, such as the FMJS or F.A.C., and through accreditation agencies.

Institutional sanitation standards ensure that the facility environment is healthy, clean, and disease free. Maintaining good standards has a positive effect on the public, staff, and inmates.

A correctional facility's sanitation plan outlines the standards and methods used to inspect and clean areas, including scheduled inspections and required documentation. One example of standards is setting heat requirements for laundry and food service to control water temperature so that chemicals successfully destroy bacteria and germs.

Sanitation equipment and supplies include soaps and cleaning compounds, detergent and scouring powders, mops, brooms, brushes, and cleaning cloths. Different levels of housing may have their own special sanitation considerations.

Part of a sanitation plan includes daily routines and schedules for:

- housekeeping, collecting trash, cleaning floors
- cleaning cells and housing areas

- cleaning and sanitizing toilets, sinks, and showers
- cleaning activity and service areas
- emptying and cleaning garbage cans
- cleaning special areas after use
- cleaning food service areas after each meal
- laundering inmate clothing and linens

Simple safety habits, such as checking to see how many times the trash is discarded or immediately cleaning up spills in areas where people may slip and fall, can strengthen your facility's sanitation plan.

Follow safety standards for serving meals in a timely manner. You can cause your facility to receive a citation if you do not follow the facility's sanitation plan. In general, look to see what needs to be done or cleaned up and see that it gets done.

ENVIRONMENTAL HEALTH PROGRAM

The components of a complete environmental health program should include:

Know the elements of a facility environmental health program

- sanitary food preparation area
- effective elimination of rodents and pests
- sanitary, adequate water supply that prevents scalding and has either a water fountain or disposable drinking cups
- adequate amount of heat, cooling, electricity, and ventilation
- adequate lighting and space
- proper sewage and liquid waste disposal
- measures to prevent the spread of communicable diseases
- clean bedding and adequate laundry
- maintenance of the facility
- facilities designed and constructed for minimum noise, to accommodate disabled people, and to minimize dangers of explosion, fire, and spread of fire
- safe storage and accountability for drugs; poisons and flammable, caustic, or toxic materials; and cleaning agents

- sanitation inspections by government health officials
- thoroughly trained inmates assigned to operate equipment in special cleaning tasks

Become familiar with your facility's environmental health program, including its requirements, methods, and schedule.

Assign inmates to sanitation tasks fairly and consistently; rotate inmates through assignments so they learn all tasks. As the inmates perform cleanup duties, supervise and conduct regular and unpredictable inspections. Cleaning supplies and equipment should be issued, inventoried, and documented. Look for unsanitary conditions and enforce housekeeping standards for cells and activity areas. You may be able to independently resolve a sanitation deficiency if resources are available. For example, if an inmate overturns a bucket of dirty mop water, you can take care of that quickly. In other cases, more formal action may be required where trained personnel will be needed to resolve the deficiency, such as a hazardous materials (hazmat) spill. Take the necessary precautions, such as sanitizing your uniform and shoes, to avoid bringing communicable diseases home.

HEALTH HAZARDS

Know the common health hazards found in a facility

The environment may pose health hazards for all who enter a facility. These hazards can include parasitic outbreaks (scabies, lice) and viral and bacterial illnesses, such as tuberculosis (TB), human immunodeficiency virus (HIV), and methicillin-resistant Staphylococcus aureus (MRSA).

Inspections can result in identifying health hazards, such as plumbing that does not work properly, broken pipes, unsanitary areas, and wet floors. If the health hazard poses an immediate danger, notify your supervisor immediately. Follow the direction of your supervisor to correct the hazard.

When inspecting for health hazards, evaluate the environment for cleanliness, the presence of unusual odors, the extent of clutter, ventilation, hazardous conditions, and possible contagion from inmates.

REVIEW ITEMS

1. *What are the elements of a facility sanitation plan?*
2. *What are the elements of a facility environmental health program?*
3. *What are the common health hazards found in a facility?*

Intake and Release

LESSON 1

INTAKE / RECEPTION AND ASSESSMENT PROCESS

LESSON GOAL

You will know the intake process in a county or state detention facility.

THINK ABOUT THIS

If you've ever been admitted to the hospital, you know that there is a specific process. You have to present a form of identification and sign documents, some of which you will be allowed to keep. Then you will be assigned a room based on the severity of your condition. This process is similar to the intake/reception and assessment process that you will learn for a correctional facility.

The intake, classification, and release processes used by county and state facilities differ in many ways. Based on the rulemaking bodies, the Florida Model Jail Standards or Chapter 33, F.A.C., each facility establishes its own guidelines and procedures. You must learn the procedures at the facility where you will be employed. You must also have knowledge of facility policies and procedures, state laws, and legal guidelines as they pertain to each part of the process.

In county detention facilities, admission to a correctional facility is known as ***intake***. In state facilities, admission to the institution is known as ***reception***.

INTAKE / RECEPTION DOCUMENTATION

Know how to verify an inmate's identity during intake / reception

During the intake / reception process, the inmate's identity is verified using various forms of identification, including the following:

- driver's license, military ID, or any other type of valid photo ID
- fingerprinting

Know how to identify arrest papers and the common features included

Identity is also verified when an inmate is moved, such as between correctional facilities or to and from court, or when moved to another area within the facility. Before an inmate can be admitted by a county or state facility, certain legal documents must be presented that support the arrest or commitment. ***Arrest papers*** are the paperwork filed by the arresting officer that results in the person being arrested and taken to a detention facility for admission. These papers may consist of arrest affidavits, warrants, and other court orders.

Common features of arrest papers include:

- personal identifying information about the inmate (name, aliases, date of birth, sex, race, current address, phone number, Social Security number, height, weight, driver's license state and number, and place of birth)

- date and time of arrest
- place of arrest
- agency-generated case number
- charges, including the statute number(s) and the number of charges
- name of the arresting officer and the arresting agency
- probable cause affidavit
- copies of warrants or court orders
- victim contact notification, if required by chapter 960, F.S.
- copies of issued citations for traffic offenses

Commitment papers are documents or orders generated by the court after an offender is found guilty of a crime and that commit the offender to a correctional facility or to a mental hospital.

Know how to identify commitment papers and the common features included

Common features of commitment papers include:

- judgment and sentence pages (signed by a judge)
- court paperwork with sentencing information and any court recommendation
- current criminal history printout from FCIC/NCIC (Florida Crime Information Center/National Crime Information Center)
- summary of inmate's behavior and adjustment to a correctional setting from the sending agency noting disciplinary issues and housing assignment while in jail
- medical transfer summary from the sending facility

Arrest or commitment papers may contain common terminology or abbreviations for different aspects of the arrest or commitment such as:

Understand the terminology used on arrest or commitment papers

- **NTA**—notice to appear. This is a summons or writ issued in place of a physical arrest and which requires a person to appear in court.
- **ROR**—release on recognizance, sometimes called a signature bond, is the pretrial release of an arrested person who promises in writing to appear for trial at a later date. No monetary bond is required before release.
- **EOS**—end (or expiration) of sentence. This date is determined by the court at sentencing and can be reduced due to gain time.
- **DOB**—date of birth as it appears on the inmate's identification
- either **"subject"** or **"arrestee"** to identify the individual

Confirming completeness of arrest or commitment papers is a critical part of the intake / reception process and includes ensuring that:

Confirm that arrest or commitment papers are complete

- all information is obtained
- all paperwork needed to complete the arrest or commitment is present, such as victim notification, traffic citations, and copies of warrants
- arrest paperwork is signed by the arresting officer and, if required, the inmate
- commitment papers have been signed by the sentencing judge

The inmate's file is created once the arrest and intake / reception documents are completed and are signed by the officer and inmate. The documents can be maintained electronically or by hard copy placed in the assigned location specific to that facility.

During the intake / reception process, the inmate is given the documents they are permitted to keep while in custody, including:

Know which documents inmates are allowed to keep while in custody

- court documents
- legal paperwork pertaining to the inmate's case
- copies of arrest papers
- copies of property receipts
- an inmate handbook for the facility in which they are incarcerated
- a copy of the Prison Rape Elimination Act (PREA)

It is the inmate's responsibility to make sure that they do not misplace these documents.

PRE-INCARCERATION ADMISSION AND MEDICAL ASSESSMENTS

COUNTY DETENTION FACILITY

Know the basic intake / reception tasks that are completed at county detention and state correctional facilities

Florida Model Jail Standards prohibit admitting unconscious, seriously ill, or injured persons into a county facility without medical clearance. Each facility has established guidelines regarding medical, suicide, and other needed screenings. The intake officer will observe the inmate for any visible injuries and drug or alcohol impairment. If an injury or impairment is present, medical staff will assess whether the person can remain at the facility or must be transported by the arresting officer to a hospital emergency room. When the inmate returns to the facility, the officer will provide written medical clearance from a physician.

STATE FACILITY

Reception is a multistep process that may take several days to complete. It is based on statewide rules along with the policies of each reception center. During reception, an inmate is assigned a unique Department of Corrections number. A health screening is done to establish immediate medical or psychological needs. The inmate is fingerprinted to get a current criminal history. The Department of Corrections reception process bases inmate evaluation and facility assignment on such factors as the nature and severity of the offense, characteristics of the sentence, and the inmate's mental and health status, age, and criminal history.

Lesson Vocabulary

arrest papers

commitment papers

intake

reception

Review Items

1. *Explain how to verify an inmate's identity.*
2. *List six common features of arrest papers.*
3. *List the common features of commitment papers.*
4. *Give examples of the terminology used on arrest or commitment papers.*
5. *Explain how to determine when arrest or commitment papers are complete.*
6. *List the documents inmates are allowed to keep while in custody.*
7. *In your own words, explain the tasks that are completed at county detention and state correctional facilities.*

LESSON 2

SEARCHING AND INVENTORYING

LESSON GOAL

You will be able to search inmates and their property and accurately document their personal property.

THINK ABOUT THIS

An inmate entered intake/reception and you conducted a search. A few hours later, you learned that a knife fell from the inmate's pocket. What went wrong? What could have happened if the inmate's knife hadn't fallen from his pocket? What should have been done differently during intake?

EXAMINING AND SEARCHING INMATE AND PROPERTY

Search an inmate during intake/reception

When admitted to a county or state facility, inmates and their property are searched thoroughly and systematically. Searches are essential to the safety and security of the facility and are conducted according to policies and procedures. Searches of an inmate are gender specific (male officers search male inmates; female officers search female inmates) unless emergency situations require otherwise. Before searching inmates and their property, you must confirm the inmate's identity using agency-approved forms of identification.

Do not assume that a prior search was conducted by another officer. Search all inmates entering the facility at intake/reception.

At county facilities, strip-searches are to be conducted only in accordance with s. 901.211, F.S. In state facilities, strip-searches may be conducted on inmates entering or exiting the facility and may be conducted at any time to discourage the introduction and movement of contraband.

To prevent the introduction of contraband, use a method of pat searching inmates. Wearing disposable gloves, search outerwear, such as jackets or layered clothing, then remove and place the piece(s) of clothing out of the inmate's reach before continuing the search. Check clothing carefully; systematically look for tears or hidden compartments in clothing and footwear in which small items or drugs could be hidden. Remove and inspect footwear insoles and the part of the shoe under the insole. Turn footwear upside down and shake or knock it against a hard object to dislodge any contraband that may be hidden inside.

Remove and inspect all items from wallets, pocketbooks, backpacks, or any other articles associated with the inmate. Instruct the inmate to take off any jewelry, including body piercings. Examine rings, necklaces, bracelets, and watches for disguised or concealed contraband. You will learn more about conducting a pat down in Defensive Tactics.

Conduct a thorough search of inmate property

Check any prescription medication containers to ensure that the name on the container is the inmate's. Treat loose medication or medication not in a labeled prescription container as contraband; handle this according to facility policy. Also check that credit cards, bank cards, driver's license, and ID cards match the inmate's name. If not, bring these items to the attention of a supervisor.

INVENTORYING AND DOCUMENTING PROPERTY

Methods of documenting inmate property vary among facilities; however, all require some type of recordkeeping for items an inmate has in their possession.

Know how to inventory and document inmate property based on the four destinations

There are four destinations for inmate property:

- destruction for items considered contraband
- retention by the inmate as specified in facility policies
- storage until the inmate is released
- mailed to the inmate's designated recipient

During intake / reception, inventory each item and note the exact number of every item. Whenever possible, inventory the inmate's property in their presence. When dealing with multiple inmates, make sure that the property being inventoried belongs to the correct inmate.

Check all non-clothing items to make sure that they are not tampered with and are in their original form. Make sure the item is not considered contraband by facility regulations. Dispose of contraband according to facility policies and procedure. The Florida Statutes allow additional criminal charges to be made against an inmate who introduces contraband into the facility.

Know the types of property inmates are allowed to keep while in custody

Inmates are limited in what property they can keep in their possession. Generally, facility policies and procedures permit inmates to keep:

- religious materials
- legal paperwork pertinent to the inmate's case (search but do not read; remove paper clips, staples, and any other contraband before returning the paperwork)
- medically necessary items as cleared by medical staff (such as artificial limbs, wheelchairs, or braces)
- photographs (allowed but limited in quantity and content, as determined by facility policies and procedure)
- personal hygiene items

Be as specific as possible when inventorying and describing property that may be stored until an inmate's release. Be sure to:

Inventory and describe property that will be stored until an inmate's release

- List all clothing by type and color.
- List jewelry by item, description, and color. Use terms such as "yellow" or "white metal with clear stones." Avoid determining value. List watches by brand name, if known. Record any missing stones, damage, or abnormalities to the property.
- Make sure that all forms of identification (for example, photo ID, Social Security card) are in the inmate's name.
- List credit and debit cards, bank cards, checks (may include check numbers but not account number), and other monetary instruments by name and issuing bank.
- Record money by denomination and amount, for example, "2 $20 bills, 1 $10 bill, 2 $5 bills, and 3 quarters for a total of $60.75." Some agencies require a second person to verify cash amount. Deposit money in the inmate's account.
- List the number of keys an inmate has in their possession and describe the key chain or key ring, if one is present.
- List cell phones or other electronic devices by brand and note the overall condition. Turn off devices and remove the battery before storing.

After you document the inmate's property, review the form with the inmate to make sure that all items are accounted for. The inmate and officer should sign and date the property inventory form. If the inmate refuses to sign the property inventory form, note the refusal; a second officer will verify the inventory and sign the form.

Once an inmate's personal property has been inventoried and documented, deliver it to a designated property room according to agency policies and procedures. Some facilities require inmates to release their property to a specific individual or mail it to a recipient away from the facility at the inmate's own expense. Many facilities have assigned property officers who are responsible for the storage and final disposition of property. The property officer is accountable for storing all property, making sure that the property room is secured at all times, inventorying property, and documenting the delivery or release of all property.

FACILITY-ISSUED ITEMS

Hygiene items such as bath soap, toothpaste, a toothbrush, shampoo, comb, and toilet paper are issued to inmates when they enter a facility. Review policies and procedures for the allowable types and amounts of agency-issued items.

Understand that hygiene items must be searched before issuing to an inmate

You must check the items issued for contraband before giving them to the inmate. Document the issuance of hygiene items in accordance with policies and procedures.

Sometimes an inmate tries to use another inmate's identification to get more hygiene items. To prevent this, check the inmate's ID card, armband identification, or wristband identification to confirm that the photo matches the inmate being issued hygiene items.

Know the importance of checking an inmate's identity when issuing hygiene items

Review Items

1. *Describe how to search an inmate at intake/reception.*
2. *Explain how to search an inmate's property at intake/reception.*
3. *Describe how to inventory and document inmate property.*
4. *Explain the possible destinations for inmate property.*
5. *List the property that inmates are allowed to keep while in custody.*
5. *Describe property that will be stored until an inmate's release.*
6. *Explain why you should check hygiene items before issuing them to an inmate.*
7. *Explain why you should check an inmate's identity before issuing hygiene items.*

LESSON 3

FINGER AND PALM PRINTING AND PHOTOGRAPHING

LESSON GOAL

You will be able to take quality finger and palm prints and photograph inmates for identification and criminal history.

THINK ABOUT THIS

An inmate's fingerprints were taken to verify her identity. However, the prints were not clear, and she was missing a finger. What would happen if these prints were submitted?

FLORIDA CRIME INFORMATION CENTER (FCIC)/NATIONAL CRIME INFORMATION CENTER (NCIC)

Know the information available in the Florida Crime Information Center (FCIC) and the National Crime Information Center (NCIC)

The Florida Crime Information Center (FCIC) is Florida's law enforcement/criminal justice information system. It maintains a computerized filing system of documented criminal justice information available to law enforcement and criminal justice agencies. FCIC also is the central repository for all criminal history records in the state of Florida, including wanted person information, missing person information, probation information, and information on offenders of special concern.

FCIC criminal histories contain the following information for people who have been arrested in Florida:

- personally identifiable information (PII) (name, race, sex, date of birth, Social Security number, and aliases)
- Florida arrest and registration history (Offender Based Tracking System [OBTS] number, date of arrest, county in which the arrest(s) occurred, arresting agency, and charge information)
- court disposition (whether the person was convicted, had adjudication withheld, etc. Note: this information is not always available for all arrests)

This information is in turn forwarded to the National Crime Information Center (NCIC), the electronic clearinghouse of crime data maintained by the FBI, where it becomes available for nationwide access by the law enforcement and criminal justice community.

NCIC provides criminal justice agencies access to criminal history records of all people arrested in the United States and its territories, including wanted persons' information (warrants nationwide). NCIC assigns the arrestee an FBI number which, when entered into the system, provides information on a specific person such as:

- PII (name, race, sex, date of birth, Social Security number, and aliases)

- arrest(s) for a person in the United States or its territories
- location of arrest (county and state)
- arresting agency
- date of arrest
- disposition of arrest (convicted, adjudication withheld, etc. Note: this information is not always available on all arrests)

Legal requirements regarding the use of FCIC/NCIC information include the following:

Know the legal requirements when using FCIC/NCIC information

- **certification**—All persons, officers, or civilians using FCIC/NCIC must be certified. Unless certified, an individual cannot use or even access the FCIC/NCIC database.
- **restriction**—Information obtained from FCIC/NCIC is for criminal justice purposes only and should not be used for personal reasons. You cannot use the system to check on family, friends, or co-workers.
- **confidentiality**—Information obtained from FCIC/NCIC is confidential and is for criminal justice purposes only. Someone outside the agency may receive certain background information through a paid public records request, although they are not entitled to everything that appears on an FCIC/NCIC printout or record.

It is important to search both FCIC and NCIC when attempting to identify an inmate, as they may have a criminal record in Florida or another state. When checking for criminal history information using FCIC/NCIC, search with as much information as possible.

FINGER AND PALM PRINTING

Fingerprint identification is the biometric standard used in the criminal justice system. Fingerprint patterns or friction ridges are unique for each individual. The ***friction ridge*** is a raised portion of the skin on the finger and palm of a hand, consisting of connected ridge units.

Fingerprints and palm prints are taken in the field and upon intake/reception to establish or verify the identity of a person. Fingerprints and palm prints are submitted to FDLE electronically via a Biometric Identification Solutions (BIS) LiveScan machine where they are searched against state and national fingerprint databases to identify an individual.

Obtain quality industry standard finger and palm prints

To capture prints at a LiveScan electronic submission machine, the fingers are rolled on a clean glass plate where each finger is scanned. The better the quality of the prints, the greater the chance that the person will be properly identified. To obtain industry standard quality prints that are sufficient to identify a person:

- roll each finger and thumb from nail to nail, then lift up and away to avoid smudging the print on the glass
- make sure the fingerprint pattern is clearly visible on the screen

- moisten a too-dry hand with water or rub against oily surfaces such as a forehead (never use lotion)
- wipe a too-moist hand with a cloth
- avoid applying too much or too little pressure, which will diminish the quality of prints
- roll prints so that they have sharp black ridges and no smudges
- capture palm impressions from the surface of the hand from fingertips down to the wrist
- place prints in proper spaces and within the borders on the LiveScan machine glass plate
- include the proper notations where applicable (missing finger, extra finger, bandaged)
- complete all PII information fully and accurately

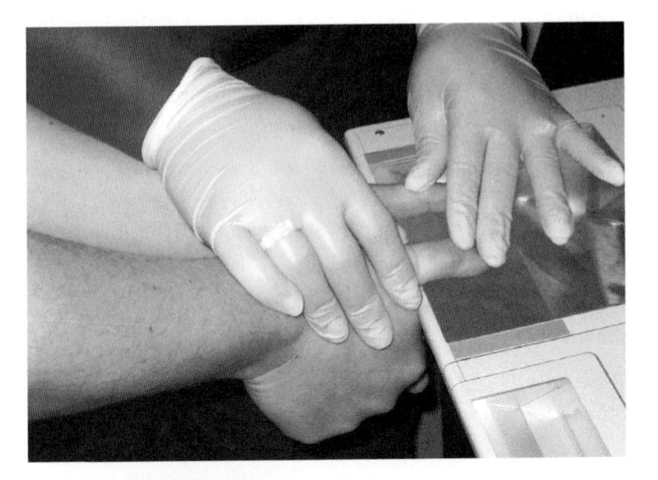

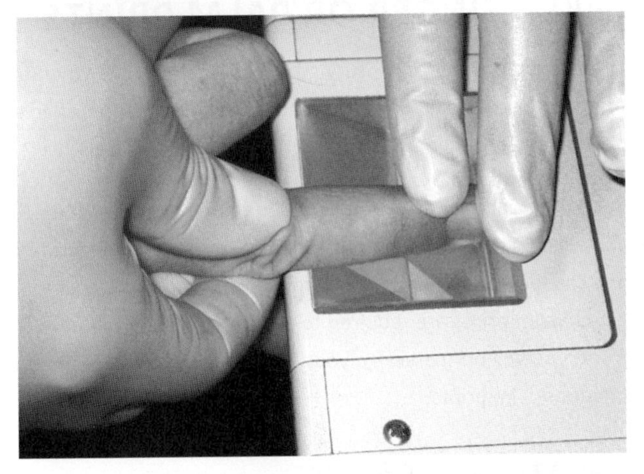

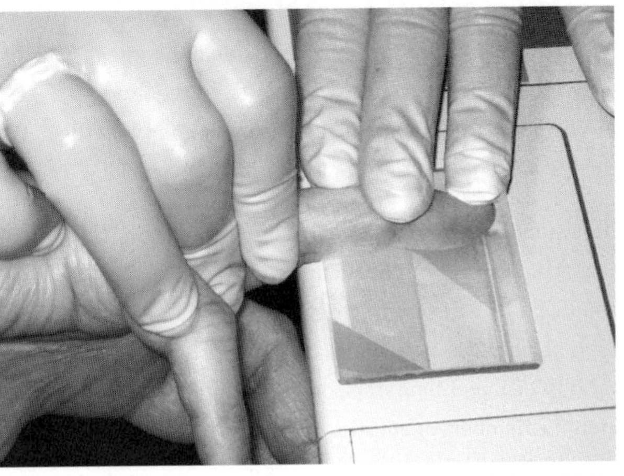

Taking fingerprints electronically *Figures 5-1, 5-2, and 5-3*

Fingers or palms must be clean and dry before fingerprinting. Depending on the officer's preference, the person should stand to the right or rear of the officer taking the prints. The weight of the finger or palm is enough to make an impression; the finger does not have to be pressed down hard. Remember officer safety when taking prints. Keep a good grip on the hand being rolled and be aware of the person's other hand and their movements throughout the process.

BIOMETRIC IDENTIFICATION SOLUTION (BIS) AND LIVESCAN MACHINES

FDLE's identification unit receives electronically submitted fingerprints through the LiveScan machine located at each criminal justice facility. The electronic system will match prints to an existing state identification number, known as a SID. If no match is found, then the system will automatically generate a new SID, indicating the person is a first-time arrestee, thus establishing their criminal history record. Many people will attempt to disassociate themselves from their records by completing official name changes or by providing aliases to avoid a new arrest. These attempts are documented in the PII of the record.

The information generated by BIS is only as accurate as the data submitted by the officers. The quality of fingerprints rolled on the LiveScan is very important for making a correct match. If the BIS database cannot read the fingerprint, it will not be able to make a positive identification. Modern LiveScan technology is designed to assist in fingerprint identification by performing checks to ensure accuracy and completeness of image quality and accompanying information. However, booking officers are ultimately responsible for the value of fingerprints taken on the LiveScan.

Understand the importance of the Biometric Identification Solution, LiveScan, and Rapid ID technologies as they apply to criminal justice agencies

Many agencies in the state now confirm an inmate's identify with a Rapid ID device—a small, often portable fingerprint scanner using less than 10 prints. Rapid ID processes a print quickly with end-to-end transaction times averaging around one minute. If identification is made, the SID number is returned, as well as the inmate's name and date of birth. Depending upon the device settings, it may also return other information, such as a Florida criminal history and a wanted person check.

INKED FINGER OR PALM PRINTS

The same principles of capturing finger or palm prints when using a BIS LiveScan machine apply when taking inked prints. Paper card submissions are used for the purposes of arrest, mandatory background checks, or personal identification and are submitted to FDLE through the postal service.

Know where signatures are required on a fingerprint or palm print card

Record personal information about the inmate on the card; this may include name, race, sex, birth date, Social Security number, criminal charges, and the local case number. Both the inmate and the officer taking the finger or palm prints are required to sign the finger or palm print card in the spaces provided: the inmate signs on the front; you will print and sign your name on the back. Follow specific agency policies and procedures when capturing finger or palm prints.

PHOTOGRAPHING

Photographs taken at intake or reception provide a visual record of each inmate and are submitted to FDLE electronically, along with finger and palm prints, as required by s. 943.052, F.S. When capturing, transmitting, and submitting facial images to FDLE, it is highly recommended that the national standards and best practice guidelines compiled by the Facial Identification Scientific Working Group (FISWG) be followed.

Know the requirements for photographing an inmate

Basic good practices include making sure the inmate's eyes are open and that their hair is not obstructing the full view of their face. Photographs should be taken from the front and from the side. It is important to photograph any bruising, injuries, bandages, or medical conditions that are present. Other photographs may also include tattoos, distinguishing scars, or marks helpful in identifying an individual. Scars, marks, or tattoos are also used to help identify members or affiliates of security threat groups (STGs). You will learn about security threat groups in Chapter 7.

Inmate photographs may be used to generate an identification wristband or ID card. Most IDs are printed from a computer and often have the inmate's photo, sex, race, date of birth, and agency-generated identification number. Inmate identification will be displayed at all times the inmate is dressed.

Know what information to include when generating an inmate identification wristband or ID card

Lesson Vocabulary

friction ridge

Review Items

1. *What information is provided in FCIC and NCIC criminal histories?*
2. *In your own words, describe the legal requirements when using FCIC and NCIC.*
3. *List six industry standards for obtaining quality prints.*
4. *Explain how the Biometric Identification Solution, LiveScan, and Rapid ID technologies are useful to criminal justice agencies.*
5. *Where do you sign an inmate's fingerprint or palm print card?*
6. *List some requirements for photographing an inmate.*
7. *List the information included on an inmate's ID card.*

LESSON 4

CLASSIFICATION AND HOUSING

LESSON GOAL

You will understand how inmates are classified for housing and work assignments.

THINK ABOUT THIS

Have you ever seen inmates working on the side of the road? If so, what was your first thought? Did you wonder why they were not in prison? Why do you think some inmates are allowed to be placed at a work camp?

CLASSIFICATION

Understand the importance of classification

Know the criteria for determining the types of classification assignments

Classification is a management tool used by facilities to assign security risk levels or custody grades to inmates. Inmates are classified when admitted to a facility as soon as practical. Classification is an ongoing process as reassessments are conducted throughout an inmate's incarceration. It may later be necessary to reclassify an inmate based on their behavior or new criminal charges. Some of the criteria that are used to establish an inmate's custody grade or security risk level include current charges, criminal history, age, sex, current and past behavior (discipline), medical and psychological needs, and degree of crime and length of sentence. Classification screening and determination of custody risk levels differ between county and state facilities.

COUNTY CUSTODY SECURITY RISK LEVELS AND CRITERIA

Minimum, medium, and maximum are county custody or security risk levels as determined by facility policies and procedures.

Know the three security levels used in county correctional facilities

Minimum security level is for inmates considered low risk: those who have adjusted well to being incarcerated, have a minimal criminal history with no violent charges in their history, or are currently charged with a non-violent crime.

Medium security level is for inmates considered moderate risk: those who have adjusted to being incarcerated in the past and have limited violence in their criminal history.

Maximum security level is for inmates considered high risk: those who have serious and violent felony charges pending or pose a threat to the safety of staff and security of the facility.

STATE CUSTODY GRADES AND CRITERIA

State facilities follow the classification grades described in Rule 33-601.210, F.A.C.: community, minimum, medium, close, and maximum.

Community custody grade refers to inmates who are eligible for placement at a community residential facility.

Know the five custody grades used in state correctional facilities

Minimum custody grade refers to inmates who are eligible for outside work assignments but not for placement in a community residential center.

Medium custody grade refers to inmates who are eligible for placement at a work camp with a secure perimeter but who are not eligible for placement in an outside work assignment without armed supervision.

Close custody grade refers to inmates who must be maintained within an armed perimeter or under direct, armed supervision when outside a secure perimeter.

Maximum custody grade refers to inmates who are sentenced to death.

HOUSING

The primary purpose for classification is to place inmates in the type of housing that best meets their needs and to provide reasonable protection for all inmates. Most facilities have designated sworn or civilian classification personnel who will complete the appropriate housing assignment documentation.

Know the categories of initial segregation

At first, inmates may be temporarily segregated from others in a holding cell during the intake / reception process, while awaiting a permanent housing assignment. Male and female inmates should be separated to prevent normal sight and sound contact. Juvenile offenders should be separated from adult inmates in the same manner. County facilities that process juveniles will follow guidelines provided by the Florida Department of Juvenile Justice. Juveniles detained in county facilities awaiting court disposition must have been direct filed, indicted, or waived. A juvenile is direct filed when they are charged as an adult and the case is transferred out of the Juvenile Division. If this criterion has not been met, a juvenile must be taken to the nearest juvenile intake facility.

Housing assignments are based on an inmate's potential or basic risk and needs. Housing assignments are provided to all inmates admitted to a facility as soon as practical. After an inmate has completed the intake / reception process, they are assigned to a housing unit based on facility guidelines. Restrictions may apply due to security concerns, high-profile cases, or medical and psychological needs, such as suicidal tendencies.

Be aware that there is a high risk of suicide for inmates within the first 24 hours of incarceration.

Lesson Vocabulary

classification

close custody grade

community custody grade

maximum custody grade

maximum security level

medium custody grade

medium security level

minimum custody grade

minimum security level

Review Items

1. *Explain why classification is important.*
2. *Describe how classification assignments are determined.*
3. *List the security levels.*
4. *List the five types of custody grades.*
5. *Explain the categories of initial segregation.*
6. *Describe how housing is assigned.*

LESSON 5
RELEASE

LESSON GOAL

You will know the process to release an inmate from a county detention or state correctional facility.

THINK ABOUT THIS

Before you are released from the hospital, you go through a process that involves verification, authorization, documentation, and, for some, transportation. This process is similar to an inmate's release from a county or state facility. You will learn about the release process and specific procedures as you read the lesson.

RELEASING AN INMATE

Know what the release process involves

Release is the process by which inmates are discharged from a county detention facility or state correctional facility. Release usually involves verification, authorization, documentation, transportation or arranging of transportation, as well as actual physical release of an inmate.

Follow common procedures before releasing an inmate

Releases are granted through a court order, posting of bond, release on own recognizance (ROR), or expiration of sentence (EOS). The posting of bond requires the arrestee to pay the court a designated fee to ensure their appearance later in court. If the defendant does not appear, any money posted is forfeited, and a warrant for arrest is issued. Release on own recognizance requires no payment for assurance.

To verify release documentation, review the order for accuracy and completeness, confirm that the release order was issued for a specific inmate, and verify that the release order was issued by the proper authority.

Common procedures to follow before releasing an inmate may include:

- checking that any special conditions have been satisfied
- notifying others within the facility as required
- assisting an inmate in obtaining a certified copy of their birth certificate and a state identification card or replacement driver's license in place of a state identification card if the inmate's identification card or driver's license has been lost, stolen, or destroyed
- notifying the inmate of their upcoming release
- notifying any victim(s), if applicable

- resolving any grievances or claims for damage or loss
- providing the inmate with a toll-free hotline for post-release referrals for community-based reentry services, and a community reentry resource directory organized by county

Obtain a DNA sample in accordance with the Florida Statutes (ss. 943.325, 925.11), which require that DNA be collected from persons convicted of or arrested for felony or attempted offenses and convicted of certain misdemeanor offenses.

Know the DNA requirements for convicted or charged felons provided in the Florida Statutes

- completing any criminal registration process (as defined by county law)
- providing instructions for criminal registration reporting (as defined by state law)

Additionally, you should check for outstanding warrants or detainers.

Follow agency policies and procedures when releasing inmate property. Begin by verifying the inmate's identity. Using the inmate's ID, locate the inmate's stored property and thoroughly search it for contraband. Once the property is searched and confirmed, it is released to the inmate.

Know how to identify and restore an inmate's stored property before release

Inmates released from a state facility may be entitled to a discharge gratuity. A ***discharge gratuity*** is money given to qualified inmates released from the custody of the Department of Corrections as indicated in 33-601.502, F.A.C. It is important to document the amount of the gratuity issued to an inmate.

Understand how gratuity applies to an inmate's release

Before release, the inmate will sign a receipt for returned money, personal property, and release papers or certificate. Return the inmate's personal property upon release, according to agency policies and procedures.

Know the process for returning an inmate's personal property upon release

Each agency has procedures for the actual physical release of inmates and their property, which includes documenting the details of the property release. The releasing officer will document all release information in the inmate's file, close out the file, and store the file as required.

Know how to document an inmate's release

Lesson Vocabulary

discharge gratuity

release

Review Items

1. *Explain what the release process involves.*
2. *Explain the common procedures to follow before releasing an inmate.*
3. *Describe the DNA requirements for convicted or charged felons according to the Florida Statutes.*

4. *When should you check for an outstanding warrant or detainer on an inmate?*
5. *Describe the process for identifying and restoring an inmate's stored property.*
6. *In your own words, define gratuity.*
7. *Describe the process for returning an inmate's personal property.*
8. *Who documents an inmate's release, and where is the information stored?*

Supervising in a Correctional Facility

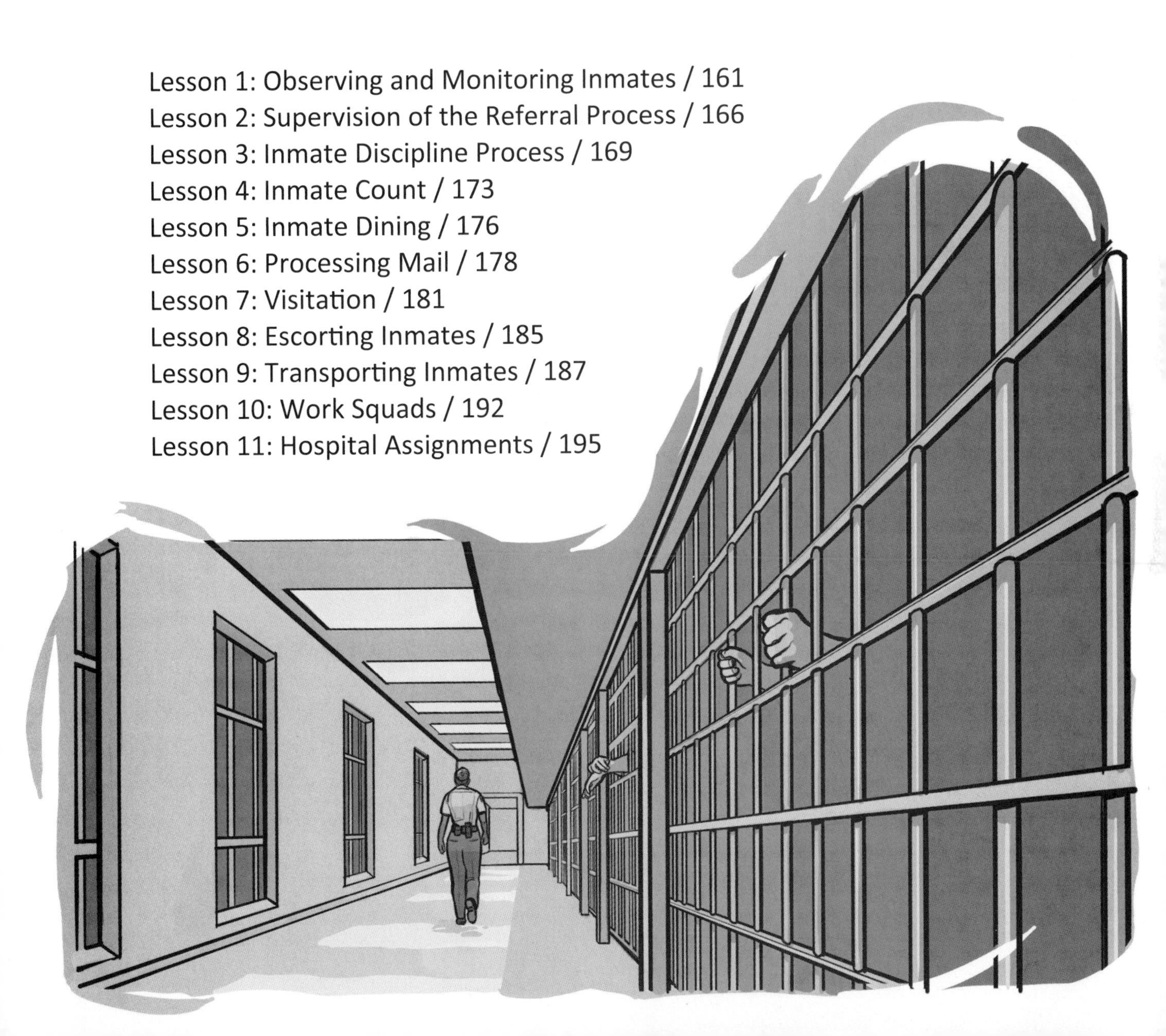

LESSON 1
OBSERVING AND MONITORING INMATES

LESSON GOAL

You will be able to monitor inmates and recognize unusual occurrences in a correctional setting.

THINK ABOUT THIS

Officer Adams is supervising his assigned day room. He has been in contact with Inmate Thompson for around six months. Inmate Thompson has been a model inmate by following the facility rules, getting along well with other inmates, and generally seeming calm. The past few days, however, Inmate Thompson has been unusually quiet and nervous. This morning, Inmate Thompson asked Officer Adams to be relocated to another day room. Should Officer Adams be concerned? Is it worth Officer Adams' time to pay attention to these changes in behavior?

OBSERVATION SKILLS

Observe inmate activity in a correctional facility

Your primary duties as a correctional officer are the care, custody, and control of inmates. Your ability to observe changes in the daily patterns and routines of your facility is an important skill in supervising inmates. Observation is being aware of your surroundings and paying close attention to details. Protect your personal safety and security by monitoring inmates at all times, such as when they enter or exit a housing area. Prevent potential threats and safety hazards to fellow officers, staff, inmates, and the public by watching your surroundings. Observe behavioral patterns of inmates to decide if a situation is normal or if it requires action.

USING THE SENSES

The first stage of observation is monitoring inmate behavior using the primary senses of seeing, hearing, touching, and smelling. Using these senses helps you detect environmental changes in the facility. When you walk your rounds in your assigned section of the facility, look for any alterations or damage to property or equipment, listen for any changes to inmate conversations or noise, and notice any changes in the regular odors of the institution, such as smelling smoke.

In the recreation yard, maintain a heightened awareness for any sudden changes in weather, any damage to the building or equipment outside, or any changes in behavior or tension among inmates. Changes in inmate behavior could include hearing a change in the noise level or observing improper contact between inmates or staff or a violation of inmate conduct, such as unauthorized dress, whistling, sexual comments, assaults, and escape attempts.

SENSE OF SIGHT

Watch the actions of inmates to observe changes in their behavior and surroundings, and to identify missing items or damage to equipment and property.

Inmates gathering in a group that keeps you from seeing what is going on could be dangerous. Disperse the group by making your presence known and giving the group verbal commands, such as telling them to break up and move on.

SENSE OF HEARING

Listening skills are an essential component of effective observation. You should be aware of the usual noises and noise levels in the facility. Changes in facility noises may indicate potential violations. It is normal for noise levels to increase when inmates are watching sporting events or participating in activities, but you should remain alert for signs of a threat. Listen to inmate communications for key words, slang, or changes in voice inflection.

During sleeping hours, excessive or unusual noise might indicate a potential problem. For example, you must investigate any loud banging or scraping noises coming from a cell, screaming, crying, or repeated flushing of toilets. These sounds could be signs of a possible fight, sexual assault, the sharpening of a shank, or an escape attempt.

SENSE OF TOUCH

There are many ways that you will use your sense of touch to make sure that your facility is secured. You will perform searches of inmates, their cells, and their possessions. You should make a thorough and accurate search, both for your safety and as a procedure for your job. While you are making your rounds, check to see if doors are closed properly by testing the knobs or handles. Perform searches in common rooms, visitor rooms, and the dining hall. Wear gloves and other PPE while searching and feeling for contraband items with your hands.

SENSE OF SMELL

Every institution has its own smell. It is a combination of industrial cleaners, laundry soap, cooking smells, and normal body odors from various inmates and staff. This smell will become familiar to you as you work in your facility. Be able to recognize the scents that do not belong in your everyday world, such as the smell of certain drugs, or of metal or wood shavings from an inmate fashioning a shank. There are other environmental scents you will recognize, such as the smell of a mattress that has been burned to distract you. Be safe and aware at all times. It is better to report an odd smell than ignoring it until it becomes a larger problem.

MONITORING INMATE BEHAVIOR

Monitor inmate behavior in the housing area of a correctional facility

Unusual activity of inmates could be an indicator that a problem is occurring or about to occur. Suspicious activities or behaviors, such as slamming a door or locker, yelling, fighting, or faking an injury could be an attempt to distract you to commit a violation. You should assess the situation and determine if additional resources are needed. If there is a threat, immediately contact a supervisor and take required action. Remember to document the situation after it has been resolved safely.

You should monitor closely any changes in inmate behavior, especially in the housing area. These changes could be the result of personal stress, such as divorce, notification of a death in the family, loss of a work assignment, or receipt of charges. Paying attention to changes in the housing area can also alert you to possible illegal activities, such as escape plans or attempts. Indicators of a possible escape include an inaccurate inmate count, missing screws, broken windows, damaged toilets (for example, a toilet being separated from the wall), evidence of digging through walls or floors, or loose security bars. Other signs of a potential escape may be inmates hoarding excessive sheets or towels, maps of facilities and the surrounding area drawn on walls, the ground, or any paper products, coded messages in the mail, or finding visitors or other inmates in unauthorized areas. Incidents such as a fire or a medical emergency, grouping of inmates, or a staged fight might be used as distractions for escape attempts or other illegal activity.

When inmates enter or exit the housing area, identify each inmate by photo ID, armband, or uniform color. Compare the identification method with the housing roster. The color of the uniform may reveal the inmate's classification, work assignment, or housing location. For example, an inmate's ID tag will confirm whether the inmate is authorized to be in that area.

Make sure that inmates clean their living areas and practice personal hygiene to minimize health hazards. An inmate practicing poor personal hygiene can draw unwanted attention, causing conflict between inmates. Showers, toiletries, personal hygiene items, and uniforms are available to inmates. Make sure that inmates follow the established housing standards, showering schedules, and uniform guidelines.

Inmates dressed according to agency policy make it easier to see concealed contraband or identify signs of security threat groups (STGs). Inmates may modify their uniforms by rolling up a pant leg, tying their shoes in a specific pattern, writing graffiti on clothes, and wearing clothes backward or inside out. An inmate's appearance can also indicate a potential security risk; for example, an inmate wearing seasonally inappropriate clothing may be concealing contraband. Inmates may alter their physical appearance with tattoos, different hairstyles, and body piercings. These security violations must be addressed and documented.

SURVEILLANCE EQUIPMENT

Know how surveillance equipment can help you monitor inmates in a correctional facility

Correctional facilities have blind spots, which are locations within a facility that have limited visibility, such as corners, closets, doorways, the rear of inmate dorms, and stairwells. These are difficult for officers to monitor for inmate activity and may pose a security or safety concern. Surveillance equipment, such as video cameras, lighting, and convex wall mirrors, help you monitor daily operations within the facility. This equipment reduces blind spots and helps officers limit the introduction of contraband, observe illegal activities, and respond to incidents safely and quickly. Surveillance equipment can also provide visual and audio evidence to support documentation for incident reports, investigations, or any additional needs.

OBSERVING UNUSUAL OCCURRENCES

Know the unusual occurrences that can disrupt the normal operations of a correctional facility

An ***unusual occurrence*** is an incident that is out of the ordinary and disrupts the normal operation of the facility. These incidents negatively affect the security of the facility, and include events such as:

- inmate or staff death
- serious injuries to inmate or staff
- suicide or attempted suicide
- escapes or attempted escapes
- criminal acts
- inability to clear inmate count
- inmates fighting
- use of force
- power or water outages at the facility
- inmate strikes (refusal to eat or work)
- riots
- hostage situations
- bomb threats or detonation

- fire
- disasters
- sexual assault
- lost or missing equipment, particularly keys

Any incident can lead to a disturbance, provoking a response from other inmates, and possibly escalating to major disturbances or riots. Handle minor incidents immediately to avoid inmates taking matters into their own hands. When inmates seek revenge, sympathetic participants could join in the conflict, and a small, containable incident can quickly grow out of control.

Look for indicators of an impending disturbance or riot and take proactive measures to prevent these incidents from occurring.

SIGNS OF POTENTIAL DISTURBANCES

Indicators of potential disturbances include when inmates:

Know the indicators of a potential disturbance in a correctional facility

- gather in a particular area
- stay in their cells
- request to be transferred or moved
- become more violent with each other
- act out to be placed in special protection or isolation
- have low morale
- avoid areas where large numbers of other inmates gather
- store food
- warn staff to stay home on particular days
- increase security threat group-related (STG) activities
- have more weapons found in searches
- who are informants share information
- separate more often along racial or ethnic lines
- make specific demands

Also avoid the distraction of long conversations, as this could be a diversion for inappropriate behavior in another area. Proactive intervention begins with being aware of surroundings and changes in inmate behaviors, dress, and social groupings. Examples may include:

- inmates wearing boots during showers and at night may indicate the occurrence of an incident
- magazines under shirts may indicate an inmate expects being stabbed or hit

- hoarding items from the commissary may indicate an inmate expects being placed in lockdown
- an increase in requests for protection or "check-in" may indicate fear of being attacked
- an increase or decrease in the normal activity or sounds of the facility may indicate a riot or escape is likely

Report these behaviors to your shift supervisor at once, call for backup if appropriate, and take immediate action to isolate the developing incident.

DOCUMENTATION

Know when to document usual and unusual occurrences that happen in a correctional facility

Officers use logs, report forms, and video recordings to document facility operations, daily activities, and unusual occurrences. Completing accurate documentation is essential for safety, security, and accountability. Examples of usual and unusual occurrences that need to be documented include:

- inmate counts
- fights
- meals
- suicide attempts
- sick call
- fire
- cell searches
- natural disasters
- clinical visits
- riots
- escapes or attempted escapes
- security checks
- workgroup assignments
- sexual assaults
- court appearances
- use of force
- visitation
- bomb threats
- transports
- medical and mental emergencies

Written reports keep the facility staff informed about developments and problem areas. It is particularly important to document inmate movement, such as moving inmates between dorms and the dining hall or to and from medical and visitation. This documentation helps verify counts and work assignments. Use forms and logs to document inmate movement, taking care to note any incidents.

LESSON VOCABULARY

unusual occurrence

REVIEW ITEMS

1. *How should you observe inmate activity in a correctional facility?*
2. *How do you monitor inmate behavior in the housing area?*
3. *What are the indicators of a potential disturbance?*
4. *What are some of the unusual occurrences that can disrupt the normal operations of a correctional facility?*
5. *When should you document usual and unusual occurrences that happen in a correctional facility?*

LESSON 2
SUPERVISION OF THE REFERRAL PROCESS

LESSON GOAL

You will be able to make a referral for an inmate with signs of distress or need.

THINK ABOUT THIS

Inmate Carter approaches Officer Williams nervously and asks, "I've been having a hard time since I got here. Is there someone I can talk to?" Officer Williams responds, "Talk to some of the other inmates. I don't have time to deal with personal problems." Weeks go by, and Inmate Carter barely talks to anyone and keeps to his cell. Being very busy, none of the officers notices that he starts hoarding bedsheets. Inmate Carter tries to use the extra bedsheets in a suicide attempt. Luckily, he is discovered and stopped. Could this have been prevented? Should Officer Williams have taken the time to help Inmate Carter through his issues, or was there someone else who could handle the situation?

REFERRAL SERVICES IN THE FACILITY

Know the different referral services available to inmates

It is critical that you effectively observe and recognize an inmate in distress and in need of referral services. You must become familiar with your agency's referral process to make sure that the inmate receives the appropriate care.

Cooperation and adequate communication between you and the service provider are vital to the proper care and treatment of inmates. Inmates may be referred to the following providers:

- medical
- dental
- psychiatric
- chaplain
- substance abuse services
- classification (for example, housing location or work assignment)
- additional services that may be provided, such as educational or legal services

Being familiar with the referral process will allow for a prompt response, needed resources for the inmate, and safety and security of the facility.

IDENTIFYING THE NEED FOR A REFERRAL

Recognize changes in inmate behavior that may require a referral

Sudden or unusual changes in an inmate's behavior may indicate the need for a referral. Being familiar with inmates under your supervision allows you to observe and recognize changes in behavior. Information used for a referral may include statements made by the inmate, observed behavior, or another reason, such as a personal crisis. Providing this information may help the service provider determine the proper treatment.

Some signs and symptoms of distress or need are illness, physical pain, odd movement, or unresponsiveness. Obvious signs or changes to observe in an inmate may include difficulty in walking, low energy, screaming, crying, weight loss, a rash, or a severe cough. It is important to be aware of changes in behavior, especially when these changes happen suddenly. Behavioral changes include giving away belongings, wanting to be alone, not eating, acting strangely, having unusual interactions with others, being restless, or showing signs of poor personal hygiene. Psychological symptoms may require more interaction to determine the severity of the need. These symptoms may include abrupt changes in demeanor, mood swings, depression, or suicidal thoughts.

Inmates may request a referral for services; treat this request in the same way as if you observed the need. Staff, friends, family members, or other inmates may report strange inmate behavior. Cell searches may also reveal suicide notes or other evidence that an inmate needs referral services.

Base your decision for an inmate referral on information you obtain and your knowledge of the facility's available services. After careful assessment, refer the inmate to the most appropriate service provider. For example, if you observe bizarre behavior, you should make a psychological referral. Illnesses and injuries require a medical referral. If the type of service the inmate needs is not obvious, contact your supervisor for further direction.

MAKING THE REFERRAL

Know the process for making an inmate referral

Once you identify the need for a referral, gather relevant facts to explain your decision. Personally observe the inmate, and interview the inmate, staff, or others.

Tell the service provider about the inmate's specific actions and behaviors, avoiding generalizations. Statements such as "acting weird" may not be helpful; instead, use more specific language such as "the inmate was talking to the wall," or the inmate was "unresponsive and staring off into space." It is essential that you take good field notes to adequately relay the information to the service provider and later document the incident.

Follow these basic steps when making a referral:

- Identify the need for a referral.
- Interview the inmate, staff, or others.
- Contact service providers.
- Request an escort if necessary.

- Make the referral.
- Document the incident.

Each agency may have different procedures for making referrals. It is your responsibility to know your agency's requirements.

OFFICER RESPONSE TO INMATE NEED

Know your responsibilities after making an inmate referral

Once you determine the need for a referral, keep the inmate under close observation. Until the inmate is in the care of the service provider, you are responsible for taking necessary action so that no harm comes to the inmate or anyone else. For example, apply first aid as necessary or intervene to prevent a suicide. Remember to use universal precautions, including PPE, as needed.

Threats to officer safety may exist when responding to inmates in distress. Be cautious; an inmate could pretend medical distress to cause a distraction. Assess the situation and determine if it is reasonably safe to respond to the inmate. From a security standpoint, recognize that an inmate might try to assume the identity of another inmate. Confirm the identity of the inmate being referred.

Always respond when an inmate reports or displays medical or psychological distress.

INMATE MOVEMENT AND DOCUMENTATION

Know who to notify and how to move an inmate after making a referral

The control room or a supervisor will coordinate movement of inmates who have received a referral inside a correctional facility. When an escort is necessary, security considerations before movement include the inmate's classification level, types of restraints used, and number of officers needed. When the inmate arrives at the destination, notify the control room or supervisor that the movement of the inmate is completed.

Any time an inmate has been referred, communicate with other appropriate staff. This communication is usually passed along verbally or through a daily log. Share details of the referral, follow-up requirements, and assessment with other shifts.

Documentation of an inmate referral varies among correctional agencies. This documentation is forwarded from the housing unit to the service provider. Typically, this documentation is a narrative report that addresses the need for the referral, the proper identification of the inmate being referred, and the service provider.

REVIEW ITEMS

1. *List the different referral services available to inmates.*
2. *What are some of the changes in inmate behavior that may require a referral?*
3. *What is the process for making an inmate referral?*
4. *What are your responsibilities as an officer after making an inmate referral?*
5. *Who should you notify after making a referral?*
6. *How should you move an inmate after making a referral?*

LESSON 3
INMATE DISCIPLINE PROCESS

LESSON GOAL

You will be able to distinguish between a minor and major rule violation, apply appropriate discipline, and complete a disciplinary report.

THINK ABOUT THIS

Many of us have seen television shows and movies that show violent fights in prisons and jails. What is not often shown is what happens after these fights have ended. How does the administration deal with the inmates involved? How are these inmates disciplined so that this behavior does not happen again? This lesson will outline the inmate discipline process and the types of rules that are violated.

INMATE DISCIPLINE

Understand the role of progressive discipline for an inmate rule violation or infraction

Discipline is the enforcement of a penalty for a violation of established rules and is used to ensure compliance with those rules. The disciplinary process is designed to correct an inmate's behavior. The goal of discipline is to maintain order and ensure the safety and security of the facility. Section 944.09, F.S., provides the authority and guidelines for enforcing rules. It allows each facility the ability to expand the guidelines for establishing rules for disciplinary processes and lets higher authorities tailor them to each situation.

You can never deny due process, but you can restrict it to meet the safety needs of a facility. For example, mail is a right, but, with the exception of legal mail, it may be withheld from the inmate until disciplinary confinement is complete.

Rule 33-601.314, F.A.C., defines the rules of prohibited inmate conduct and the penalties for violations or infractions in state correctional facilities. A list of these rules is included in every inmate's handbook. The Florida Model Jail Standards govern rules in county facilities, and inmates are also given a copy of these standards in their inmate handbook.

In a correctional facility, the disciplinary process is an administrative function that addresses minor and major rule violations; it does not follow the same rules as criminal procedures. This disciplinary process is sometimes called progressive discipline. The process increases the penalty if the inmate does not correct their behavior. Officer discretion may be applied when determining a disciplinary action, considering the severity of the rule violation or any violations of the law. If an inmate is involved in a disciplinary process, and a pending outside criminal charge may apply, *Miranda* warnings must be given before questioning the inmate.

A ***rule violation or infraction*** is an activity or behavior that is not permitted in the correctional facility. For example, an inmate steals a radio that belongs to another inmate. While this is technically petit theft, the offending inmate may be disciplined only within the facility and not prosecuted in a court of law.

Collect and analyze all relevant information about an observed or reported rule violation. Ask the inmate and other observers open-ended questions to obtain more information about the violation. Ask follow-up questions and take complete and accurate notes on the information you receive. During questioning, look for inconsistencies in inmate responses, body language, or physical evidence.

MINOR AND MAJOR RULE VIOLATIONS

Understand the process of progressive discipline for minor and major rule violations, including inmate isolation

When you observe inappropriate inmate behavior, begin the documentation process of progressive discipline. Be familiar with and refer to your facility's inmate handbook or agency's rules and regulations manual. After determining if it is a minor or major rule violation, respond based on the severity of the incident.

Minor infractions are violations of rules for which a disciplinary report is not necessary. A minor violation is any rule violation resulting in a consequence that goes beyond a verbal warning, but the violation would not justify maximum disciplinary sanctions. Some unacceptable behaviors generally considered to be minor rule violations include wearing a uniform improperly, rough horseplay, and gambling. Some rule violations may be considered major or minor depending on the circumstances, the severity or the degree of the violation, and other considerations.

Major rule violations are any disruption so significant that maximum disciplinary sanctions may be imposed. Incidents like disorderly conduct, disrespectful behavior, violence, use of a weapon, sexual activity, use of drugs or intoxicants, battery, and extortion are considered major rule violations. As soon as you become aware of a major rule violation, obtain approval from the shift supervisor to begin the disciplinary process.

It may be necessary to isolate the inmate in a holding area to maintain the order and security of the facility, as well as the safety of staff, visitors, and inmates. If you need to place an inmate who has committed a major rule violation into isolation, follow these steps:

- Contact a supervisor or control room.
- Request backup if necessary.
- Secure the inmate and separate them from other inmates.
- Secure the scene (if there is a suspected crime scene).
- Move the inmate to a holding cell.
- Have medical perform a pre-confinement physical (depending on agency policies and procedures).
- Move the inmate to confinement.
- Document the incident.

In most facilities, officers must notify their supervisor of any major rule violations. The supervisor will evaluate the incident and make sure that any additional action is taken as needed. A higher authority, such as a duty warden or sheriff, may also be notified, as well as outside agencies. There may be a crime scene, evidence may need to be preserved and protected, and coordination with other agencies may be required. The supervisor must approve any action taken, verify that proper documentation is completed, and make sure that the disciplinary process is carried out in a fair and unbiased manner.

CORRECTIVE ACTION

Understand the corrective action an officer can take as part of the inmate discipline process, to include writing a disciplinary report (DR)

Corrective action is taken to eliminate the cause of inappropriate or unlawful behavior to prevent it from happening again. Given the nature of a correctional facility and inmates in general, inappropriate inmate behavior will occur. Officer presence discourages rule violations.

When you observe inappropriate conduct, give a verbal warning or counseling to the inmate to stop the behavior immediately. A majority of disciplinary issues can be handled at this level. If the inmate immediately corrects the behavior, no other action is required. If the behavior continues, you may escalate your response.

The discipline process involves counseling and may also result in:

- verbal warning
- corrective consultation (incident report or mid-level written warning)
- formal disciplinary report

Counseling is an in-depth explanation of a rule violation, including suggestions on how the inmate can correct their behavior. Before counseling an inmate, refer to the inmate's handbook or rules and regulations manual. Separate the inmate from others during counseling and communicate professionally. Make sure the inmate has a clear understanding of the rules they have broken. Explain the disciplinary process if the inmate's behavior continues. This process could include a disciplinary report, possible loss of privileges, a change in custody level or work assignment, confinement, or loss of gain time.

A ***verbal warning*** is a statement to the inmate that they have committed a rule violation and should correct the behavior immediately. Explain your observations to the inmate and describe the unacceptable behavior and steps to correct it. An inmate's behavior is unacceptable if it clearly violates the facility rules. You can document a verbal warning in a variety of ways, including incident reports, daily logs, computer logs, an inmate's permanent disciplinary record, or specific agency forms.

A ***corrective consultation*** (incident report or written warning) is usually an agency-specific form that documents an inmate rule violation. You will counsel the inmate about the offense and then document it on the form. Document the corrective consultation as soon as possible, and include the details of the incident, including your name, the inmate's name and identification number, and the date, time, and location of the violation. Basically, include the who, what, where, when, why, and how of the violation and the specific corrective actions you took. You and the inmate must sign the form. If the inmate refuses to sign the form, document the refusal on the form, and provide the inmate with a copy within 24 hours of your completion of the form. An additional copy will be placed in the inmate's institutional file. This documentation may serve as a basis for future reference or formal disciplinary action. Some agencies do not require written warnings and immediately issue a disciplinary report.

A ***disciplinary report (DR)*** is a detailed report of the facts surrounding an inmate's rule violation and sets in motion a series of events that ensures due process. A DR is normally reserved for major rule violations; however, when an inmate frequently commits minor rule violations, a DR could be issued. Prior documented rule violations should be included in the report. You must write a disciplinary report within 24 hours from when the incident is discovered. A DR should include the following:

- officer name; inmate name and number, if applicable; and place, date, and time of the discovered incident
- formal statement of the specific violation (the charge)
- a narrative that contains a detailed explanation of the events and supports the specific violation
- statements from any known witnesses or participants
- a description of physical evidence and its disposition
- action taken
- signature of involved staff
- supervisor's approval

Lesson Vocabulary

corrective action

corrective consultation

counseling

disciplinary report (DR)

discipline

rule violation or infraction

verbal warning

Review Items

1. *What is the role of progressive discipline for an inmate rule violation or infraction?*
2. *What is the process for placing an inmate in isolation?*
3. *What is the process of progressive discipline for minor and major rule violations?*
4. *What corrective action can you take as part of the inmate discipline process?*
5. *What should you include when writing a disciplinary report (DR)?*

LESSON 4

INMATE COUNT

LESSON GOAL

You will be able to safely and accurately conduct different types of inmate counts.

THINK ABOUT THIS

A single correctional officer is often responsible for monitoring many inmates. While it may seem simple, an effective way to keep track of these inmates is by counting them. Counts can alert you to an issue if the ending shift count was 50, and the beginning shift count was 49. Keeping these counts helps maintain the safety and security of the facility.

TYPES OF COUNTS

Know the main types of inmate counts

One of the primary duties of correctional officers is counting inmates. Counts verify and account for every inmate within a facility or off-site area and are vital to security and safety. Counts are conducted at housing or cell assignments, work details, and any other location where an inmate may be, such as at the clinic, court, or dining hall.

Informal Count

An informal count verifies the number of inmates in an area. These counts are done randomly by the supervisor of inmates who are on-site or off-site, such as the medical center, court, or work details, or during transport. A body count is a type of informal count that is a custody count of all of the inmates under your supervision and is only reported if an inmate is missing.

Formal Count

A formal count verifies the total number of inmates at a facility, accounting for all gains and losses during the day. A formal count is performed at least once per shift, and may be conducted at the beginning and end of your shift. A computer-generated roster is used to determine the actual number of inmates in a specific unit or housing assignment.

Out Count

This count provides accountability for the location of inmates outside their assigned housing area. Some examples are the canteen area, the dining area, workgroups (laundry, kitchen, or warehouses), the hospital, and court. These inmates are counted as part of the formal count.

Master Count

In a master count, positive identification of each inmate is verified through various items, such as armband identification or photo identification cards that include the facility number, and the inmate's name, date of birth, sex, and race. This count is conducted a minimum of once a day at a specified time and accounts for all inmates admitted, released, returned, or detained in the facility during the previous 24-hour period. Use a current computer-generated roster and compare it to the inmates' personal identification cards or armbands. Record and document this information according to agency policies.

Emergency Count

Emergency counts are conducted when unusual situations arise, such as a possible escape, a disturbance, an evacuation, or when the total count of inmates, regardless of the type of count, is not confirmed or verified with the facility total. Some agencies refer to an emergency count as a recount.

COUNT PROCEDURES

Conduct an inmate count

Depending on the design of the facility, a count may require two officers. You will conduct a formal count at least once per shift. You should complete a count in a timely, systematic, and accurate manner following facility policies and procedures. You must document all types of counts except informal counts.

The inmates are aware that counts occur throughout the day and that the counts can be random. You will receive an order to begin the count. The inmates will know that a count is to occur by the audible notification alarm. The inmates should report back to their assigned area for the count to begin. Common steps in the count process inside the facility include:

1. The control room, a supervisor, or the daily facility schedule will begin a count.
2. The inmates will return to their assigned housing area.
3. There is a physical count of each inmate.
4. The physical count is verified by armbands or ID cards matched against a computer-generated roster.
5. The officers making the count will document and report the totals to a supervisor or the control room staff.
6. The supervisor or assigned staff members (control room) will verify the count.
7. If every inmate was present for the count, then a clear count is announced to the staff and the inmates.
8. The facility will resume its normal operations.

You must physically verify the identity and presence of each inmate. Cross-check their armbands or ID cards with facility documentation. If an inmate is in their bunk with the covers pulled up, preventing you from seeing their face or verifying their identity, you must confirm that there is a live person in the cell.

The inmates' cooperation is required for an accurate count; however, there are occasions when inmates will try to disrupt the process. Some inmate behaviors that may interfere with proper count procedures include, but are not limited to, inmates talking, tapping on walls, not being at their assigned bunks, wearing inappropriate attire, going to the bathroom, listening to the radio, and switching identification cards.

While performing a count, enforce the rules and regulations in a firm, fair, and consistent manner. Given the close proximity of the inmates during a count, stay alert and aware of your surroundings. Maintain attention to detail to ensure an accurate count.

If two officers conduct a count together, they should make sure that their count numbers match. If there is a difference, they should immediately recount the inmates in their count area before reporting the count. Report the count when the totals agree. If counts are reported from all areas in the facility and a difference is found, a recount will be conducted.

If the recount does not resolve the difference, an emergency master count procedure will be announced and initiated. Use extreme caution during a recount, as an inmate may be hiding or attempting an escape. Report all count information to the appropriate supervisor or personnel for verification.

Once the numbers are accurate, a clear count will be announced over the communication system of the facility. Once the count is cleared, the facility will resume normal operation.

COUNT SLIP

Document an inmate count using a count slip

A count slip is a form used to document inmate counts. There may be two types of count slips: a dormitory count slip and a formal count slip. The dormitory count slip includes the total number of inmates in a housing area, and your signature.

The formal count slip may include the following information: facility name, date, time, location, officer signature, total number of inmates counted, and time cleared. The results may be documented through either an electronic or handwritten form and forwarded to appropriate personnel. The count slip cannot contain erasures, strikeouts, or alterations. Verifying count slips completes the inmate counting process.

REVIEW ITEMS

1. *Describe the main types of inmate counts.*
2. *How do you conduct an inmate count?*
3. *How do you document an inmate count using a count slip?*

LESSON 5
INMATE DINING

LESSON GOAL

You will be able to maintain security and follow dining procedures during mealtime in a correctional facility.

THINK ABOUT THIS

Officer Blair watched the line of inmates as they got their food. He noticed that Inmate Franklin was carrying his lunch tray very low, and to the left. Suspicious, Officer Blair halted the line and asked Inmate Franklin to lift his tray high. Inmate Blair's left pocket was bulging. After searching, Officer Blair discovered that Inmate Franklin was attempting to leave the dining area with several utensils. This could have led to a serious breach in security for the facility. This lesson will show how important it is to monitor inmates during meal-times.

SECURITY CHECK BEFORE MEALS

Conduct a security check of the dining area prior to mealtime

The dining area should be inspected for cleanliness and order to ensure health and safety. Designated inmate dining areas may include a dining hall, dayroom, cell, or workgroup areas.

If inmates are served in cells or other common areas, a pre-mealtime security check is not necessary; regular searches will go on as usual. When serving meals in a dining hall, conduct a thorough and systematic security check before opening the dining facilities to inmates. Document the results on the appropriate form.

The security check includes examining locations where contraband can be concealed. These areas include tables and chairs, heaters, ceiling fans, beverage containers, and trash cans. Document and report any equipment that poses a safety hazard; its use must be restricted until the equipment is repaired or replaced.

Be aware that the dining area is a common location for inmates to obtain and distribute contraband. Some examples of contraband include food, utensils, drugs, and sensitive items (food such as sugar, yeast, and fruit can be used to produce alcohol). Thoroughly search concealable areas, such as jackets, medical devices (casts, wheelchairs, or prosthetics), napkins, and containers. Make sure you account for all issued utensils, glasses, and trays. If you locate contraband, you should confiscate and process it.

INMATE MONITORING DURING FOOD DISTRIBUTION

Monitor food distribution during mealtime

Depending on the type of facility, meals may be served in a dining hall or in a housing area. If meals take place in a dining facility, when mealtime is announced, inmates will report directly to the dining hall. Other inmates may need to be escorted to the designated dining area. The security level of the inmate determines the type of escort.

In most facilities, inmates serve the meals. Enforce all sanitation standards, making sure food handlers are properly attired in gloves, hairnets, and aprons. Observe and ensure the proper distribution of food, making sure each inmate receives only one tray of food and the proper number of utensils. Be aware of what foods are being served on a daily basis and ensure inmates receive the correct menu items. Also document the number of inmates and food trays served.

Some inmates may have special dietary requirements because of diabetes, religious restrictions, allergies, or a need for more portions. Be aware of those differences and ensure that the correct inmate receives the proper prescribed meal. Identify, address, and correct any discrepancies. Facilities that house juveniles may have child-specific nutrition guidelines that must be followed.

Compare the number of inmates who received food trays during the distribution of meals with the number of meal trays returned. The mealtime process should be orderly to ensure compliance with safety, security, and sanitation standards.

INMATE MONITORING DURING MEALS

Monitor inmates during mealtime

Disturbances and riots may occur in the inmate dining area. Officer positioning and patrolling are essential for effective observation of all inmate activity in the dining area. By walking around the dining area and making your presence known, you will be able to observe the inmates' behavior and prevent rule violations. Also monitor and supervise specific areas, such as the entrances, serving lines, seating areas, tray return windows, and exits.

Conduct a security check of the dining area after mealtime

Each agency establishes a policy on dining procedures. This may include searching inmates who enter and exit the dining area. At the conclusion of a meal, clear the area of inmates. A security check of the dining area is then conducted to ensure the security of the facility. Conduct a post-mealtime security check in the same manner as a pre-mealtime security check. This check includes serving utensils. Following these policies ensures a safe and secure dining area.

REVIEW ITEMS

1. *How do you conduct a security check of the dining area before mealtime?*
2. *How do you monitor food distribution during mealtime?*
3. *How do you monitor inmates during mealtime?*
4. *How do you conduct a security check of the dining area after mealtime?*

Lesson 6

Processing Mail

Lesson Goal

You will be able to process mail in a correctional facility.

Think About This

A college professor wanted to send surveys to inmates for a research project. The mail packets were simple: they contained only the paper survey and a prestamped envelope to return the survey. The facility's mail processor caught the mistake immediately. What was the problem? Inmates would use the stamps from the return envelopes as a form of currency within the facility, making them contraband. It is important to safety and security to monitor all types of mail coming into and out of the facility.

TYPES OF INMATE MAIL

Inmates are allowed to receive three types of mail: routine, legal, and privileged.

Know the types of mail an inmate may receive in a correctional facility

Routine mail: Routine mail is the most common type of mail in a correctional facility, and it comes directly through the postal service. Routine mail may consist of letters, magazines, newspapers, periodicals, and book subscriptions that have not been tampered with and were received directly from the publisher or supplier.

Legal mail: Legal mail contains confidential information concerning legal matters. It includes mail to and from municipal, county, state, and federal courts, state attorneys, private attorneys, public defenders, and legal aid organizations.

Privileged mail: Privileged mail is defined as correspondence to and from public officials, government agencies, and the news media. Privileged mail is delivered to a facility by the U.S. Postal Service.

PROCESSING MAIL

There is no limit to the amount of mail that an inmate may receive, but there is a limit to the amount of mail that an inmate may possess. All mail must be sent through the U.S. Postal Service.

Process inmate routine mail to include inspecting for contraband

When mail is received by the mailroom or mail clerk, it must be logged. All mail is opened by designated staff and is examined for content and to prevent introduction of contraband. People inspecting mail should use PPE to prevent exposure to contaminants, such as fecal matter, blood, and body fluids or other hazardous materials that may be found inside or outside of mail. Some hazardous materials are harmful if inhaled, but they may not be easily recognized. One example is fentanyl, which, in a fine-powdered form, can be fatal if inhaled and left untreated. Use caution when opening the mail, and never smell the contents to identify it.

The content of the mail is scanned for pornography, information about criminal activity, codes, threats to the facility, threats or evidence of extortion against staff or other inmates, and escape plans, including dates, times, or arrangements for clothing and transportation. It is also scanned to ensure victims or witnesses are not contacting the inmate.

When inspecting mail for contraband, check the texture of the mail to determine if it is brittle or stained. An odd texture could indicate the presence of drugs, body fluids, or hidden messages. Inspect stamps or stickers placed on paper and envelopes to determine if any alteration has been made. These are potential concealment sites for contraband and can be laced with drugs. Drugs or other substances can be concealed in the glue of the stamp and envelopes, in the folds of the paper, as watermarks, between two pieces of paper glued together, or in concealed areas within poly-bubble envelopes. No mail is delivered directly to the inmate before inspection.

Once the mail is cleared, it is sent to the housing area. The identification of the inmate is verified, and the mail is delivered. Delivery methods vary between agencies and must be handled according to agency policies and procedures.

Process inmate legal mail

Legal and privileged mail is handled differently than routine mail. While you may inspect the outside of the envelope, you can open it only in the presence of the inmate to whom it is addressed. When the inmate opens the envelope or package, you can inspect it for contraband, but you must not read the content of legal or privileged mail. Document that the inmate received the legal or privileged mail on the Incoming Legal or Privileged Mail Log.

Legal mail cannot be withheld from an inmate for disciplinary action and must be delivered within 24 hours of receipt. To ensure that the legal mail is authentic, confirm the letterhead has the proper return address and a raised seal or watermark, and verify that the correspondent is a legitimate legal source.

Inmates can receive packages only with special permission. The packages must be sent through the U.S. Postal Service. All packages should be thoroughly searched for items such as drugs, cell phones, money, and inappropriate photographs.

OUTGOING MAIL

Process inmate outgoing mail

In the same manner as incoming routine mail, outgoing routine mail should be inspected for contraband and security violations. Mail should be scanned for adequate postage and proper address format of the sender and recipient. Inspect the mail to make sure the correspondence is allowed and that the address is legitimate. Mail may be held to make sure it is legitimate.

Forward approved outgoing mail in accordance with agency policies and procedures for delivery. Mail should be processed only through the U.S. Postal Service and never personally carried out of the facility.

CONFISCATION OF MAIL

Know how to confiscate incoming and outgoing mail in a correctional facility

Any mail that violates agency policies or threatens security may be confiscated. If the mail contains unauthorized items (such as too many photographs), return it to the sender with a copy of the mail rules. Confiscate any illegal items found in mail. Disciplinary action could follow, and the confiscated item may become evidence in a disciplinary hearing or criminal case. Make sure to use proper evidence-handling procedures.

If you confiscate outgoing inmate mail due to a rule violation, contact your supervisor. All mail—routine, legal, and privileged—must comply with facility rules.

An inmate may correspond only with approved people. Inmates must receive special permission to contact one another by mail. For example, a husband and wife who are both incarcerated must get permission before corresponding. However, correspondence with victims or witnesses and between codefendants and security threat group members is prohibited. Depending on the circumstances, other legal restrictions may apply to inmate communication.

Kickback or three-way mail is a common method inmates use to send illegal communications to each other. The sender uses the intended inmate's location as the return address on the envelope and includes a deficiency such as insufficient postage, requiring the envelope to be returned. The envelope is thus returned to the intended inmate instead of the sender. Check the return address before returning mail to an inmate and note if the return address is for another housing unit or facility.

Lesson Vocabulary

kickback or three-way mail

legal mail

privileged mail

routine mail

Review Items

1. *What are the types of mail an inmate may receive in a correctional facility?*
2. *How do you process inmate routine mail to include inspecting for contraband?*
3. *How do you process inmate legal mail?*
4. *How do you process inmate outgoing mail?*
5. *Why do you confiscate incoming and outgoing mail in a correctional facility? What is the process for confiscating incoming and outgoing mail?*

LESSON 7
VISITATION

LESSON GOAL

You will be able to supervise inmate visitation while maintaining officer, visitor, and inmate safety and facility security.

THINK ABOUT THIS

A visitor comes to the facility to meet with one of the inmates. She is visibly sweating, and her voice sounds nervous as she asks to sign in. Her eyes dart back and forth. Is this behavior a problem for the facility? Should she be allowed to continue her visit?

Visitation is a privilege and not a right for inmates and visitors (Rule 33-601.714, F.A.C.). Visitors and inmates can lose this privilege because of inappropriate conduct, rule violations, or by introducing contraband.

TYPES OF INMATE VISITS

Know the difference between contact visits and non-contact visits

Visitors may not understand the operation of a correctional facility. When subjecting visitors to security measures, speak clearly and courteously to make sure the visitor understands any directions you give.

All visits within a correctional facility can be classified as either contact or non-contact visits. ***Contact visits*** are visits in which both the visitor and the inmate are in the same room, without a physical barrier, and can have limited physical contact. ***Non-contact visits*** are visits in which the inmate and visitor are physically separated by some type of barrier or communicate through electronic means, such as an audio and video communication system.

An inmate may receive two types of visitors, social and professional. Social visitors may include friends and family. Some agencies require social visitors to be preregistered and screened for criminal histories or active warrants. Agencies may also limit the number of social visitors an inmate may receive at one time or within a specified period of time.

A professional visitor may include attorneys and staff employed by attorneys, investigators, bail bondsmen, parole and probation officers, law enforcement officers, social service agency staff, and clergy. Professional visitors are processed in a manner similar to social visitors.

Training academies, schools, or self-help or religious groups visiting a correctional facility may be subject to the same search procedures. These are usually preapproved visits with staff escorts to a designated area or for a tour of the facility.

Most visits occur at the correctional facility. However, occasionally inmates being treated at outside medical facilities could receive visitors. These visits are usually for inmates who are terminally ill, and are receiving social visitors at the discretion of the correctional agency.

FACILITY SECURITY AND VISITOR IDENTIFICATION AND AUTHORIZATION

Know the valid forms of identification and security equipment required for different types of visitors in a correctional facility

Visitation and entry requirements vary considerably from state correctional institutions to municipal and county facilities. Confirmation of visitor identification is necessary for authorized entry into all facilities. All visitors must present valid photo identification. Valid forms of identification include government-issued photo identification, driver's license or identification card, military identification, agency-issued identification, or passport. It is a crime to present a false ID (s. 944.39, F.S.).

The purpose of the person's visit will determine the types of security equipment issued. You will need to determine if a visit is social or professional. Social visits are conducted on a specific schedule on designated days and times, whereas professional visits may be permitted at any time. Any special equipment or requirement for professional visitors varies from agency to agency. Some agencies may use closed-circuit television systems to monitor visitor movement, while others may issue personal body alarms that the visitor can activate in an emergency, alerting security personnel to potential threats and the need to respond immediately. Some agencies provide security escorts for visitors throughout the facility.

When a visitor requests to meet with an inmate, verify the reason through either a published schedule or a shift supervisor's authorization according to facility policies. Direct any question regarding the validity of the purpose for the visit to the supervisor. Once a visitor is approved, direct them to the visitor registration area.

As part of the registration process, the visitor's identification information is recorded, along with the date and time of entry and exit, the purpose of the visit, and the person visited. Visitors must sign in and should be told what items are permitted in the visitation area. Correctional agencies maintain visitor registration logs as a permanent record. These logs are for accountability purposes to prove that an inmate's rights have not been violated (such as for attorney visits), and for emergency evacuation purposes.

Search the visitation area for safety hazards and security issues before a visitation

Conduct a systematic search of the visiting area before allowing inmates or visitors access. The area should be free of contraband and any potentially hazardous material. Inspect the equipment and furniture in the visitation area to make sure they are in working order. Search the restrooms in the same manner. Resolve any issues before allowing visitation to occur.

Search visitors for contraband before admitting them to the visitation area

Visitors are searched to control the introduction of contraband into the facility. This search is accomplished by various methods, such as metal detectors, pat down searches, and visual inspection. All objects a visitor brings are subject to search, whether visually, with an X-ray machine, or by other electronic means.

Contraband is commonly found on visitors. Not all items that are considered to be contraband in a correctional facility are criminal in nature or pose an immediate threat to the safety or security of the facility. For example, most facilities consider personal keys as contraband, since keys are sharp implements and could be dangerous. The visitor will likely be told to return the keys to their car or place them in a secure location until they leave. If a visitor is found with contraband that poses an immediate threat to the facility's safety or security, it will be confiscated and may be processed as evidence. Confiscate all contraband of a criminal nature, such as unauthorized cell phones, weapons, drugs, and intoxicants. The visitor is then subject to criminal prosecution, and visitation privileges may be terminated. All confiscated property will follow the chain of custody. Take necessary precautions to preserve evidence that would aid in an investigation.

Direct visitors to the visitation area while maintaining facility safety and security standards

After registering and searching, visitors are either verbally directed or escorted by an officer to the visitation area. In either instance, you must maintain the safety of the visitor and the security. Visits may occur in other designated areas as approved by the officer in charge. These may include a medical center or confinement area. In such instances, it may be necessary to escort the visitor to the alternate location. Remember attorney-client visits are privileged and must follow approved guidelines.

INMATE NOTIFICATION OF VISIT AND SEARCH

Know the process for notifying an inmate of visitor arrival in the designated visitation area

When visitors arrive at the facility and have been approved for visitation, the inmate is properly identified and informed of the visit. The inmate may either accept or decline the visit. Document if the inmate declines the visit. If the inmate declines the visit, the visitor registration area is advised, and the visitor is informed and asked to leave.

Search an inmate before entering the visitation area

For inmates accepting visitors, search the inmate for contraband before the visit. Visually inspect inmates to make sure they comply with the facility dress code. Depending on the facility layout and agency policies or procedures, verbally direct, monitor, or escort the inmate to the designated visitation area.

MONITORING THE VISIT

Monitor an inmate and visitor during a visitation

Continually observe the conduct of the inmate and visitor for general rule violations such as excessive noise, vulgarity, sexual misconduct, introduction of contraband, and altercations. Take immediate action if you observe a rule violation.

Even though all visitors are searched before entering the visitation area, contraband can still be introduced to the facility during visitation. For example, visitors may smuggle contraband through security checkpoints by "ballooning," which is when contraband is placed in a sealed balloon and concealed in a body cavity or swallowed for later expulsion. You should pay particular attention to inmate and visitor activity after a visitor exits a restroom. While in the restroom, the visitor may retrieve the concealed contraband and later pass it to an inmate or hide it in the visitation area. If you observe a visitor with contraband, the visitor may be detained.

If an issue arises that you cannot control or that is beyond your authority, call for backup. You may end the visit, permanently restrict the visitor from the facility, and discipline the inmate. Document any actions taken. During and after visitation, monitor inmates for emotional reactions that require referral to service providers, such as a mental health professional or chaplain.

EXITING THE VISITATION AREA

Complete inmate visitation while maintaining facility safety and security standards

At the end of visitation, ensure the inmates and visitors are separated. Explain to the visitors where and how to exit the visitation area. Verify that all visitors have left the visitation area, and confirm the identity of each visitor before they exit the facility. Update the visitation log to reflect that the visitor has departed.

Be aware that contraband could be concealed in the visitation area to be recovered by an inmate at a later time. Systematically search the visitation area and restrooms upon conclusion of the visit. The area should be free of contraband or any potentially hazardous material. If you discover contraband, confiscate it, maintain chain of custody, and contact your supervisor.

At the conclusion of the visit, the inmates should be segregated and monitored pending a thorough search. Inmates exiting a contact visit are searched to make sure no contraband enters the facility. Process any contraband found according to agency policies and procedures. When done with the search, direct or escort the inmate back to their assigned area and complete the search documentation.

LESSON VOCABULARY

contact visits

non-contact visits

REVIEW ITEMS

1. *What is the difference between contact and non-contact visits?*
2. *What are the valid forms of identification and security equipment required for different types of visitors in a correctional facility?*
3. *How should you search the visitation area for safety hazards and security issues before visitation times?*
4. *How do you search visitors for contraband before admitting them to the visitation area?*
5. *How do you direct visitors to the visitation area while maintaining facility safety and security standards?*
6. *What is the process for notifying an inmate of visitor arrival in the designated visitation area?*
7. *How do you search an inmate before entering the visitation area?*
8. *How do you monitor an inmate and visitor during visitation times?*
9. *How should you conclude inmate visitation while maintaining facility safety and security standards?*

LESSON 8

ESCORTING INMATES

LESSON GOAL

You will know how to safely escort an inmate within and outside of a correctional facility.

THINK ABOUT THIS

Escorting inmates requires the use of officer safety procedures to ensure the safe and timely movement of an inmate from one location to another. Escorting may be as simple as walking with a single unrestrained inmate from different locations or as complex as accompanying a group of fully restrained inmates.

ESCORT CONSIDERATIONS

Count and search inmates to begin the escorting process

An ***escort*** is the movement of an inmate from one point to another accompanied by an officer or staff member. You may conduct two types of escorts in a correctional setting. Internal escorts are conducted within the facility's secure perimeter. External escorts occur outside the secure perimeter of the facility.

You will receive oral or written instructions to escort inmates, including which inmates will be escorted and their destination. Inmates must be positively identified before departing. Take an accurate count of the inmates and notify appropriate staff of the number of inmates to be escorted and their destination. The reason for an escort, the number of inmates, and the inmate classification may determine the number of officers needed for the escort and the level of physical restraint required. Reasons for an escort may include medical, workgroup assignments, mental health services, and visitation. Additional staff may also be necessary.

Before escorting an inmate, conduct a frisk for weapons or contraband. Some facilities require strip searches when inmates are escorted outside of or returning to the facility. To ensure the safety of the inmates, consider any limitations and the physical condition of the inmate to be escorted, such as missing limbs, paralysis, obesity, prosthetic devices, crutches, or wheelchairs. All medical equipment or prosthetic devices require a search for contraband. You should not, however, pay attention only to disabilities, as extraordinarily physically fit inmates should also be of concern. Inmates who have acute or chronic medical conditions or serious injury may require additional specialized equipment during an escort. Examples include inmates with respiratory illness, broken limbs, gunshot wounds, cardiovascular diseases, and mental illness.

Escort inmates while maintaining facility safety and security standards

Stay aware of your surroundings at all times while escorting an inmate. Position yourself to the rear and slightly to one side of the inmate to control movement. Escorting officers should be familiar with diversionary tactics of inmates. During movement, contraband may be introduced, the inmate may commit battery, or the inmate may attempt to escape. Some equipment that officers may use while escorting inmates includes handcuffs, leg-irons, waist chains, and restraint chairs. Escort techniques and equipment are further discussed in the Defensive Tactics portion of the curriculum.

Complete escorting inmates to include documentation

After completing the escort, confirm that the number and identity of the inmates arriving at the destination match the original record of the inmates departing. Contact the appropriate staff member to notify them of the escort's completion, and document the escort as required.

External escorts could be an outside work detail, a chase vehicle following an ambulance, or any other escort outside the security perimeter of the facility. Follow agency policies and procedures with external escorts.

LESSON VOCABULARY

escort

REVIEW ITEMS

1. *How do you begin the escorting process?*
2. *How do you escort inmates while maintaining facility safety and security standards?*
3. *How do you complete the escorting process?*

LESSON 9
TRANSPORTING INMATES

LESSON GOAL

You will be able to transport inmates of all classifications while maintaining safety and security standards.

THINK ABOUT THIS

Moving an inmate from one area to another, even if only from the facility to a courtroom, presents a potentially dangerous situation. Many inmates try to use the time between locations, and outside of the facility's gates, to attempt an escape. You will need to know the security issues that arise with transporting inmates to prevent risk to yourself and the community.

Transport is defined as moving an inmate from the confines of a secure facility to another location outside the facility. Inmate transport is a routine operation. Be continually aware of your surroundings during inmate transport, including inmate behaviors, the public, the transport vehicle, other vehicles, traffic, and the security at the destination. Other potential security issues you may encounter include vehicle accidents, mechanical failure, or interaction with the general public. Reasons for inmate transport include medical treatments at local facilities or offices, transfers, work assignments, confinement, and required court appearances within and between jurisdictions.

CHOOSING A TRANSPORT VEHICLE

Know the function of each type of inmate transport vehicle

There are several types of transport vehicles with specialized security or accommodation equipment. These may include:

- a transport bus or van with cages, extra locks, and isolation seats
- a van with negative pressure ventilation and wheelchair accessibility
- a car with cages

Interior of a transport van *Figure 6-1*

Determine what type of transport vehicle is required by considering how many inmates are to be transferred; the custody levels, gender, and special needs of the inmates; and the purpose of the transport. You may need to segregate inmates in separate vehicles or separate compartments within the transport vehicle.

Example of a typical transport vehicle with partitions and screens

Figure 6-2

The following groups of inmates must be transported in separate compartments: male and female inmates, juveniles and adults, high-profile inmates, and violent inmates (who must be separated from others). Whenever possible, transport inmates in secure compartments without access to the driver.

Lower-custody inmates, such as those assigned to workgroups or squads, may be transported in vehicles without cages and partitions. Certain custody levels require transport vehicles with secure cages and partitions; these types of transports may also require trailing or chase vehicles.

A ***trailing or chase vehicle*** is an armed escort vehicle following or trailing a transport vehicle to provide additional security. These vehicles are often used when the transport is a high-level threat, such as when transporting a death-row inmate.

TRANSPORT VEHICLE INSPECTION AND SEARCH

Inspect an inmate transport vehicle for safety and contraband

It is your responsibility to systematically inspect the transport vehicle for mechanical deficiencies and possible security breaches, and to make sure the vehicle is properly equipped and in good working order. Make sure that the vehicle is fueled, fluid levels are sufficient, and tires are properly inflated. Check that all equipment functions properly, including the radio, issued cell phone, brakes, spare tire and jack, horn, lights, seat belts, wipers, mirrors, security equipment, and locks. Some agencies may require equipment such as safety reflectors, a fire extinguisher, or a first-aid kit. Document the inspection results on the designated agency-approved form. Note any deficiencies and, if necessary, submit a work order. Notify your supervisor if further instructions are necessary. Any discrepancies should be corrected. Do not use the vehicle until repairs are performed.

Apply systematic area search techniques to the inside and outside of the transport vehicle. These searches are done to make sure there is no contraband present before and after inmate transport. Pay particular attention to the secure compartments where the inmates will be or have been seated. Common components of the vehicle, such as bolts, screws, and parts of seat belts, can be removed quickly and without notice. Such items can be made into weapons or other contraband.

SECURITY ISSUES

When the vehicle has entered the designated area, such as a sally port, secure the inmates in the vehicle. When loading or unloading inmates from a non-secure area, such as a hospital, tactically position the vehicle to prevent escape or ambush. If you observe security concerns, contact a supervisor or local law enforcement for assistance.

Park an inmate transport vehicle while maintaining safety and security standards

Generally, keep all inmates restrained during transport. However, you must not restrain inmates to the vehicle except by the use of standard seat belts and shoulder harnesses. An inmate's custody level will determine the level of restraint required during transport. You must take the limitations and physical attributes of the inmate into consideration when determining the types of restraints to use. The various security restraint devices that can be used on an inmate when in transport include hand or ankle cuffs, waist chains or cuffs, black boxes (hard interlocking cover for handcuffs and waist chains), leg braces, and an electronic control belt. Transport vehicle security devices, such as security cages, partitions, and screens, are all physical barriers installed in vehicles to segregate the various types of inmates as well as separate the inmates from the officers.

Know the functions of the different types of inmate transport vehicle security devices

Examples of typical security restraint devices used on inmates during transport

Figure 6-3

TRANSPORT DOCUMENTATION

Before departing, make sure you have the proper authorization and documentation to transport the inmate(s). These documents may include a court order, court docket, face sheet, transport request, or TWIX (a Department of Corrections computerized message). A ***face sheet*** is a document with a current picture of the inmate, name, inmate identification number, physical description, incarceration date, date of birth, end of sentence date, and custody level.

Know the role of inmate transport documents

Once you have verified transport documents, confirm the identity and total number of inmates. Check the count at departure and again at arrival. You must make certain that all required transport documentation goes with you to the destination.

SECURING THE INMATE AND STAFF NOTIFICATION OF TRANSPORT

Secure the inmate in the transport vehicle while maintaining safety and security standards

An important part of the transport process is searching the inmate. Remove the inmates identified for transport from the general population and move them to a secured area. Verify that they wear proper attire, search each individual inmate before transport, and secure the inmates. Once you have properly applied security restraint devices, place the inmates in the transport vehicle. Situate the inmates in segregated compartments if required. Apply seat belts to all inmates. Officers and inmates must adhere to the Florida Safety Belt Law, and the number of inmates transported cannot exceed the vehicle passenger capacity.

According to agency policies and procedures, you may be assigned a firearm and duty gear. Make sure that the firearm is in good condition and has ammunition. You should also wear available body armor.

Transport the inmate while maintaining safety and security standards

A transport plan should include a primary and an alternative route. Be aware that inmates may create diversions to provide opportunity for escape. Routine routes should be varied to reduce the risk of outside assaults.

During transport, if an inmate becomes non-compliant, combative, or disorderly or complains of a medical condition, do not stop the transport.

Many doctors' offices will not see disruptive inmates. The courts are also hesitant to hold legal proceedings with inmates who cannot conform to courtroom decorum. Immediately contact your agency with all appropriate information and follow instructions.

If the transport vehicle encounters any unforeseen situations, such as a vehicle crash, mechanical failure, or a problem with the primary route, immediately make sure that the inmates are secure. In such cases, contact the local law enforcement agency for assistance and notify your supervisor for further instruction. When contacting local agencies, provide as much information as possible.

Maintain communication with the facility and provide necessary information during transport, such as the direction of travel, the primary and alternative routes, the number of inmates, the time of departure, the beginning and ending mileage, the destination, and the predicted time of arrival. Provide status updates and time of arrival at the destination. Information provided by the transport officer will be documented by the agency's control room. Document any unusual occurrences on an agency form (incident report) and include all relevant information.

In some circumstances, a transport could result in a transfer. A ***transfer*** is movement of an inmate from one housing location to another. For example, an inmate's routine medical appointment could result in hospitalization. If this occurs, contact your agency for specific instructions.

Upon conclusion of the transport, again perform a vehicle inspection and note any damage. Check the vehicle's fluids, and make sure that the vehicle is clean, refueled, and parked in the designated area. Complete the vehicle inspection documentation as required.

Lesson Vocabulary

face sheet

trailing or chase vehicle

transfer

transport

Review Items

1. *What are the different features and uses of each type of inmate transport vehicle?*
2. *How do you inspect an inmate transport vehicle for safety and contraband?*
3. *How will you park an inmate transport vehicle while maintaining safety and security standards?*
4. *What are the functions of the different types of inmate transport vehicle security devices?*
5. *What is the role of inmate transport documents?*
6. *How do you secure the inmate in the transport vehicle while maintaining safety and security standards?*
7. *How will you transport the inmate while maintaining safety and security standards?*

LESSON 10
WORK SQUADS

LESSON GOAL

You will know how to monitor inmates during an inside or outside work detail.

THINK ABOUT THIS

As difficult as it is to monitor inmates within a facility, you can imagine how difficult it is to monitor inmates without the help of walls, gates, and cameras. This is a correctional officer's responsibility when they are supervising an outside work detail.

Many inmates have work responsibilities within the correctional system. Classification is responsible for assigning inmates to a work detail. Medical will screen, approve, and train the inmate for job assignments. These assignments could be inside or outside the correctional facilities. Work crews or squads that do not go beyond the security perimeter of a facility are considered inside. Any squad or detail that works beyond the perimeter is considered an outside work squad.

INSIDE AND OUTSIDE WORK SQUADS

Know the differences between inside and outside work squads

Correctional facility work squads perform a variety of services that provide a cost benefit to state and local governments. Inside work squads assist with maintenance, sanitation, food service, library, medical, laundry, and other duties as assigned. Inmates on outside work squads usually perform road maintenance, grounds maintenance, sanitation, farming, and other assigned duties. In certain circumstances, some inmates are allowed to leave the facility without supervision for work. These inmates may be on a work release or continued employment program.

Verify an inmate's identity for inside or outside work details

Verify an inmate's identity on an inside or outside work squad by comparing the inmate's issued ID card with the work squad roster and the inmate. Officers assigned to outside work squads are required to verify each inmate's identity before they exit the facility. You should inspect the identification for obvious signs of tampering, making sure that the identification card is valid. If you suspect that the identification card is altered or the inmate is concealing their actual identity, confiscate the card and immediately contact a supervisor for further instruction.

Search an inmate before and after an inside or outside work detail

Search inmates for contraband before and after the work assignment. The type of search may depend on the type of work assignment, the location, and the equipment used during the work detail. Perform a pat down or strip-search, depending on the agency's policies. While conducting a search, make sure the inmates are properly dressed for the work squad. Inmates who fail to comply with rules and regulations, such as dress codes, will be subject to disciplinary action. If an inmate cannot perform the assignment, notify your supervisor.

The officer supervising the work squad must maintain an ongoing count of the inmates under their supervision. This count begins when you take custody of the inmates for the work assignment. Counting is particularly important when changing work locations. The specific reporting procedure varies from agency to agency. Count, document, and report the number of inmates when leaving the facility, as you arrive at the destination, after any other change in location, when leaving the work site, and upon arrival back at the facility. Document the inmates' names, numbers, work location, and the total number of inmates in the workgroup.

Maintain accountability of an inside or outside work detail

Search the work area to provide safety and security before allowing inmates access. Vary the method and timing of searches conducted for regularly scheduled work locations so as not to set a pattern or routine. When searching, you should remove any potentially hazardous material. Work areas outside the facility are potential contraband drop-off sites, especially when the work assignment extends beyond one workday. If a work assignment is regularly scheduled, inmates can arrange for contraband to be dropped off at a predetermined location. The inmate will then return to the site and retrieve the contraband.

INSTRUCTIONS FOR WORK DETAILS

Before each new job assignment, conduct and document safety training for the inmates. Ensure you issue the proper work and safety equipment to all inmates assigned to the work detail. Safety equipment may include safety goggles, hearing protection, or gloves. Before allowing the inmates to work, inspect equipment to ensure proper working order and verify the item has not been altered. This inspection should take place both before issuing the equipment to the inmate and after it has been returned. It is the work squad officer's responsibility to maintain accountability for equipment used by inmates at all times.

Maintain inmate safety and security during an inside or outside work detail

Explain the boundaries of the work site and remind inmates in the work area of the rules regarding inmate behavior. Demonstrate how to use any work equipment and answer any questions the inmates may have concerning the assigned work. It is your responsibility to supervise work performance, maintain safety and security of the squad, notify your supervisor of any problems that arise, and document all training.

MONITORING INMATES DURING WORK DETAIL

While monitoring a work detail, ensure the inmates are doing the following:

Monitor inmates during an inside or outside work detail

- completing the work assignment in a timely manner
- operating the equipment as trained
- not damaging or altering the equipment or other items in the work area
- wearing issued safety equipment properly
- not interacting with the public
- wearing proper clothing
- staying within the assigned work area

Immediately correct any deviation from the instructions given and document as necessary. Report any injuries or illness at the work site immediately and ensure the inmate receives appropriate treatment. In the event of a life-threatening emergency, immediately request local emergency medical services, notify your agency, and request additional support as needed.

Allow for required rest periods, proper hydration, meal breaks, and restroom use. Search restroom facilities before use and verify the locations to discourage possible escape attempts and introduction of contraband. During work periods or restroom breaks, secure and monitor the vehicle constantly to ensure no contraband is introduced.

If an inmate becomes non-compliant, combative, or disorderly during a work assignment, contact the control room or local law enforcement for assistance and use the amount of force necessary to control the inmate and protect the public. In the event of an escape, immediately assemble the remaining inmates and notify the facility that an escape has occurred. Do *not* abandon the remaining inmates in an attempt to capture the escaping inmate.

COMPLETION OF WORK DETAIL

Maintain facility and inmate safety and security at the end of an inside or outside work detail

At the end of the work detail, instruct the inmates to secure all equipment and thoroughly search the work area to ensure they have not left any tools, materials, notes, or contraband behind.

The ease of obtaining contraband during a work assignment requires that you conduct a thorough search of each inmate upon return to the facility. Remove the inmates from the transport vehicle and escort them into a secure area to conduct the searches. Some facilities require that returning inmates are strip-searched.

Review Items

1. *What are the differences between inside and outside work squads?*
2. *How do you verify an inmate's identity for inside or outside work details?*
3. *How do you search an inmate before and after an inside or outside work detail?*
4. *How do you maintain the safety and security of an inside or outside work detail?*
5. *How do you monitor inmates during an inside or outside work detail?*
6. *How will you maintain facility and inmate safety and security at the end of an inside or outside work detail?*

LESSON 11
HOSPITAL ASSIGNMENTS

LESSON GOAL

You will maintain custody of an inmate during a hospital assignment.

THINK ABOUT THIS

Security measures continue for an inmate who is taken to a hospital outside of a correctional facility. Consider this example of an escape attempt. Officer Harris was monitoring Inmate Foster during a hospital assignment. Inmate Foster asked to use the restroom. Officer Harris removed Inmate Foster's restraints and stood guard outside the restroom door. Inmate Foster climbed through the roof of the restroom and attempted an escape. Fortunately, the inmate fell through the ceiling and was recaptured. Did the officer here do anything wrong? Was there another way that this could have gone?

COMMUNICATING SECURITY CONCERNS WITH MEDICAL STAFF

Communicate with medical staff about inmate security concerns

When you arrive at the hospital, give any accompanying medical records to hospital staff. Speak with medical staff if you have security concerns that may affect the care of the inmate. These concerns may include:

- unauthorized visitation
- safety and suicide precautions
- unauthorized phone access
- access to items that are considered contraband in a correctional facility

Hospital staff may assist with moving the inmate throughout the facility. However, it is your responsibility to maintain security.

GENERAL OFFICER RESPONSIBILITIES

Maintain inmate safety and hospital security during hospital assignments

When you are assigned hospital duty for an inmate, upon arrival or start of a shift notify your supervisor or control room staff of the arrival, room number, and the inmate's condition. Survey the area in which the inmate is being held for potential security threats. Remove unnecessary medical equipment, furnishings, and hospital personnel from the immediate area if possible. Conduct a visual search of the inmate, the room, and any adjacent rooms, such as bathroom facilities that the inmate may use during their stay. Systematically inspect and secure all windows and secondary exits if possible. Inspect all restraints used on the inmate to ensure proper security. Correct and immediately report any discrepancies to your supervisor.

When applying, removing, or checking restraints, be aware of your weapon retention techniques, as you are near the inmate. Stand strategically between the inmate and other people or the door. If the inmate is in isolation, station yourself outside the door. If the inmate is in the operating room or intensive care unit (ICU), follow the direction of hospital staff, but do not violate correctional agency policies or procedures. Contact your supervisor immediately if a conflict occurs between hospital and agency policy.

Do not allow the inmate to have contact with the public. If the security of the inmate is compromised due to public contact, notify your supervisor immediately to determine what additional security measures may be necessary. Inmate deathbed visit requests by family members will be addressed by agency administration on a case-by-case basis.

RESTRAINT ISSUES

Know the role of security restraint devices during hospital assignments

Security restraint devices, such as shackles, handcuffs, or flex cuffs, may be used to secure an inmate in the hospital. It is common practice for officers to apply one leg restraint to the inmate and the other to the bed frame and not the bed rail, to prevent unauthorized movement. Security restraint devices may be removed temporarily, with the approval of the facility officer-in-charge, to conduct medical tests or procedures. Removing handcuffs and leg restraints at the same time is not recommended unless medically necessary; however, in such cases, take additional security measures. Reapply restraints once the test, procedure, or examination has been completed.

Restraints may not be used on a prisoner who is known to be pregnant during the third trimester, or during labor, delivery, and postpartum recovery unless you make a determination that the prisoner presents a substantial flight risk or some other extraordinary medical or security circumstance that dictates restraints should be used. There are restrictions on the types and placement of restraint devices on pregnant prisoners. Follow your agency's policy. If a licensed health care professional requests all restraints be removed, inform them of all pertinent security concerns regarding the inmate.

Know the role of clinical restraints and clinical seclusion during hospital assignments

Inmates may also be controlled through other methods. ***Clinical restraints*** are ordered by the attending physician and are used to keep inmates from injuring themselves in a medical facility. ***Clinical seclusion*** is used to isolate the inmate from the general population at a medical facility for medical and safety reasons. This may include placing the inmate in a padded room or a straightjacket for their safety. The attending physician has sole discretion on the application or removal of clinical restraints and placement in or out of clinical seclusion based on specific medical needs.

INMATE MEDICAL EMERGENCIES

Maintain inmate safety and hospital security during inmate medical emergencies in a hospital setting

Notify the nearest medical personnel for assistance if the inmate exhibits:

- any signs of medical distress, such as difficulty breathing, extreme sweating, nausea, extreme bleeding, or paralysis

- any dislodging of medical devices or equipment, such as intravenous (IV) lines or monitors
- any medical situation beyond your training and abilities

Inmate medical emergencies are chaotic events, and multiple medical personnel may respond to the situation. Security measures must not interfere with medical life-saving intervention. Monitor all activity and maintain a balance between security and medical treatment. You must complete an incident report as soon as possible after the medical emergency has been resolved.

Lesson Vocabulary

clinical restraints

clinical seclusion

Review Items

1. *How and in what situations should you communicate with medical staff about inmate security concerns?*
2. *How do you maintain inmate safety and hospital security during hospital assignments?*
3. *What is the role of clinical restraints and clinical seclusion during hospital assignments?*
4. *How do you maintain inmate safety and hospital security during inmate medical emergencies in a hospital setting?*

Supervising Special Populations

UNIT 1 DIVERSITY IN THE CORRECTIONAL SETTING

LESSON 1
INMATE SOCIETIES

LESSON GOAL

You will understand the range of special populations that could be living in a correctional facility.

THINK ABOUT THIS

On a daily basis, you will interact with a variety of inmates. Special populations are inmates or groups of inmates with characteristics you should be aware of, so you can respond appropriately when supervising them.

Although Florida has a very diverse population, inmates that make up Florida's incarcerated population reflect large numbers of particular groups. Knowing how to monitor the more diverse populations in a correctional facility is important for your safety, visitor safety, and the well-being of inmates.

SPECIAL POPULATIONS

Know the range of special population inmates

Special populations are groups of inmates who have unique mental, physical, or social characteristics that distinguish them from the general population. Officers, management, and administrative staff will need to respond to these inmates in non-traditional and innovative ways. Agencies have specific procedures, strategies, and approaches to managing special populations, which may include:

- members of gangs
- people with substance abuse issues
- people with mental illness or an intellectual disability
- people with long-term medical conditions or physical disabilities
- women
- the elderly
- juveniles
- LGBTQ+ people
- inmates in special confinement or on death row

SOCIETIES

By nature, humans are social beings, even in a correctional setting, and tend to identify with people with similar beliefs and backgrounds. Inmate societies tend to form around race, religion, medical needs, geographical identity, ethnicity, cultural background, and socioeconomic status. An inmate's social and financial status, physical size, crimes committed, number of repeat offenses, and length of sentence can also play a part in these associations. These societies bond together because of a common background or interests and sometimes for protection. Inmates might align with others they think have power, imitating them and wanting to be more like them.

Know the reasons that inmates form unique types of societies

Having knowledge of some of the characteristics of these five basic societies will help you better understand the inmate population.

Know the common types of societies inmates form

- Racial societies are often hybrids of multiple racial groups and may not reflect a single race.
- Groups focused on religious practice may guide an inmate's daily activities, such as praying five times a day, carrying a rosary, or fasting.
- Inmates with similar medical issues, such as diabetes, HIV, and cancer often sympathize with their own social group, sharing medical experiences and hardships.
- Geographical societies are coming to the forefront of inmate populations. Inmates from the same geographical region often group together. They use identifiers, such as the telephone area code, and name of the major city or county in which they lived.
- Some inmates from similar socioeconomic groups will cluster and sometimes control certain activities within the inmate population with money, contraband, and influence. Inmates on the lower end of the social ladder often struggle to gain protection from inmates with greater influence.

Inmate societies may follow a hierarchical leadership where there is a clearly defined leader, sub-leaders, and followers. Elderly inmates typically do not have a leader. Youthful offender societies often do not maintain the discipline required to keep a leadership structure. Different situations, such as fights, releases, intakes, changes in the availability of assets, or politics can frequently alter the hierarchy of an inmate society.

Know the structural dynamics of inmate societies

LESSON VOCABULARY

special populations

REVIEW ITEMS

1. *What are special populations?*
2. *Why do inmates group into five basic societies?*
3. *What are the characteristics of the five basic inmate societies?*
4. *Describe how two different inmate societies are structured.*

UNIT 2 SECURITY THREAT GROUPS

LESSON 1
STG CHARACTERISTICS

LESSON GOAL

You will understand the basic characteristics, symbols, graffiti, colors, signs, tattoos, codes, and slang of security threat groups (STGs) in a correctional facility.

THINK ABOUT THIS

Gang activity causes many of the problems in a facility. Because of this, the Department of Corrections formed the Security Threat Group (STG) Initiative. The main goal of the STG Initiative is to reduce gang activity in facilities and keep staff, visitors, and inmates safe and secure. This lesson will help you identify and respond to gang activity in your facility.

SECURITY THREAT GROUP

Understand the link between a criminal gang and an STG

According to s. 874.03, F.S., a criminal gang is a formal or informal ongoing organization, association, or group. The primary activities of a criminal gang are to commit criminal or delinquent acts. Criminal gangs consist of three or more people who have a common name or common identifying signs, colors, or symbols. Criminal gangs include, but are not limited to, terrorist organizations and hate groups.

A ***security threat group (STG)*** is a criminal enterprise or an organization of a continuing nature that engages repeatedly in acts of crime individually or collectively, and poses a safety or security threat within, as well as outside of, a correctional facility. STG is a term officers use to remove any glamour from being a member of a criminal gang and to diminish the power associated with being a gang member. Some inmates idolize the lifestyle of gang members and the term STG makes being a member less appealing.

STGs are a threat to the orderly operation of a correctional facility, because the roots of their operations are criminal. STGs can influence inmates and usually control the bulk of the contraband flow because of the extent of their membership. STGs can commit the same crimes in the facility they commit outside of the facility, such as extortion, gambling, prostitution, battery, assault, money laundering, drug smuggling, escape plots, robbery, and murder.

STGs represented in a correctional setting can include:

Know the names of some common STGs

- 5%er
- Aryan Brotherhood
- Aryan Nations
- Black Gangster Disciples
- Black Guerrilla Family
- Bloods
- Crips
- Folk Nation
- Gangster Disciples
- Insane Gangster Disciples
- MS-13
- Ñeta
- Sur-XIII or Sur-13
- White Supremacists
- Zoe Mafia

TRADITIONAL STGs

Know the basic characteristics of STGs

Traditional STGs have a documented history, a written set of laws or codes, and can have an organizational structure. Some examples include the Latin Kings, Bloods, Crips, Aryan Brotherhood, Ku Klux Klan, MS-13, and SUR-13. These STGs often have a leadership structure (implicit or explicit), codes of conduct, colors, special dress, signs, and symbols. A traditional STG may vary in characteristics of age, gender, community, ethnicity, or generation, as well as in the scope and nature of its criminal activities.

NON-TRADITIONAL/HYBRID STGs

Non-traditional STGs that do not fall under the criteria of a traditional STG can be without laws or code, but still have an organizational structure. Some examples include Haitian STGs, Jamaican Posse, Asian Pride, and Taking Over Your Shit (TOYS).

Hybrid STGs form within schools, neighborhoods, or regions, and in youthful offender, juvenile, and adult correctional facilities. They are composed of members from other STGs, united to form one group, and associated with specific geographic areas or neighborhoods. Examples include Money Over Bitches Boyz (MOB Boyz), 704 (or local area codes), Zoe Mafia, and Guatemalans Taking Over (GTO).

TRANSITIONAL STGs

Transitional STG members are individuals or a group of criminal gang members who come to prison and realign themselves with traditional and non-traditional STGs, or they can be hybrid STG members recruited by larger, traditional STGs.

FEMALE STGs

Female inmates can be members of a typically male STG or members of an all-female STG. Female STGs can be similar to male STGs in structure. The female STG crime rate is low; however, when female STG members commit a crime, it is often violent. As the population of female inmates increases, so does the female STG population.

PRISON-BASED STGs

Prison-based STGs originate within the prison system, as opposed to most STGs that begin as gangs outside of prison, and predominantly base their operations from within the prison system. Some examples include Mexican Mafia / LA EME, Aryan Brotherhood, Black Guerilla Family, Ñeta, Texas Syndicate, and Nuestra Familia.

EXTREMISTS

Extremists may act solo or as a group, follow an extreme ideology, such as faith- or belief-based, or anti-establishment, and are usually very tight-knit, unpredictable, and exclusive. There are similarities and differences among inmate behaviors displayed as religious belief, religious fanaticism, and extremism. Some examples of religious fanaticism and extremism include sovereign citizens, Jihadists, and Posse Comitatus. A solo or a lone inmate that subscribes to a specific extremist ideology can cause significant security concerns when they commit criminal acts individually, or individually as part of a group within or from outside the facility.

STG SYMBOLS, GRAFFITI, COLORS, SIGNS, TATTOOS

Know the symbols, graffiti, colors, signs, and tattoos of STGs

Most correctional facilities have an STG coordinator who can provide additional information related to the symbols, graffiti, colors, signs, and tattoos of specific STGs. Officers using these STG symbols, gestures, graffiti, or alphabets as communication can potentially place themselves in a compromising or dangerous situation. Some STG symbols, graffiti, colors, signs, and tattoos may include:

- forming hand signs with the left or right hand
- wearing hats cocked or tilted to the left or right
- rolling up one pant leg
- untying one shoe
- resting the hand in a specific pocket
- wearing jewelry turned at an angle
- wearing specific color combinations (such as black / brown or blue / red)
- wearing identifiers or icons that appear in combination, such as a star and a crown, revealing both the inmate's alliance and the specific STG to which the inmate belongs
- using a common phrase, such as "All is one" or "All is well"
- using hand signals or graffiti in a certain direction, such as upside down or sideways as a sign of disrespect
- using hand signals or graffiti properly as a sign of respect
- using non-verbal communication, such as tugging on a shirt

People Nation *Figure 7-1* *Folk Nation* *Figure 7-2* *Nuestra Familia* *Figure 7-4*

Aryan Brotherhood 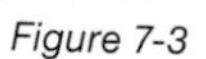 *Figure 7-3* *Mexican Mafia* *Figure 7-5*

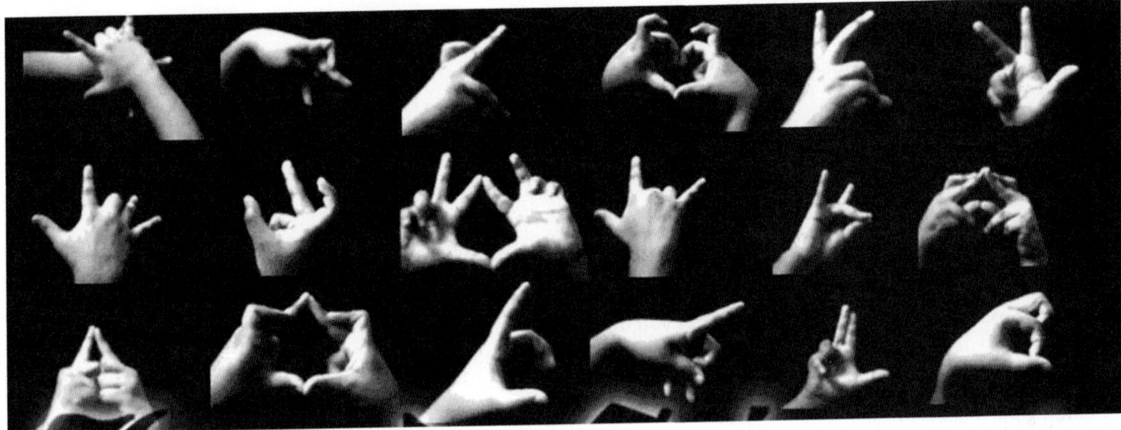

Gang Hand Signals Table

Figure 7-6

Top: People's Nation Alliance, Allport Lovers, Almighty Popes, Maniac Latin Disciples, Gangster Party People OR Party Players, Vice Lords

Middle: Two Two Boys, Gangster Disciples, Insane Deuces, Latin Kings, Insane Dragons, Imperial Gangsters

Bottom: Crazy Gangsters, Spanish Gangster Disciples, Latin Counts, Familia Stones, Latin Lovers, Bishops OR Almighty Brazers OR Insane Latin Brothers

STG SLANG

Know the codes and slang of STGs

13: sure or no

187: to kill someone; California penal code for murder

911: police

B.K.: blood killer

B.O.S.: Brothers of the Struggle

bang / gang bangin': being involved in gang activity

banger: gang member

beef: complaint, dispute

behind the wall: in prison

blade: knife

bogart: to con or trick

bolt: run

book: run, get away, leave

bounce: to leave an area

buck: prison-made alcoholic beverage

buck: to not comply

buck, buck: sound of a handgun

C.K.: Crip Killer

call the shots: give orders

catch a V: punishment for breaking a gang rule or code

cellie: person who shares a cell with another inmate

check yourself: watch what you say or what you do

check-in: an inmate that requests protection from staff or other inmates

chief: gang leader

chill out: stop what you are doing

claim: announce your gang affiliation, represent

colors: specific color scheme used by the gang

crab: derogatory name for Crip members used by Bloods

creepin': a married or committed person going out to have an affair

dissin': disrespecting someone

down: loyalty or allegiance to someone or something

drop a dime: to snitch or tell on someone

dropping the flag: leaving the gang

false flaggin': representing a gang that you don't belong to

fishing: sending small notes using fishing line by slinging under the door

flag: gang handkerchief

kite: letter

latching / jumped: placing a heavy object in a sock to use as a weapon

rag: gang handkerchief

set: group or gang that one is affiliated with

shiv / shank: prison-made weapon, usually a knife

shot caller: person in charge

slob: derogatory name for Bloods used by Crips

violation: the punishment given to a gang member who breaks a rule

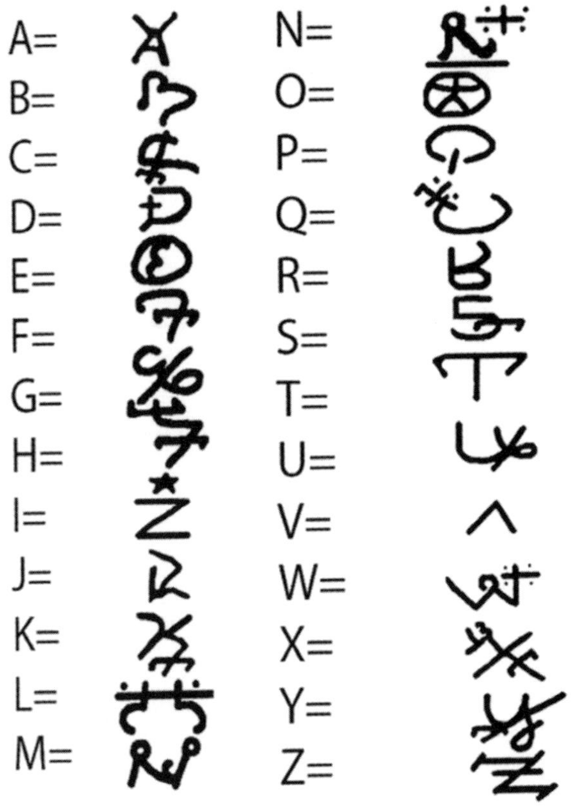

Bloods alphabet

Figure 7-7

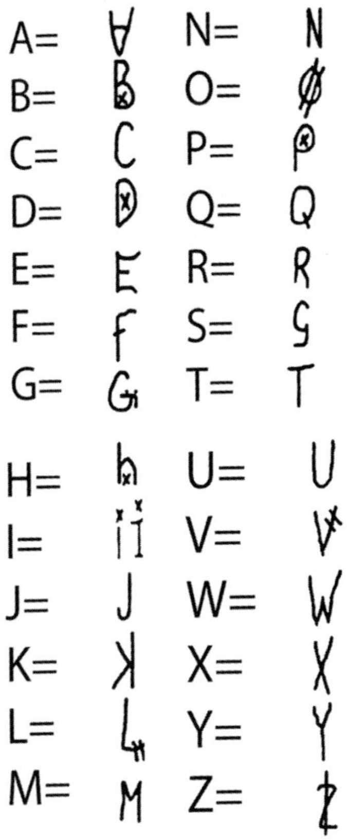

Crips alphabet

Figure 7-8

Inmates can deliver messages through sign language and written code sent by fishing (passing paper messages using a string) or through the U.S. Postal Service. STG code is a form of cryptic communication using written symbols and letters, broken by matching the letter with the symbol. Notify a supervisor when you find these types of communications and explain the circumstances under which you found them, and from whom and where you found them.

Lesson Vocabulary

security threat group (STG)

Review Items

1. *Why do you call a criminal gang an STG in the facility?*
2. *How do you know the difference between a traditional STG, a non-traditional STG, and a hybrid STG?*
3. *What is different about the crimes female STGs commit from other STG crimes?*
4. *What is different about a prison-based STG from other STGs?*
5. *Why are extremist STGs so dangerous?*
6. *What are some of the symbols, graffiti, colors, signs, and tattoos STG members may use?*
7. *How do some inmates communicate within the correctional facility?*

Unit 2 Security Threat Groups

Lesson 2

STG Structures and Activities

Lesson Goal

You will be able to deter STG activity in a correctional facility.

Think About This

Now that you know what STGs look like and how they communicate, let's learn how they can behave in a correctional facility. Some STGs act as if they have power over other STGs. Within an STG, some inmates behave as if they have power over other inmates. What does it look like when this organizational structure changes? Can this be a threat to your safety and the security of your facility? What are some of the things that STGs do when they are planning an incident? Can they plan a disruptive event outside the facility from inside the facility? Often these disruptions result in injuries to inmates, officers, and sometimes to visitors. Your role is to deter STG activity and help maintain the safety and security of your facility.

STG Structures

Understand the different ways that STGs may structure themselves

There are several ways that STGs structure themselves within a correctional setting. The pyramid structure contains one inmate, who is a strong leader, with at least two or more sublevels of command. The pyramid structure is usually the strongest and most organized structure and is common to the more traditional, national gangs.

The linear structure contains a single leader representing each clique; however, the leaders do not answer to a higher command. The leaders will often meet to consult with one another. This structure is common to the more non-traditional or local street gangs.

The flux or circular structure has a continually changing leadership. Stronger or more charismatic people enter this type of STG structure. These STGs will usually evolve into the linear or pyramid structure as they work toward establishing a strong leader; some examples of the flux or circular structure include school-based gangs and some hybrid gangs.

Some STGs have an organization based on length of commitment or tenure. The STGs rule by committee, there is no leader, and members make all decisions by consensus. If a member disagrees with the group's ideas, that member will not participate. When a member initiates a criminal activity, all of the participating members must commit the crime. These STGs have specialists (not leaders) in specific crimes who consult with members on how to carry out each crime.

It is common for the formal leader of a street gang to control the street gang while in prison, and this is the case for most of the national gangs. The leader, similar to other inmates, usually has phone and visitor privileges. The leader will issue orders from inside the institution, and the next in command outside of the institution will carry these orders out to the street.

STG INDICATORS

Understand inmate behaviors that may indicate a pending escalation in STG activities

Some of the indicators of STG activity in a correctional setting can be an increase in crime, inmate-on-inmate violence, and taggings. A ***tagging*** is a marking on a wall, a fence, or the ground that identifies STG territory. You could notice an increase in rule violations, differences in inmates gathering, new STG tattoos, and an increase in recruitment, fights, injuries, and requests for personal protection or housing reassignment. The main way you will learn about STG activity is through an increase in confidential disclosures from inmates who want to avoid association with the STG plans.

Understand the indicators you may find of a pending escalation in STG activity when conducting cell or area searches

During cell or area searches, look for a shift in the types of contraband items, such as weapons, cell phones, gang literature, and a change in the quantity of commissary items. STG leaders will often have the largest amount of commissary items without receipts, which they will pass along to other inmates. Look for an increase in the allowable items, such as an extra lock, a pair of shoes, and excessive amounts of facility-provided items.

Understand inappropriate mail items that can indicate a pending escalation in STG activity

Often inmate mail can indicate pending escalation in STG activity. The mail-room staff should filter inappropriate items when monitoring inmate mail. They should look for STG-related symbols, codes, phrases, and photos that can be a direct or indirect threat of STG activity or hidden contraband.

MONITORING

Know how to deter STG activity inside and outside of a facility

Monitoring inmate behavior is critical to the safe and secure operation of the facility, and it discourages STG activity. You could observe changes in inmate cliques or groupings that indicate a shift in alliances, authority, and influence over other STG inmates. Alliances and conflicts between STGs are constantly changing and can result in an argument or a major fight that can spread throughout the facility. Awareness of likely or forthcoming STG activity within the facility is the most effective tool to deter STG activity. Observation of STG activity can also mirror gang activity that is happening or about to happen outside of the facility. Do not underestimate the ability of an STG member to get things done inside or outside of a facility. With input based on your observations, the STG coordinator at your facility should maintain a flow of STG information to law enforcement outside of the facility, which can deter activity both inside and outside of the facility.

An additional deterrent to STG activity is recognizing and seizing STG contraband. This process can be as simple as viewing the item, seizing it, and determining what to do with it. However, you may encounter STG contraband that requires further review by the STG coordinator, supervisor, or investigating authority.

DOCUMENTATION

Know how to document STG activity inside and outside of a facility

Documenting STG activity can help you statutorily identify an inmate as a potential STG member. This can increase their criminal penalties or change their classification and housing status. Photograph their clothing, tattoos, and any other observable identifiers. Many inmates are proud of their STG affiliation and will pose for photographs while showing hand signs. Documenting these activities can aid in developing a roster of STG members. If you find tagging in the facility, photograph it, and report the information to the STG coordinator. Remove or cover tagging quickly, as other inmates are likely to be encouraged to add tagging of their own, and the effect will multiply. Thoroughly document all suspected STG activity immediately to provide additional information for STG databases.

LESSON VOCABULARY

tagging

REVIEW ITEMS

1. *What are the differences among the following ways STGs organize themselves: pyramid, linear, flux or circular, tenure based, and outside control?*
2. *What are some of the things inmates do that may indicate they are planning a disruptive STG event?*
3. *What items should you look for during a cell or area search that may indicate inmates are planning a disruptive STG event?*
4. *Why is monitoring inmate mail important to prevent STG activity?*
5. *What are two of the most important things you should do to prevent STG activity?*
6. *Why is it important to document STG activity?*

UNIT 3 SUBSTANCE ABUSE AMONG INMATES

LESSON 1

SUBSTANCE ABUSE AMONG INMATES

LESSON GOAL

You will be able to monitor inmates with a substance abuse issue.

THINK ABOUT THIS

Some of the inmates in your facility will have substance abuse or drug addiction issues. As they may be new to the facility, inmates may be going through the withdrawal and detoxification process. These issues can compromise the inmate's safety, health, and well-being while under your supervision. Having a solid understanding of what these symptoms look like and how to respond should better prepare you to supervise these types of inmates.

DEFINITION

Know the difference between substance abuse and drug addiction

Substance use disorder or drug addiction covers a range of conditions and practices and can include the use of alcohol, narcotics, or prescription medication, or the use of any drug without medical justification. ***Substance abuse*** is a pattern of substance use that leads to significant impairment or distress, as displayed by at least one of the following behaviors:

- failure to fulfill major obligations at work, school, or home
- repeated substance use in situations that are physically hazardous, such as driving a car
- frequent substance use-related legal problems
- persistent or repeated social or interpersonal problems caused by the effects of the substance, such as domestic violence

Not everyone who has a substance abuse problem becomes a drug addict; however, many suffering from substance abuse tend to evolve to addiction. ***Drug addiction*** is a chronic, relapsing brain disease. A person with drug addiction constantly seeks drugs despite the harmful consequences. The drugs change the structure of the brain and how it works. These brain changes can be long lasting and can lead to many harmful, often self-destructive, behaviors.

SIGNS AND SYMPTOMS

Inmates may display the following physical and health signs of substance abuse:

Know the physical, behavioral, and psychological signs of an inmate with substance abuse issues

- bloodshot eyes, pupils that are smaller or larger than normal
- frequent nosebleeds
- changes in appetite or sleep patterns
- sudden weight loss or weight gain
- seizures without a history of epilepsy
- a decline in personal grooming or appearance
- unusual smells on breath, body, or clothing
- shakes, tremors, incoherent or slurred speech, impaired or unstable coordination

Inmates may display the following behavioral signs of substance abuse:

- silent, withdrawn, engaging in secretive or suspicious behaviors
- sudden change in relationships
- frequently getting into arguments, fights, accidents

Inmates may display the following psychological signs of substance abuse:

- unexplained changes in personality or attitude
- sudden mood changes, irritability, angry outbursts, or laughing at nothing
- periods of unusual hyperactivity or agitation
- a lack of motivation; an inability to focus, appearing lethargic or "spaced out"
- appearing fearful, withdrawn, anxious, or paranoid, with no apparent reason

Know the physical, emotional, and acute symptoms of substance withdrawal an inmate may experience during the detoxification process

Inmates who are going through the process of detoxification, or ridding their bodies of a drug, may experience symptoms of withdrawal. Withdrawal from some substances, such as alcohol, opiates, and tranquilizers, produces a physical withdrawal. Some substances, such as cocaine, marijuana, and ecstasy, produce a more emotional withdrawal. Every person with addiction issues has a different physical and emotional withdrawal pattern. Treat acute withdrawal symptoms as a medical emergency and immediately notify your supervisor and medical staff. Symptoms of the different types of withdrawal include:

Physical Withdrawal Symptoms	Emotional Withdrawal Symptoms	Acute Withdrawal Symptoms
• sweating • racing heart • palpitations • muscle tension • tightness in the chest • difficulty breathing • tremor • nausea, vomiting, diarrhea	• anxiety • restlessness • irritability • insomnia • headaches • poor concentration • depression • social isolation • mood swings • fatigue	• grand mal seizures • heart attacks • strokes • hallucinations • delirium tremens (DTs), violent tremors

Withdrawal symptoms may last several days to several weeks. Treating the symptoms of withdrawal with medications treats only the symptoms and is not the same as treating the addiction.

MONITORING

Know the housing considerations for an inmate with substance abuse issues

Agencies should screen all inmates to identify substance abusers, determine the severity of the substance abuse, and provide the appropriate substance abuse program service for drug addiction treatment. Substance abuse services include prevention, outpatient treatment, intensive outpatient treatment, and aftercare services, as well as education and vocational services.

Inmates who identify as substance abusers have a high potential to hurt themselves by banging their heads on hard objects, biting or hitting themselves, or attacking others. Their behavior can be unpredictable. They may be calm one moment, unstable the next, and will need increased monitoring and observation to ensure their safety. This may include a shift in housing or management that places an inmate in an environment more favorable to preventing self-harm. This may also include the restriction of personal property and facility-provided items. The Florida Comprehensive Drug Abuse Control Act, chapter 893, F.S., states that agencies will house separately from the general population and under close supervision any inmate with a substance abuse issue that poses safety concerns. When a physician, practitioner, or medical personnel determine that an inmate no longer poses a threat to themselves or others, that inmate can relocate to the general population.

Know your role when monitoring an inmate participating in a court-ordered substance abuse treatment program

If an inmate is court-ordered into a substance abuse treatment program, allow every opportunity for them to attend the program. Increase the number of inmate searches to discourage them from introducing contraband into the housing area. Document any refusal, denial, or lack of attendance at a substance abuse treatment program.

Lesson Vocabulary

drug addiction

substance abuse

Review Items

1. *Why is it important to know whether an inmate has a substance abuse issue or a drug addiction?*
2. *List at least three characteristics for the following symptoms of substance abuse:*
   a. *Physical*
   b. *Behavioral*
   c. *Psychological*
3. *List at least three characteristics for the following symptoms of withdrawal:*
   a. *Physical*
   b. *Emotional*
   c. *Acute withdrawal*
4. *Why is it important to place inmates with substance abuse issues in the most appropriate housing?*
5. *Why is it important to actively monitor inmates with substance abuse issues?*

Unit 4 Mentally Ill Inmates and Inmates With Disabilities

Lesson 1

Americans With Disabilities Act

Lesson Goal

You will be able to understand the role of the Americans with Disabilities Act when supervising a disabled inmate.

Think About This

A disabled inmate in your housing section is continually delayed in the shower and often misses the time for an inmate count. Will you treat him any differently than the other inmates? How will you manage this issue?

Know the terms associated with the Americans with Disabilities Act (ADA) definition of disability

The Americans with Disabilities Act (ADA) defines a ***disability*** as a physical or mental impairment that substantially limits one or more of a person's major life activities. Major life activities include caring for oneself, performing manual tasks, walking, seeing, hearing, speaking, breathing, learning, and working. A physical impairment is any physical disorder or condition, disfigurement, or anatomical loss affecting one or more body systems. A mental impairment is any mental or psychological disorder, such as intellectual disability, organic brain syndrome, emotional or mental illness, or specific learning disabilities.

Know the physical or mental conditions that the ADA regards as impairments that contribute to a disability

Specific impairments may include:

- contagious and non-contagious diseases and conditions
- orthopedic, visual, speech, and hearing impairments
- cerebral palsy
- epilepsy
- muscular dystrophy
- multiple sclerosis
- cancer
- heart disease
- diabetes
- intellectual disability

- emotional illness
- specific learning disabilities
- HIV disease (with or without symptoms)
- tuberculosis
- drug addiction, alcoholism

The term disability does not include the following:

- cross-dressing, gender identity
- pedophilia, exhibitionism, voyeurism, or other sexual behavior disorders
- compulsive gambling, kleptomania (the urge to steal), pyromania (the urge to set things on fire)
- substance use disorders resulting from current illegal use of drugs

APPLY THE ADA

Understand how a facility complies with the ADA when providing a reasonable accommodation for an inmate with a disability

The ADA provides guidelines for housing and monitoring disabled inmates. Facilities must have a certain percentage of housing units with accessible mobility features to areas used by inmates for visitation, dining, recreation, educational programs, medical services, work programs, religious services, and participation in other programs that the facility offers. Housing for inmates with disabilities must be in the most integrated setting appropriate to the needs and security classification of an inmate.

A physician should assess and diagnose any inmates who have limitations in daily living activities that need a reasonable accommodation. A ***reasonable accommodation*** refers to any modification or adjustment that will allow a qualified inmate with a disability to participate in the programs, services, or activities of an institution or facility. When determining any reasonable accommodation, public safety and the health, safety, and security of all inmates and staff are the overriding considerations. A service plan should outline the reasonable accommodations to meet an inmate's medical and mental health needs, and housing consistent with the inmate's custody level and medical status.

Specific institutions may provide custody and care for inmates who are blind or deaf, who require a walker or a wheelchair, or who have more specialized housing or service needs. Agencies may provide auxiliary aids for blind or deaf inmates, such as:

- qualified interpreters on site
- note takers, written materials, exchange of written notes
- telephone handset amplifiers, telephones compatible with hearing aids
- closed caption decoders, closed captioning
- voice and text telecommunications products and systems
- qualified readers, taped texts, audio recordings, Braille materials, large print materials

Some inmates will require health-care appliances, such as:

- wheelchairs
- manually powered mobility aids, such as walkers, crutches, canes, orthopedic prostheses or braces
- hearing aids
- prescription eyeglasses

It is the joint responsibility of the agency and an inmate to maintain all health-care appliances in good repair and operation. Avoid removing any health-care appliance that the disabled inmate has properly obtained while in custody unless there are legitimate documented safety or security reasons.

Know the methods of deception used by a disabled inmate to manipulate the accommodation request process for a disability determination

Inmates may try to use medical conditions or disabilities to manipulate staff by requesting additional health-care appliances beyond their personal needs, avoiding undesirable job assignments, or receiving unnecessary medications. Exaggerating illness or disability is difficult to prove; however, it is a common method of manipulation. Agency medical staff determines whether an inmate has a disability, based on an inmate's record of an existing physical or mental impairment or qualified evaluation. When denied unnecessary supplies, an inmate may go to such extremes as exaggerating an existing disability or illness and creating frivolous lawsuits, or even self-injury to achieve desired results.

Lesson Vocabulary

disability

reasonable accommodation

Review Items

1. *List some of the impairments associated with the ADA definition of disability. What impairments are not included?*
2. *How does an agency comply with the ADA when providing a reasonable accommodation for an inmate with a disability?*
3. *What are some of the methods of deception that inmates use to manipulate the accommodation request process for a disability determination?*

UNIT 4 MENTALLY ILL INMATES AND INMATES WITH DISABILITIES

LESSON 2

INMATES WITH MENTAL ILLNESS

LESSON GOAL

You will be able to communicate with and de-escalate situations involving inmates with mental illness.

THINK ABOUT THIS

According to the Florida Department of Corrections, an increasing number of inmates are people with mental illness. Rates of inmates with serious mental illnesses are four to six times higher in jails and three to four times higher in prisons than the general population. More than two-thirds of jail inmates and half of prison inmates also have a substance use disorder. Paying close attention to this lesson can provide the foundation for supervising these inmates with a patient, non-confrontational approach.

Know the rights of mentally ill inmates in a correctional setting, according to the Florida Statutes

As defined in s. 394.455, F.S., ***mental illness*** is an impairment of the mental or emotional processes that exercise the conscious control of one's actions. Mental illness interferes with a person's ability to perceive or understand reality. You will encounter inmates with mental illnesses during your career. According to s. 394.459, F.S., inmates with mental illness have the right to individual dignity and treatment. Procedures, facilities, vehicles, and restraining devices used for criminals do not apply to a person who has a mental illness, except for the protection of the person or others.

Mood disorders, thought disorders, and personality disorders are categories of mental illness. An inmate can display one or multiple behaviors associated with these disorders. Having an awareness of how these disorders display in inmates and how to respond to these behaviors can make supervising these inmates less challenging.

PSYCHOTIC DISORDERS

Know the characteristics of an inmate with a psychotic disorder

When an inmate has a psychotic disorder, their thoughts seem disorganized and not logically connected. An inmate may hallucinate, a sensory experience in which someone can smell, taste, or feel something that is not there. An inmate may have delusions, false beliefs firmly held despite obvious proof or evidence to the contrary. A common psychotic or thought disorder is schizophrenia, a brain disorder caused by a chemical imbalance that distorts the way a person thinks, acts, expresses emotion, and perceives reality. Psychotic inmates (those hearing voices, for example) are sometimes preoccupied with internal voices, do not hear you, and cannot follow commands.

MOOD DISORDERS

Know the characteristics of an inmate with a mood disorder

Major depressive disorder (MDD) is one of the most common mood disorders that you may encounter. MDD is different from the brief, situational depressive episodes that most people commonly experience with the loss of a loved one, the loss of a job, or a financial loss. MDD is a clinically diagnosed mental illness for a person having multiple, major depressive episodes. Symptoms may be severe, can last for several weeks, and do not include periods of persistent high moods (mania). You may notice an inmate is profoundly sad; cries uncontrollably; is unable to concentrate, to eat, or to sleep; or is suicidal.

Bipolar disorder (BD) is another common mood disorder. Formerly known as manic-depressive illness, BD is a clinically diagnosed mental illness with alternating episodes of depression and mania. Symptoms of a manic episode include loud, quick, uninterrupted speech, racing thoughts, fidgeting, and hyperactivity. A person in a manic episode feels charged up, high, or excitable. Usually, persons with mania have previously experienced one or more episodes of major depression.

Inmates may also have a substance-induced mood disorder from drug and alcohol abuse and can be easily distracted or may have an exaggerated sense of self, powers, and abilities. Inmates with psychotic or mood disorders do not react the same way other inmates do when you give them orders.

ANXIETY DISORDERS

Know the characteristics of an inmate with an anxiety disorder

The characteristics of an anxiety disorder include excessive nervousness, tension, apprehension, "fight or flight" behavior, excessive fear, or anticipation of looming danger, flashbacks, or ritualistic behavior, such as excessive hand washing. Anxiety disorders can range in intensity from mild to debilitating. Some people with anxiety disorders can have panic attacks that are so severe that they mimic a heart attack. You may encounter four main types of anxiety disorders in the correctional setting.

- An inmate who has a panic disorder can experience an extreme panic attack with a racing heartbeat, sweating, tension, and a feeling that something terrible is about to happen. Chest pain or discomfort, sweating, trembling, choking, or a feeling that one is going to die could accompany a panic attack.
- An inmate who has obsessive compulsive disorder (OCD) has intrusive thoughts and impulses resulting in ritualistic behavior, such as an excessive need to count, excessively wash their hands, or an extreme need to avoid dirt.
- A traumatic event, such as war, natural disaster, sexual or physical assault, or the unexpected death of a loved one, can cause post-traumatic stress disorder (PTSD). Characteristics of PTSD are lasting thoughts and memories of terror causing emotional numbness. An inmate with PTSD may not have had the traumatic experience but may have witnessed it or been affected by another's trauma.

- Phobia is an intense fear of a specific object or situation, such as a fear of heights, spiders, or leaving home.

PERSONALITY DISORDERS

Know the characteristics of an inmate with a personality disorder

A personality disorder is a deeply ingrained, non-psychotic, inflexible pattern of relating, perceiving, and behaving. It is serious enough to cause distress to the people around an inmate with the disorder. Depending upon the specific disorder, a person may display anxiety, fear, drama, emotion, unpredictable behavior, or impaired function. You may encounter three common personality disorders in a correctional facility. Inmates with these disorders may display some of the following behaviors:

Antisocial Personality Disorder	Narcissistic Personality Disorder	Borderline Personality Disorder
• a lifelong pattern of violating rules, social norms, and the rights of others • little capacity for empathy, guilt, remorse	• an inflated sense of importance • a need for admiration, or a desire to be feared or notorious	• significant emotional instability • unawareness of and inability to control their behavior
• persistent lying and exploiting for personal gain and pleasure • disregard for right or wrong • unnecessary risk-taking • homicidal actions	• dramatic emotional behaviors • difficulties with relationships • a lack of empathy for others • aggression when challenged	• rapid and intense mood swings typically involving angry, erratic, self-destructive, and impulsive acts toward themselves and others • impulsive and risky acts • inappropriate anger that escalates into physical fights

Know the different ways an inmate with a mental illness may gain access to mental health services

Inmates will often lie about their mental health status; however, you should not try to diagnose whether an inmate is faking a mental health disorder. If you have any doubts about an inmate's mental status, refer or escort the inmate to the mental health clinic and fully explain your observations to the mental health clinician.

Inmates may access mental health services in several ways. An inmate may request an appointment, explain briefly the nature of the problem, and request confidentiality. An inmate may also request mental health services due to an emergency that cannot wait. You may refer an inmate for services; also, the Florida Commission on Offender Review or health services staff at a previous institution may refer an inmate.

COMMUNICATION

Know how to communicate with a mentally ill inmate to de-escalate a situation

When communicating with inmates with mental illness, be respectful. When someone feels respected and heard, they are more likely to return respect and consider what you have to say. You can diminish or avoid a serious negative incident, reverse any escalation of the symptoms, and provide immediate protection and support to the mentally ill inmate and those in the immediate environment.

> **Good communication can help de-escalate a serious negative incident and provide immediate protection and support to the mentally ill inmate and those nearby.**

If an inmate is experiencing an event, such as a hallucination, be aware that the hallucination or the delusion is their reality. You will not be able to talk them out of that reality. Effective communication with an inmate experiencing active symptoms of their illness is particularly important because the external environment can so easily overwhelm them. When communicating with an inmate with a mental illness:

- Solve problems using a plan and in a definite order of actions from beginning to end. Make changes gradually. Work on one thing at a time.
- Avoid continuous eye contact and touching, if possible.
- Consider temporarily going along with reasonable requests that are not endangering or beyond reason. This gives an inmate the opportunity to feel somewhat "in control."
- Avoid agitating the situation.
- Let some things slide. Ignore what you cannot change and focus on the most concerning behaviors. Pay attention to any violent behavior.
- Keep it simple. Say what you have to say clearly, calmly, and positively.
- Lower your expectations, temporarily, when an inmate shows symptoms of mental illness.
- If needed, set limits with them as you would others. For example, "I only have five minutes to talk to you," or "If you scream, I will not be able to talk to you."
- Call for backup if you feel physically threatened or need help de-escalating the situation.
- Listen to an inmate and try to understand what they are communicating. Find out what reality-based needs you can meet.

DO NOT:

- threaten—this may increase fear or may prompt assaultive behavior
- shout—an inmate is not listening; other "voices" are probably interfering
- criticize—it will make matters worse; it cannot make things better
- bait an inmate into acting out wild threats; the consequences could be tragic
- crowd an inmate—for officer safety, provide adequate space, as an inmate may be paranoid
- block the doorway—but position yourself for safety

- assume an inmate is not smart and will believe anything you tell them—mental illness has nothing to do with intelligence level
- lie—it will usually destroy any rapport you are trying to establish
- pass them on to another officer or staff member—this may save you time in the short run but may come back to haunt you later or cause problems for someone else. Refer them to someone else only if it is an appropriate referral.

Understand the use of force options that can de-escalate a situation involving a mentally ill inmate

Mental illness alone does not increase the risk of violent behavior; however, when mental illness combines with other risk factors, such as substance or sexual abuse, it increases the risk of inmate violence. Whether an inmate has mental illness or not, they do not just snap. There is a progression of behaviors toward violence. Recognize those behavioral warning signs and communicate your concerns to your supervisor or the mental health provider. Warning signs can include sleeplessness, ritualistic preoccupation with certain activities, suspiciousness, and unpredictable outbursts.

During a violent incident involving a mentally ill inmate, avoid using batons, chemical agents, electronic immobilization devices (EIDs), specialty impact munitions, and other authorized non-lethal weapons. Following agency policy, refrain from using these weapons unless attempts to de-escalate and resolve the situation are unsuccessful and it appears reasonably necessary to prevent an inmate from taking control of a unit, taking a hostage, or escaping. Use these types of weapons to stop any assault on staff or other inmates when other interventions are ineffective or pose a risk of injury. In addition, use these weapons to disarm an inmate who has a weapon capable of causing injury to staff when other possible means of disarming an inmate pose a risk of injury to the staff involved. Agency policy may involve having a qualified mental health professional provide crisis intervention and attempt to de-escalate the situation and prevent the use of force.

Based on your agency policy, a mentally ill inmate may receive a medical examination and treatment after they have been subject to an application of an EID or non-lethal weapon.

THE BAKER ACT

Know the role of the Baker Act as it relates to inmates with mental illness

In a detention setting, you or a health professional may apply the Baker Act at the end of an inmate's sentence if the inmate displays behavior(s) indicating the need for evaluation. The ***Baker Act*** provides for emergency service, temporary detention for evaluation, and voluntary or involuntary short-term community inpatient treatment, if necessary. According to s. 394.463, F.S., a law enforcement officer may take an inmate to a receiving facility for involuntary examination if you believe the inmate has a mental illness, and because of their mental illness, the inmate is unable to care for him- or herself, or to protect the inmate from harming him- or herself or others.

Lesson Vocabulary

Baker Act

mental illness

Review Items

1. *List some of the characteristics of an inmate with a psychotic disorder.*
2. *List some of the characteristics of an inmate with a mood disorder.*
3. *List some of the characteristics of an inmate with an anxiety disorder.*
4. *List some of the characteristics of an inmate with a personality disorder.*
5. *How does an inmate access facility mental health services?*
6. *What are some of the things you should do or say to calm a mentally ill inmate and avoid or reduce a negative situation?*
7. *What are some of the things you should never do or say to a mentally ill inmate who is upset?*
8. *How are you going to de-escalate the violent behavior of a mentally ill inmate using the right amount of force?*
9. *When should you consider using the Baker Act for a mentally ill inmate who has reached the end of their sentence?*

UNIT 4 MENTALLY ILL INMATES AND INMATES WITH DISABILITIES

LESSON 3

INMATES WITH AN INTELLECTUAL DISABILITY

LESSON GOAL

You will be able to communicate with an inmate who has an intellectual disability.

THINK ABOUT THIS

People who have an intellectual disability become involved not only as victims of crime but also as offenders. This happens more often than people who do not experience forms of disabilities. The Florida Department of Corrections estimates that about 3% to 9% of the inmate population has an intellectual disability. Inmates with an intellectual disability are more likely to have communication difficulties. Often there is a co-occurring disorder, such as ADHD, depression, anxiety, bipolar disorder, or autism spectrum disorder. Knowing the characteristics of an intellectual disability should help you communicate better with these inmates.

CHARACTERISTICS

Know the differences in the causes of mental illness and intellectual disability

Intellectual disability is a type of developmental disability, a lifelong condition characterized by slow intellectual development. An inmate with an intellectual disability will not benefit from taking psychiatric medication, as opposed to an inmate with a mental illness. Mental illness is the result of biological diseases or chemical imbalance in which brain chemistry does not work normally and requires medication to correct the imbalance. By contrast, an intellectual disability may be the result of a childhood illness or injury that causes permanent and irreversible brain damage.

Know the characteristics of an inmate who has an intellectual disability

Inmates with a severe level of intellectual disability have very slow motor development and communication skills. The majority of inmates with an intellectual disability function at a mild disability level that may not be easily identifiable, and they may develop coping skills to cover up their disability in an attempt to appear non-disabled.

Inmates with a mild intellectual disability might not understand long-range consequences or might not be able to make appropriate choices. They may have trouble describing events in chronological order and may not understand cause and effect. While they may understand that they have done something wrong, they may not grasp the significance of their actions.

People with intellectual disabilities may not be able to distinguish between abstract and concrete thought and might confess to crimes they did not commit. They may recognize their own needs and wants but not easily identify the needs and wants of others, and they may have few relationships outside of family members and caregivers. They can be independent in familiar surroundings but may be easily frustrated with unfamiliar surroundings and circumstances. Most of these inmates have difficulties with problem solving, have high anxiety levels, and are easily frustrated when faced with simple tasks. Inmates with an intellectual disability are more comfortable with routines and become agitated when routines vary. Often, they display self-soothing behaviors, such as rocking or clicking their fingers, and they may become upset when interrupted. An inmate may be easily intimidated and eager to please and may generally be in agreement with all authority figures. Intellectual disabilities are incurable; however, appropriate modifications and accommodations may enhance an inmate's capabilities.

COMMUNICATION

Know how to communicate effectively with an inmate who has an intellectual disability

Some, but not all, inmates with an intellectual disability have difficulty communicating. Determine an inmate's language skills and choose the level of language to use. Talking with an inmate with a mild communication difficulty is very different from talking with an inmate with a moderate or severe communication difficulty.

When an inmate with an intellectual disability does have difficulty with communication, allow additional time to exchange information. Some inmates may be delayed in responding to questions; so much so, that their answers may seem to "come out of nowhere." An inmate may give the impression that they comprehend; however, that may not be true. Determine if an inmate understands. If you are in a busy area with many distractions, consider moving to a quieter location. Speak directly with an inmate and avoid talking to them as if they were a child. Avoid shouting. Use plain language and short, simple sentences. Listen to what an inmate says and let them know when you do or do not understand.

Should you find yourself in a situation where use of force or a non-lethal weapon is required to maintain inmate safety, officer safety, and the security of the facility, refer to the previous lesson on communicating with mentally ill inmates. During a violent incident involving an intellectually disabled inmate, avoid using batons, chemical agents, EIDs, specialty impact munitions, and other authorized non-lethal weapons. Agency policy may involve having a qualified mental health professional provide crisis intervention and attempt to de-escalate the situation and prevent a use of force.

REVIEW ITEMS

1. *What are the differences between mental illness and intellectual disability?*
2. *List some of the characteristics of an inmate with an intellectual disability.*
3. *How should you communicate with an intellectually disabled inmate?*
4. *How will you de-escalate the violent behavior of an intellectually disabled inmate using the right amount of force?*

UNIT 4 MENTALLY ILL INMATES AND INMATES WITH DISABILITIES

LESSON 4

PHYSICALLY DISABLED INMATES

LESSON GOAL

You will be able to monitor a physically disabled inmate.

THINK ABOUT THIS

The Florida Department of Corrections reports that 11% of inmates have a physical disability. The risk of having a disability increases the older we get. As the number of inmates growing old in a facility is increasing, the number of inmates with a disability increases as well.

MONITORING

Know how to monitor a disabled inmate who has a health-care appliance or personal care attendant

A disabled inmate may use their assigned medical appliance (wheelchair, cane) to move contraband from one location to another, or sell medications or portable accessories to other inmates. Use the same search techniques and frequency with disabled inmates as with the general population, including searching their property and specially issued medical appliances. Some medical appliances have detachable parts, which a disabled inmate can use as a weapon. Check medically issued passes that allow inmates to have medical appliances and additional medical supplies, such as diapers and catheters.

A significantly disabled inmate may have a personal care attendant, who is also an inmate. If applicable, check and make sure that an inmate assigned as a personal care attendant is performing their duties within the allowable scope, such as pushing a wheelchair, changing linens, providing bowel care and hygiene assistance, and feeding. The assigned personal care attendant is not responsible for handling or having access to medical devices, such as needles, medications, surgical instruments, or other health care activities or records.

REVIEW ITEMS

1. *How do you monitor a disabled inmate who has a health-care appliance or personal care attendant?*
2. *Provide some examples of how an inmate with a disability can conceal contraband.*
3. *What is the role of a personal care attendant in a facility?*

UNIT 4 MENTALLY ILL INMATES AND INMATES WITH DISABILITIES

LESSON 5

INMATES WITH MEDICAL NEEDS

LESSON GOAL

You will be able to monitor inmates with chronic or communicable diseases.

THINK ABOUT THIS

The nature of a correctional facility as a closed environment contributes to and increases the likelihood that inmates will "share" communicable diseases. This can influence the health of staff, visitors, and the overall well-being of the people associated with a facility. Although chronic disease is not transferable to others, the inmate population reflects that part of a community's population with limited access to health care and little experience with a healthy lifestyle. When supervising inmates, your role is to balance the medical needs of individual inmates with the overall welfare and safety of the facility you work in.

CHRONIC AND COMMUNICABLE DISEASES

Know the chronic and communicable diseases an inmate can bring into and acquire in a corrections setting

Like senior citizens outside the facility, older inmates are more susceptible to chronic medical conditions, including dementia, impaired mobility, and loss of hearing and vision. In prisons, these ailments require more staff, more officer training, and special housing. Medical experts say inmates typically experience the effects of age sooner than people outside prison do. This can happen because of a substance use disorder, inadequate preventive and primary care before incarceration, and stress linked to the isolation of prison life.

Physical health, mental health, and substance abuse problems often are more apparent in jails and prisons than in the community. Most inmates have not had regular access to any form of health care before incarceration and suffer from preexisting conditions, such as alcohol and drug addiction, mental health issues, and chronic diseases. Chronic disease is a long-lasting medical condition in which medicine can control the symptoms but not cure the disease. Common inmate chronic diseases or conditions include:

- arthritis
- asthma
- cancer
- diabetes

- heart disease
- high blood pressure
- stroke recovery

Communicable disease spreads through direct contact with an infected person or indirectly through such means as a biting insect or drinking glasses. You will learn more about communicable diseases in the First Aid portion of your training. Communicable disease control policies must protect inmates from infection while not interfering with the rights of the infected prisoners. Facilities should have comprehensive policies for control of certain communicable diseases found in the corrections setting, including:

- hepatitis
- HIV/AIDS
- MRSA
- sexually transmitted diseases
- tuberculosis
- novel influenza A virus (H1N1)

PREVENTION

Know how to prevent the spread of communicable diseases within a correctional facility

Encourage all inmates within the facility to cover their cough or sneeze with a tissue. Throw all tissues in the trash after use. Maintain good hand hygiene by washing with soap and water, or using an alcohol-based hand sanitizer, especially after coughing or sneezing. Avoid touching eyes, nose, and mouth without cleaning hands.

The facility should have appropriate hand cleansing readily available, including intake areas where inmates are booked and processed, visitor entries and exits, visitation rooms, common areas, and staff-restricted areas, in addition to lavatories and food preparation and dining areas. The means for hand cleansing are ideally running water, soap, and hand-drying machines or paper towels and wastebaskets; alternatively, except in lavatories and food preparation areas, alcohol-based hand sanitizer.

Keep all common areas within the facility routinely clean and immediately, when visibly soiled, clean with the cleaning agents normally used in these areas. Eating utensils should be washed either in a dishwasher or by hand with water and soap. Cups and utensils should not be shared until after washing. Always apply PPE whenever you anticipate or suspect the presence of body fluids.

MONITORING

> **Know how to respond to and monitor an inmate with an emergency or non-emergency medical need**

An inmate might self-declare a medical emergency or request non-emergency care. You need to recognize changes in an inmate's physical manner or behavior that shows a need for medical, dental, or mental health intervention. In some facilities, medical passes are available to bring to your attention that an inmate has a medical issue. Make sure that the pass is valid, and follow the procedures outlined in the pass. If an inmate declares an emergency medical need, apply officer safety, obtain backup, and respond immediately.

Complaints of respiratory distress, chest pain, new onset of change in mental status, and abnormal function of a specific body area, such as the inability to speak, should receive immediate attention and evaluation. Based on the evaluation of the problem, medical staff will make a referral or will treat an inmate within the scope of their practice. Some inmates may require additional meals, snacks, and supplements, or increased observation to prevent unintentional self-injury during seizures or dizzy spells. Take reasonable steps to make sure that all health care encounters, including medical and mental health interviews, examinations, and procedures respect an inmate's privacy.

TERMINALLY ILL

> **Know how to monitor a terminally ill inmate within the corrections setting**

Most facilities define inmates as terminally ill if they are known to have a fatal disease and have less than six months to live. Some facilities release terminally ill inmates and provide end-of-life services, such as prison-based hospice programs. Some terminally ill inmates are able to remain within the general population while others may need a more protected housing arrangement. These inmates tend to cycle in and out of infirmaries and hospitals. Because terminally ill inmates may experience increased anger and depression, they are at increased risk of suicide. Increasing security checks and involving clergy, mental health professionals, and others who can offer supportive counseling is essential. Administration may permit the family, clergy, or authorized visitor of a terminally ill inmate to visit an inmate under close, isolated supervision.

CHEMICAL RESTRAINT AGENTS OR EIDS

> **Know the different medical conditions that the use of chemical restraint agents or EIDs may aggravate**

Identify any changes in an inmate's medical condition, documented by health care staff, which may affect the use of chemical restraint agents or EIDs.

The use of chemical restraint agents may aggravate the following medical conditions:

- asthma
- chronic obstructive pulmonary disease (lung disease)
- emphysema (shortness of breath)
- chronic bronchitis
- tuberculosis
- congestive heart failure

- dysrhythmia (irregular heartbeat)
- angina pectoris (severe chest pain)
- cardiac myopathy (heart muscle disease)
- pacemaker
- pregnancy
- unstable hypertension (high blood pressure)
- multiple sclerosis, muscular dystrophy (genetic disorders that weaken muscles)
- epilepsy

The use of an EID may aggravate the following medical conditions:

- seizure disorder
- multiple sclerosis
- muscular dystrophy
- pacemaker
- pregnancy

Review Items

1. *List the types of chronic diseases commonly found in a correctional facility.*
2. *List the types of communicable diseases commonly found in a correctional facility.*
3. *What should you do to prevent the spread of communicable diseases in a correctional facility?*
4. *How should you respond to an inmate with a non-emergency medical need?*
5. *How should you respond to an inmate with an emergency medical need?*
6. *What special considerations should you make for a terminally ill inmate?*
7. *What medical conditions get worse after using a chemical restraint agent or EID?*

UNIT 5 JUVENILE INMATES AND YOUTHFUL OFFENDERS

LESSON 1

JUVENILE INMATES AND YOUTHFUL OFFENDERS

LESSON GOAL

You will be able to monitor juvenile inmates and youthful offenders.

THINK ABOUT THIS

Being a teenager comes with its own set of challenges. Add involvement with the criminal justice system, and you have a unique set of constraints, legal obligations, and disciplinary issues. Facilities that offer quality services and positive experiences can reduce the odds of a juvenile offender re-entering the system and your correctional facility. Being positive, patient, and using good judgment, not impulsive reaction, can provide these juveniles with the positive adult role model they need.

DEFINITIONS

Know the terms juvenile adjudication, juvenile inmate, and youthful offender

Juvenile adjudication occurs when the court charges, sentences, judges as delinquent, and commits a juvenile younger than 18 to the Department of Juvenile Justice. This includes a juvenile who accepts a conviction as if entering a guilty plea but does not admit guilt.

A ***juvenile inmate*** is an inmate who is not legally an adult or judged as an adult and who the court may assign to the Department of Juvenile Justice.

A ***youthful offender*** is any offender younger than 24, who the court sentences as an adult or who the Department of Corrections assigns youthful offender status, according to ss. 958.03 and 958.04, F.S.

Know the different ways a juvenile can be remanded to the Department of Corrections as a youthful offender

Sometimes when the court incarcerates an adjudicated juvenile within the juvenile justice system, the placement is unsuccessful or not appropriate for the juvenile's rehabilitation program. When this happens, the court remands (reassigns) the juvenile to the Department of Corrections as a youthful offender. A juvenile can be remanded to the Department of Corrections as a youthful offender in four ways.

Declared by the court when:

- the offender is not sentenced to prison for more than six years,

- the offender was younger than 21 on the date the sentence was imposed for offenses committed on or after 10/01/2008, and
- the offender has not previously been classified as a youthful offender.

Designated by the Department of Corrections when:

- the total length of the juvenile's prison sentence does not exceed 10 years,
- the offender is younger than 24, and
- the offender has not previously been classified as a youthful offender.

Declared by the Department of Corrections when:

- the offender is not otherwise qualified as a youthful offender, but is housed at a youthful offender facility by virtue of their mental or physical vulnerability, or
- the offender's mental or physical vulnerability would significantly jeopardize their safety in a non-youthful offender facility.

Young adult offender when:

- the offender is not a youthful offender, but housed at a youthful offender facility by virtue of their age at the time of the crime and the time of admission to prison.

CHARACTERISTICS

Know the characteristics of a juvenile inmate or youthful offender

The courts incarcerate youthful offenders primarily for person and property crimes, and technical violations of probation. Females account for a small yet growing proportion of juveniles held in custody, while minority youth account for 75% of juveniles held for a violent offense. Juveniles or youthful offenders can also have one or more of the following characteristics:

- be impulsive and unpredictable
- act first and think about the consequences later
- be unable to accept responsibility for their behavior, blaming others for their inappropriate behavior
- be oppositional, defiant, and resentful of authority
- join gangs in an attempt to find an identity and for personal safety
- cave to peer pressure, be easily manipulated, and be concerned about what other inmates think about them
- come from households with a history of abuse and criminal activity or generations of gang members and whose value systems clash with common social norms
- have few positive adult role models
- not be a high-school graduate; not have a formal education but have street smarts

- if diagnosed with learning disabilities, continue to have those challenges, which may also affect their ability to respond appropriately in a variety of situations
- have a lot more sexual curiosity issues and an increased incidence of lewd and lascivious behavior
- have no moral compass
- depersonalize other inmates, correctional officers, and people on the outside
- be insensitive, lack regret for what they do, and not see their behavior as antisocial or criminal

Know disciplinary issues associated with the juvenile inmate or youthful offender

These young inmates need a structured, predictable environment that is consistent from one shift to another. You can become a positive role model for young inmates, demonstrating professional behavior, and being consistently firm and fair. Young inmates will constantly test a new officer, looking for weakness and vulnerability. It is important that officers new to the facility understand policies and procedures, enforce them, and appear competent. Juvenile inmates and youthful offenders may need frequent disciplining to correct inappropriate behavior and are in confinement more often than adult inmates. Major infractions can include fighting, battery, STG activity, rioting, setting fires, theft, and lewd and lascivious behavior. Minor infractions can include an unmade bunk or failure to wear an ID or follow proper dress code.

LEGAL REQUIREMENTS

Know the legal requirements for incarcerating juvenile inmates and youthful offenders

The federal Juvenile Justice and Delinquency Prevention Act sets the standards for state and local juvenile justice systems for incarcerating youth. It provides for the following:

- Juveniles who commit status offenses (skipping school, running away, breaking curfew, and possession or use of alcohol) may not be held in secure detention or confinement, but receive community-based services, such as day treatment or residential home treatment, counseling, mentoring, alternative education, and job development support.
- Juveniles may not be detained in adult jails except for limited periods before release or transporting them to an appropriate juvenile placement (six hours), in rural areas (24 hours plus weekends and holidays), or when weather and travel conditions prevent authorities from transporting them.
- When adult jails hold juveniles under the exceptions listed above, they may not have any sight or sound contact with adult inmates. Juveniles cannot be housed with adult inmates or next to adult cells, share dining halls, recreation areas, or any other common spaces with adult inmates, or be placed in any circumstances in which they could have any visual or verbal contact with adult inmates.
- Disproportionate minority contact (DMC) requires states and localities to develop oversight committees that plan and implement data-driven approaches to ensure fairness and reduce racial and ethnic disparities.

According to s. 985.265, F.S., juveniles are housed separately from adult inmates to prohibit sight and sound contact with incarcerated adults. Separation of juveniles from adults permits no more than random or accidental contact. The receiving facility must contain a separate section for juveniles and have adequate staff to supervise and monitor the juvenile's activities at all times. Supervising and monitoring juveniles includes physical observation and documented checks by facility supervisory staff at intervals of no more than 10 minutes. The facility can place two or more juveniles in the same cell; however, under no circumstances will a juvenile and an adult be in the same cell.

SERVICES AND PROGRAMS

List the types of required programs, and other programs and services available to juvenile inmates and youthful offenders

Juvenile inmates or youthful offenders are required to participate in:

- an Extended Day Program providing work assignments, educational (academic and vocational) programs, substance abuse programs, counseling, behavior modification, military-style drills, systematic discipline, and other programs that reduce inmate idleness and improve a young offender's chance of becoming a law-abiding resident upon re-entry into the community
- vocational and job training
- life and socialization skills training (including anger / aggression control)
- pre-release orientation and planning
- suitable transition services

Juvenile inmates or youthful offenders qualify for the nutritionally adequate menu that provides uniformity of food items and meets the requirements of the National Child Nutrition Program.

LESSON VOCABULARY

juvenile adjudication

juvenile inmate

youthful offender

REVIEW ITEMS

1. *What are some of the primary characteristics of juveniles who end up in the criminal justice system?*
2. *Match the following terms with the associated definition:*

   Juvenile Inmate _____ Juvenile Adjudication _____ Youthful Offender _____

   a. occurs when the court charges, sentences, judges as delinquent, and commits a juvenile younger than 18 to the Department of Juvenile Justice, includes a juvenile that accepts a conviction as if entering a guilty plea but does not admit guilt

   b. an inmate who is not legally an adult or judged as an adult and who the court may assign to the Department of Juvenile Justice

   c. any offender younger than 24, who the court sentences as an adult or the Department of Corrections assigns youthful offender status

3. *Describe the four ways a juvenile can be remanded to the Department of Corrections as a youthful offender.*
5. *What are some of the infractions juveniles tend to commit while in a corrections facility?*
7. *Describe the four legal requirements for incarcerating juveniles set by the Juvenile Justice and Delinquency Prevention Act.*
6. *List the programs and services in which juvenile inmates and youthful offenders are required to participate.*

UNIT 6 ELDERLY INMATES

LESSON 1

ELDERLY INMATES

LESSON GOAL

You will be able to monitor an elderly inmate who may have health issues, physical limitations, or mental health issues.

THINK ABOUT THIS

The number of elderly inmates in the state prison system has increased steadily. The Florida Department of Corrections expects the elderly population to increase from the current 21.6% to 26.5% of the total population by 2021. This projection emphasizes why it is important that you know how to recognize when an elderly inmate cannot perform the daily activities for living and how to monitor and communicate with an elderly inmate who may have health issues, physical limitations, or mental health issues.

CHARACTERISTICS

Know the characteristics of an elderly inmate

At some time in your career as a correctional officer, you will likely interact with older inmates. This will require you to be aware of the special needs of elderly inmates to make sure that you monitor them appropriately. Understanding the aging process and the characteristics of the elderly population will help you relate in a positive and effective manner. Elderly inmates are 50 years of age and over; however, elderly inmates' life experiences before and while in prison can contribute to a lower life expectancy.

Almost every elderly inmate experiences normal physical and physiological changes and can develop certain medical conditions. They may experience changes in their eyesight and hearing. These changes may limit an inmate's mobility, increase the likelihood of accidents, or lead to fear, isolation, and victimization by other inmates.

Older inmates may also experience a change in their sense of touch. Damage to nerves may make them less likely to feel surface pain and less likely to notice injuries. They are more prone to rips, tears, and bruising to their skin from everyday activities. They are more likely to suffer loss of balance, which increases the risk of falls. Because older people often experience an increased sensitivity to weather, they are more susceptible to heat stroke, heat exhaustion, and hypothermia.

Another result of aging is the loss of muscle flexibility and strength, which makes performing daily tasks more difficult. Joints may stiffen due to arthritis, making movement extremely painful. Older inmates may also lose some cognitive ability, which is the ability to think, learn, and remember. They may experience slowness in thinking, finding the right words, or identifying objects. Be patient when supervising elderly inmates, as it may take them longer to explain themselves than younger inmates.

HEALTH ISSUES

Know the health issues that elderly inmates may experience

Some elderly inmates have chronic medical conditions, such as incontinence, bedsores, and dehydration. Elderly inmates may also experience a variety of mental health issues, such as depression and anxiety. Depression and anxiety can cause great suffering and lead to impaired functioning in daily life.

Some inmates will suffer from dementia or Alzheimer's disease and require long-term management or care. Dementia and Alzheimer's are progressive mental disorders characterized by loss of memory, impairment of judgment and abstract thinking, and changes in personality. These inmates appear confused, and may use violent behavior as they experience progressive declines in mental functions. Due to the onset of Alzheimer's and dementia, another condition known as sundown syndrome may set in. This condition is most notable after dinner hours or sundown. Inmates with sundown syndrome become active after dark, have a tendency to wander, and may have mood swings or become demanding, suspicious, or disoriented. Not all inmates with Alzheimer's or dementia will exhibit sundown syndrome.

COMMUNICATION

Know the elements of effectively communicating with an elderly inmate

When communicating with an elderly inmate, always treat them with dignity, respect, and patience. Speak directly to an inmate, establish and maintain eye contact, and speak loudly only if the inmate indicates they cannot hear you. Include the elderly inmate in all discussions concerning their welfare and adjust the manner of communication based on any disabilities or limitations.

Some elderly inmates are submissive and more apt to follow the rules. They are less apt to play games; however, elderly inmates can be good at manipulating officers through sympathy.

MONITORING

Know the special considerations to make when monitoring elderly inmates

Increase the number of rounds when monitoring elderly inmates. Observe if an inmate is moving around. If the inmate is in bed, observe if their chest is rising and falling, which shows that they are breathing. Monitor the restrooms and showers more often as some elderly inmates have difficulty using the facilities or can slip and fall.

You may find that elderly inmates have items in their locker that are different from the general population such as:

- hearing aid batteries
- varicose vein socks
- adult diapers, catheters
- prosthesis (artificial arm or leg)

Some elderly inmates tend to hoard food beyond the expiration date and then get sick after eating it. Pay attention to expiration dates on packaged foods and encourage an inmate to dispose of expired food items.

PHYSICAL LIMITATIONS

Know when to make special considerations for an elderly inmate with physical limitations

A physician should assess and diagnose any inmates who have limitations in daily living activities. A service plan is designed to meet their medical and mental health needs, and housing consistent with their custody level and medical status. You will encounter elderly inmates with physical limitations that may include, but are not limited to, missing limbs, the inability to move about due to physical defects or malformations, deafness, and blindness or near blindness. Inmates who cannot walk will require a walker or wheelchair. Some will need adapted eating and drinking utensils.

Make an effort to reasonably accommodate an inmate when asking them to perform tasks or follow directions and give them more time to get where they need to be because of mobility challenges. Be aware that instances might arise where standard physical control measures, tactics, and even verbal directions used with younger populations may not work for elderly inmates. Examples include:

- an inmate who has a prosthesis that restricts movement of the knee cannot kneel before getting into a prone position
- an inmate that cannot see or hear well may have trouble understanding verbal directions, which may make an inmate appear to refuse to obey an order
- an inmate with physical limitations may be unable to perform a task; assign jobs based on the physical limitations and on the inmate's medical grade and classification

An elderly inmate might falsely claim to have a physical limitation in an attempt to avoid following commands or to obtain sympathy. They may claim they cannot perform the actions as directed or refuse to comply with the direction. Give the inmate another action to perform or task that will achieve a similar result.

REVIEW ITEMS

1. *List some of the characteristics of an elderly inmate.*
2. *List some of the health issues of an elderly inmate.*
3. *How will you adapt the way you communicate with an elderly inmate?*
4. *What special considerations will you need to make when monitoring an elderly inmate?*
5. *What special considerations will you need to make for an elderly inmate with physical imitations?*

UNIT 7 INMATES AND GENDER

LESSON 1

FEMALE INMATES

LESSON GOAL

You will be able to monitor female inmates.

THINK ABOUT THIS

Supervising female inmates and supervising male inmates can be similar in some ways and very different in others. Men and women are different, and they bring these differences into the correctional setting as inmates and as officers. Some supervision techniques used by a female officer supervising a female inmate may not be appropriate for a male officer to use when supervising a female inmate.

CHARACTERISTICS

Know the common characteristics of female inmates within the corrections setting

The courts incarcerate the majority of female inmates because of drug-related charges and economic crimes, such as passing worthless checks, forgery, fraud, and other non-violent crimes; however, the incidence of younger females committing violent crimes is on the rise. Female inmates are the fastest growing criminal population.

Women, especially older female inmates, are less likely to join STGs. They tend to be more concerned with relationships, form small groups, and maintain the same roles they had outside the correctional environment. They do, however, tend to create surrogate families. These surrogate families take the place of their families on the outside and contain hierarchies with mother, father, child, and grandparent figures. Female inmates tend to form relationships based more on companionship than for sexual reasons.

Female inmates tend to struggle more with depression, guilt, and worry about their children, if they are mothers. They freely express their fear, anger, and affection verbally, while men tend to express their feelings physically. Female inmates tend to base their self-esteem on what others think about them rather than what they think about themselves. They can have a lower self-esteem than male inmates do because of issues related to sexual abuse and domestic violence before incarceration. Female inmates have higher instances of relieving stress through self-mutilation and self-harm than male inmates.

Many female inmates have a higher tolerance for others entering their personal space until an unwelcome person attempts to put their hands on them. This can lead to a physical fight. They are frequently more concerned with cleanliness and having a neat environment.

Female inmates have a high tendency to manipulate staff. Common methods of manipulation include using sex to form a relationship with a staff member or another inmate. They also tend to be more inclined than male inmates are to provide false information to achieve an agenda.

Know the common methods of manipulation officers may encounter when supervising female inmates

PROGRAMS AND SERVICES

Generally, female inmates are more willing to participate in programs available in custodial settings than males, because these present additional opportunities to bond and socialize with other inmates.

Know the types of programs and services available to female inmates

Some of the programs available to both male and female inmates include:

- career and technical education
- character awareness and motivation
- special education
- boot camp
- faith-based residential
- services, if available, and child visitation as indicated in a Department of Children and Families case plan

Some of the career and technical education programs available to female inmates include:

- web development
- automotive technology career services
- technology support services
- cosmetology
- drafting
- equine care technology
- commercial foods and culinary arts
- fashion design services
- air conditioning
- refrigeration and heating technology

Medical services available to female inmates are gynecological, obstetric, and prenatal.

Review Items

1. *What are some of the characteristics that are unique to female inmates?*
2. *What are some of the common methods of manipulation that female inmates use?*
3. *List some of the services that may be available to female inmates.*

LESSON 2

TRANSGENDER INMATES

LESSON GOAL

You will be able to monitor transgender inmates according to the Prison Rape Elimination Act (PREA) standards.

THINK ABOUT THIS

Transgender inmates can be vulnerable to violence and harassment in a correctional facility; however, PREA provides regulations to protect them. PREA requires every state to consider transgender inmates when making decisions regarding housing, supervising, searching, and medical and mental health care.

TRANSGENDER INMATES

Know the term transgender according to the American Psychological Association and the Prison Rape Elimination Act (PREA)

PREA defines ***transgender*** as a person whose gender identity is different from the sex they were assigned at birth. The American Psychological Association notes that many transgender people live part time or full time as members of another gender. Anyone whose identity, appearance, or behavior falls outside of conventional gender norms can be described as transgender. However, not everyone who may appear or behave as another gender will identify as a transgender person.

Know how PREA affects conducting searches of transgender inmates

An inmate might be in the process of transitioning their gender or sex characteristics, and you may have difficulty determining their gender or sex. PREA states that officers cannot search or physically examine a transgender inmate for the sole purpose of determining an inmate's genital status. If an inmate's genital status is unknown, it may be determined during conversations with them, by reviewing medical records, or, if necessary, by learning that information as part of a broader medical examination conducted in private by a medical practitioner. Conduct cross-gender pat-down searches, and searches of transgender inmates, in a professional and respectful way and in the least intrusive manner possible, while still applying officer safety.

Know the housing, programming, and safety issues unique to transgender inmates

Housing issues may arise with inmates who have changed their sex through treatment with hormones, surgery, or both, or who are in any stage of the transitioning process. When deciding whether to assign a transgender inmate to a facility for male or female inmates, and in making other housing and programming assignments, consider each on a case-by-case basis. Consider an inmate's health and safety and if the placement would present management or security problems based upon the behaviors of other inmates. Transgender inmates should be able to shower separately from other inmates. Transgender inmates are at risk for victimization and abuse, which requires serious considerations to the safety of their living conditions.

Lesson Vocabulary

transgender

Review Items

1. *What is the meaning of the term transgender according to the American Psychological Association and PREA?*
2. *How does PREA affect conducting searches of transgender inmates?*
3. *What are the housing, programming, and safety issues unique to transgender inmates?*

UNIT 8 INMATES AND SEXUALITY

LESSON 1

INSTITUTIONAL HOMOSEXUALITY

LESSON GOAL

You will be able to understand the meaning of sexual orientation and the reasons for and characteristics of institutional homosexuality.

THINK ABOUT THIS

Homosexual behavior in a corrections setting might seem to occur naturally, something almost expected and tolerated. Heterosexual inmates claim that they are not homosexual but are meeting a physical need, and they try to keep it secret. Inmates engage in same-sex activity for power, control, or sexual release because they are in a place where heterosexual activity is not possible.

SEXUAL ORIENTATION

Know the three main types of sexual orientation an inmate can have upon entering the corrections setting

Sexual orientation describes the group of people with which a person is most likely to find satisfying and fulfilling romantic relationships. This can become an essential part of a person's identity. You may encounter inmates with various sexual orientations. Some of the most common are:

- heterosexual—having emotional, romantic, or sexual attraction to someone of the opposite sex
- gay/lesbian—having emotional, romantic, or sexual attraction to someone of the same sex
- bisexual—having emotional, romantic, or sexual attraction to both men and women

INSTITUTIONAL HOMOSEXUALITY

Know the characteristics of institutional homosexuality

Homosexual and bisexual inmates who do not experience same-sex attraction before incarceration might begin same-sex relationships when confined together for long periods of time without access to the opposite sex. Institutional homosexuality can begin as sexual abuse through intimidation and coercion, sometimes as repayment for a debt or favor. Among both male and female inmates, the dominant inmate will often protect the submissive inmate from violence, including sexual abuse. Sometimes an inmate will take on a more dominant inmate partner for the sole purpose of protection. Fellow inmates sometimes will regard the dominant inmate as not homosexual, but will regard the submissive inmate (who may or may not be consenting) as homosexual regardless of their actual sexual orientation. Heterosexual inmates will often hide institutional homosexuality inside and outside of the correctional setting. Inmates with institutional homosexual behaviors have not necessarily changed their sexual orientation.

Review Items

1. *What are the three main types of sexual orientation an inmate can have upon entering the corrections setting?*
2. *What are the characteristics of institutional homosexuality within the corrections setting?*

UNIT 8 INMATES AND SEXUALITY

LESSON 2

SEXUAL ABUSE

LESSON GOAL

You will be able to prevent and respond to sexual abuse and sexual harassment according to the Prison Rape Elimination Act (PREA) standards.

THINK ABOUT THIS

According to a 2008 report by the U.S. Department of Justice, one in 10 inmates suffered sexual abuse while in a correctional facility or jail. "In popular culture, prison rape is often the subject of jokes; in public discourse, it has been at times dismissed by some as an inevitable—or even deserved—consequence of criminality." The PREA standards provide guidelines to prevent sexual abuse among inmates. It provides a grievance reporting system, increased staff monitoring, prompt medical and mental health treatment for victims, and discipline for inmate or staff perpetrators.

APPLYING PREA

Know the meaning of the term sexual abuse in a corrections setting

PREA defines *sexual abuse* as sexual abuse of an inmate, detainee, or resident by another inmate, detainee, or resident, staff member, contractor, or volunteer. Sexual abuse occurs when the victim:

- does not consent,
- is coerced by open or implied threats of violence, or
- is unable to consent or refuse.

The following sexual acts are sexual abuse of an inmate, detainee, or resident by another inmate, detainee, or resident:

- contact between the penis and the vulva or the penis and the anus, including penetration, however slight
- contact between the mouth and the penis, vulva, or anus
- any penetration of the anal or genital opening of another person by a hand, finger, object, or other instrument
- any other intentional touching, either directly or through the clothing, of the genitalia, anus, groin, breast, inner thigh, or the buttocks of another person, excluding contact incidental to a physical altercation

The following acts, in addition to the above, are sexual abuse of an inmate, detainee, or resident by a staff member, contractor, or volunteer when there is the intent to abuse, arouse, or gratify sexual desire:

- contact between the mouth and any body part
- contact unrelated to official duties
- any attempt, threat, or request to engage in the sexual acts described above
- any display of a staff member's, contractor's, or volunteer's uncovered genitalia, buttocks, or breast in the presence of an inmate, detainee, or resident
- voyeurism

Voyeurism is an invasion of privacy of an inmate, detainee, or resident by staff for reasons unrelated to official duties, such as:

Know the meaning of voyeurism in a corrections setting

- peering at an inmate who is using a toilet in their cell to perform bodily functions
- requiring an inmate to expose their buttocks, genitals, or breasts
- taking images of all or part of an inmate's naked body or of an inmate performing bodily functions

PREA mandates that correctional facilities have a zero tolerance for sexual abuse and sexual harassment. ***Sexual harassment*** includes:

Know the meaning of sexual harassment in a corrections setting

- repeated and unwelcome sexual advances, requests for sexual favors, or verbal comments, gestures, or actions of a derogatory or offensive sexual nature by one inmate, detainee, or resident directed toward another
- repeated verbal comments or gestures of a sexual nature to an inmate, detainee, or resident by a staff member, contractor, or volunteer, including demeaning references to gender, sexually suggestive or derogatory comments about body or clothing, or obscene language or gestures

PREA addresses the safety and treatment of inmates who have been victims of non-consensual sex acts, and disciplines and prosecutes those who commit or promote these acts. It provides guidelines for the first responding officer and the investigator of a suspected sexual abuse incident, as well as for housing the involved inmates before, during, and after the initial investigation.

Know the role of PREA in reducing the prevalence of sexual abuse in the corrections setting

CHARACTERISTICS OF VICTIMS

Targets of sexual abuse and sexual harassment in a corrections setting include inmates who:

Know the characteristics of inmates who can be targets of sexual abuse in the corrections setting

- identify as LGBTQI (lesbian, gay, bisexual, transgender, queer, or intersex)
- are younger
- have disabilities (mental health, developmental / intellectual, physical)

- are biracial or multiracial
- have been victims of previous sexual abuse

Possible physical signs that an inmate has experienced sexual abuse include:

Know the common physical and behavioral signs of inmates who are victims of sexual abuse

- sexually transmitted infections
- unexplained pregnancies
- stomach or abdominal pain
- anal, penile, or vaginal discharge, bleeding, or pain
- difficulty walking or sitting
- unexplained injury

Possible behaviors that a sexually abused inmate may display include:

- acting out
- anger, anxiety, depression
- difficulty with daily routines and concentrating
- fear, numbness, denial
- suicidal thoughts

Some of the reasons that a sexual abuse victim might not report the abuse may include one, several, or all of the following reasons:

- feeling embarrassed or ashamed
- lack of knowledge about how to report
- afraid of being written up for misconduct
- fear of retaliation by inmates or staff
- fear of not being believed

Understand the association between trauma and sexual abuse, and the effect of trauma on inmates who are victims of sexual abuse

Victims usually have ongoing contact with the perpetrator(s), increasing the likelihood of revictimization. Often separating the victim from the general population to avoid this scenario isolates an inmate, who feels punished, limits access to services, and leaves the victim with no support system. In addition, the corrections environment is not conducive to expressing emotions. Sexual abuse is traumatic for the victim, which changes how an inmate's brain responds to stress or any stimuli that can induce an emotional response. Inmates who are victims of sexual abuse can display the following behaviors associated with experiencing trauma:

- hypervigilance (being constantly on guard to a degree that makes it difficult to disengage from stressful situations)
- acting without thinking
- inability to calm down
- intense or prolonged anxiety
- irritability, aggressiveness, impulsiveness

The long-term effects of the trauma of sexual abuse can include:

- flashbacks and nightmares
- mood swings
- social withdrawal
- sudden and unexplained changes in behavior or personality
- PTSD

RESPONDING TO SEXUAL ABUSE

Know the role of screening and housing inmates to prevent sexual abuse and harassment

Screening for risk of victimization and abusiveness is an important piece of the intake/reception process. All inmates should be assessed during an intake screening and upon transfer to another facility for their risk of being sexually abused by other inmates or sexually abusive toward other inmates.

Inmates at high risk for sexual victimization should not be placed in involuntary segregated housing unless an assessment of all available alternatives has been made and there is no means of separation from likely abusers. If a facility cannot conduct an assessment immediately, the facility may hold an inmate in involuntary segregated housing for less than 24 hours while completing the assessment.

Know the reporting processes for inmates, and officers' requirements for reporting sexual abuse and harassment

Inmates should have ways to privately report sexual abuse and sexual harassment, retaliation by other inmates or staff for reporting abuse, and staff neglect or violation of responsibilities that may have contributed to the abuse. This includes the ability to report abuse or harassment to a public or private entity.

Accept all inmate reports of sexual abuse or harassment made verbally, in writing, anonymously, and from third parties. Treat all sexual abuse allegations seriously and promptly document the sexual abuse incident. Do not reveal any information related to a sexual abuse report to anyone unless it is specific to an investigation, treatment, or security or management decisions.

Upon learning of an allegation that an inmate was sexually abused, the first responding officer should separate the alleged victim and abuser and preserve and protect any crime scene until appropriate steps can be taken to collect any evidence.

Know the appropriate response to an inmate allegation of sexual abuse the first responding officer should make to preserve any physical evidence

If the abuse occurred within a time period that still allows for the collection of physical evidence, ensure that the alleged victim does not take any actions that could destroy physical evidence, such as washing, showering, brushing teeth, changing clothes, urinating, defecating, smoking, drinking, or eating.

Lesson Vocabulary

sexual abuse

sexual harassment

voyeurism

Review Items

1. *What is the meaning of the term sexual abuse in a corrections setting according to the Prison Rape Elimination Act (PREA)?*
2. *What is the meaning of the term voyeurism in a corrections setting according to PREA?*
3. *What is the meaning of the term sexual harassment in a corrections setting according to PREA?*
4. *What is the role of PREA in reducing the prevalence of sexual abuse in the corrections setting?*
5. *What are the characteristics of inmates who can be targets of sexual abuse in the corrections setting?*
6. *What are the common physical and behavioral signs of inmates who are victims of sexual abuse?*
7. *What is the association between trauma and sexual abuse and the effect of trauma on inmates who are victims of sexual abuse in the corrections setting?*
8. *What is the role of screening and housing inmates to prevent sexual abuse and harassment?*
9. *What is the reporting process for inmates and officers' requirements for reporting sexual abuse and harassment in the corrections setting?*
10. *What is the appropriate response to an inmate allegation of sexual abuse?*
11. *What should the first responding officer do to preserve any physical evidence?*

UNIT 9 INMATES IN CONFINEMENT OR ON DEATH ROW

LESSON 1
INMATES IN CONFINEMENT OR ON DEATH ROW

LESSON GOAL

You will be able to understand why an inmate is in administrative confinement, protective management, or disciplinary confinement, or on death row and the associated inmate conditions, privileges, and monitoring routine.

THINK ABOUT THIS

As a new correctional officer, you will rarely be responsible for supervising inmates in confinement or on death row. However, having a basic understanding of the types of confinement and some of the conditions and privileges may be useful should your correctional facility experience an incident where you may be temporarily monitoring these types of inmates.

ADMINISTRATIVE CONFINEMENT

Know the reasons for administrative confinement and inmate behaviors that can result in this type of placement

Administrative confinement is the temporary removal of an inmate from the general population to provide for safety and security until a more permanent inmate management process is in place. This may limit an inmate's conditions and privileges as a means of promoting the security, order, and effective management of the facility. An inmate should understand the reason and be able to present verbal comments or a written statement about the placement. An inmate can be placed in administrative confinement for the following reasons:

- There are pending disciplinary charges for the inmate.
- There are pending outside charges for the inmate.
- The inmate is waiting on approval for protective management.
- The inmate presents a signed written statement alleging that they are in fear of staff and provide specific information to support this claim.
- An investigation, evaluation for change of status, or transfer is pending—the presence of the inmate in the general population might interfere with that investigation or present a danger to the inmate, other inmates, or to the security and order of the institution.
- The inmate is received from another institution, and classification staff is not available to review their file and classify them into the general population.

Inmates in administrative confinement may have the following conditions and privileges:

Know the possible inmate conditions and privileges when in administrative confinement

- clothing, bedding and linen, personal property, comfort and personal hygiene items
- normal meals, canteen items, exercise
- counseling interviews, access to legal resources
- visitation, telephone, correspondence, writing utensils, reading material, library access

Inmates in administrative confinement may require additional officers and restraints for escorting to exercise, medical or disciplinary call-outs, telephone calls, recreation, and visits.

PROTECTIVE MANAGEMENT

Know the possible inmate conditions and privileges when in protective management

Protective management is a special management status for the protection of an inmate from other inmates. It is not disciplinary in nature; inmates are not under punishment nor in confinement. The treatment of inmates in protective management should be similar to that of the general population, as the individual inmate's safety and security concerns permit. An inmate can request protective management or an officer can recommend the classification change. The request receives a review, and there can be an inmate interview to assess their potential risk to or from other inmates in the unit. Throughout this process, an inmate can be in administrative confinement awaiting a final decision to resolve their protection issue.

Housing for inmates in protective management should be physically separate from other housing units when possible. Inmates in protective management may have the following conditions and privileges:

- clothing, bedding and linen, personal property, comfort and personal hygiene items
- normal meals, canteen items, exercise
- counseling interviews, access to legal resources
- visitation, telephone, correspondence, writing utensils, reading material, library access
- religious activities, self-improvement programs, work assignments

Inmates in protective management are subject to searches in the same manner as general population inmates, and they have the same restraint and escort requirements.

DISCIPLINARY CONFINEMENT

Know the reasons for disciplinary confinement and the possible inmate conditions and privileges when in disciplinary confinement

Disciplinary confinement is a form of punishment in which an inmate, found guilty of committing violations, is in confinement for a specified period to an individual cell, based upon authorized penalties for prohibited conduct. Medical staff should give the inmate a preconfinement medical evaluation, including weighing the inmate, before placement in disciplinary confinement. Disciplinary confinement cells should be physically separate from other confinement statuses whenever possible, and should receive frequent inspections to ensure the inmate's welfare and to determine if they are ready for release.

Inmates in disciplinary confinement may have the following conditions and privileges:

- clothing, bedding and linen, personal property, comfort and personal hygiene items
- normal meals, canteen items, exercise
- counseling interviews, access to legal resources
- visitation, telephone, correspondence, writing utensils, reading material, library access

Any privilege listed above, except essential health items (including prescribed medication) and receiving and sending legal mail or grievance forms, can be subject to restriction when an inmate's conduct and behavior become unmanageable. Inmates in disciplinary confinement may require additional officers and restraints for escorting to exercise, medical or disciplinary call-out, telephone calls, recreation, and visits.

MONITORING

Know how to adjust the monitoring routine of inmates who are in confinement or protective management

Specific support staff is assigned to routinely evaluate inmates in confinement; however, you should vary the time between intervals of monitoring these inmates, not to exceed 15- or 30-minute rounds. Be aware of how inmates in confinement communicate with each other through hand signals, fishing, kites, or talking through air ducts connecting the cells.

INMATES ON DEATH ROW

Know the housing and monitoring requirements unique to a death row inmate

About one-third of inmates on death row have a mental illness or an intellectual disability. Many suffer from depression and anxiety, aggravated by the conditions of confinement. These inmates are not housed with the general population and do not have access to the same conditions and privileges available to other inmates. An inmate on death row is housed in single-cell special housing after being sentenced to death for a capital felony. Inmates on death row are reviewed every year to determine their overall adjustment to confinement and are monitored regularly by officers, supervisors, chiefs of security, wardens and assistant wardens, health care staff, and a chaplain. They have strict restraint and escort requirements and limited conditions and privileges.

LESSON VOCABULARY

administrative confinement

disciplinary confinement

protective management

Review Items

1. *What are the reasons for administrative confinement and inmate behaviors that can result in this type of placement?*
2. *What are the possible inmate conditions and privileges when in administrative confinement?*
3. *What are the possible inmate conditions and privileges when in protective management?*
4. *What are the reasons for disciplinary confinement and the possible inmate conditions and privileges when in disciplinary confinement?*
5. *How would you adjust the monitoring routine of inmates that are in confinement or protective management?*
6. *What are the housing and monitoring requirements unique to a death row inmate?*

RESPONDING TO INCIDENTS AND EMERGENCIES

UNIT 1 IDENTIFYING EMERGENCY SITUATIONS

LESSON 1

RESPONDING TO AN EMERGENCY SITUATION

LESSON GOAL

You will be able to identify emergency situations and resolve them.

THINK ABOUT THIS

As soon as you arrive at work, you smell something burning. When you walk around the corner, you notice an inmate's mattress is on fire. How would you respond?

One of the most important duties of a correctional officer is to apply knowledge, training, and reasonable judgment during an emergency. Your first priority is the safety and security of everyone. Any incident can develop into an emergency, and you are expected to be effective in the use of equipment, crime scene control, chain of custody procedures, and documentation of involvement. Be aware of agency policies, procedures, and emergency plans, as well as post orders (job-specific documents that outline how to handle daily responsibilities and operations).

When you respond to an emergency, you need to assess the situation, isolate or evacuate people, if needed, and resolve the issue. If you are knowledgeable and prepared, you will be able to fulfill your responsibilities during emergencies. You are responsible for the care, custody, and control of inmates, safety of staff and visitors, and security of the facility. Properly responding to an incident or emergency requires a variety of procedures, techniques, and equipment.

An emergency requires a strict, urgent, and immediate response. When an emergency happens, you must use good judgment to respond effectively. You and other staff must stay flexible and adapt to changes without having a negative impact on facility operations.

Emergencies often occur because of a disturbance, a disaster, or an escape attempt. Escape attempts usually happen during work details inside or outside the correctional facility, inmate transports, and recreational activities.

When an emergency disrupts the normal operations within a facility, you should recall the agency's emergency plan, facility layout, and evacuation routes.

You should know the locations of emergency exits, equipment, and keys to properly respond. Tasks assigned during an emergency could include setting perimeters, using a radio to communicate, conducting evacuations, and applying use of force.

VERIFY THE INCIDENT OR EMERGENCY

When verifying the type of emergency, properly assess the threat while using discretion and caution as you approach the scene. While identifying the type of emergency, communicate with control room staff, command post personnel, and supervisory staff to coordinate a response in line with the emergency plan. Assess the severity of the emergency. Is it a major or a minor incident? Communicate with the control room, and be prepared to describe the nature and location of the emergency. For example, be ready to give the number of people involved, describe the nature of any injuries, and report if hazardous materials or weapons are involved.

Know which staff to notify during an emergency

SETTING UP A PERIMETER

Secure and isolate the situation so that it does not spread to other areas. Limit movement of inmates, such as locking down the cell block or dorm. Restrict the isolation to a limited area if possible, depending on the severity of the incident. For example, an inmate suicide may require a facility-wide lockdown, with correctional officers ordering all inmates to return to their individual cell areas or bunks. Begin the process of setting up a perimeter by using structures, such as internal gates, sally ports, roll gates, doors, and cross fences. You may also need to evacuate everyone, including non-essential personnel, as soon as it is safe to do so.

Know how and why to set up a perimeter during an emergency

EVACUATIONS

Evacuation routes should take evacuees as far away from the threat as necessary and be accessible by the quickest and easiest route possible. Evacuations may not always be possible due to time constraints or other factors. You may not have enough time to properly restrain inmates or may need to group inmates together that are not normally combined. In such cases, it may be necessary to wait to begin an evacuation. Evacuating or isolating people from a threat may involve a lockdown. Lockdown can differ from agency to agency, as it relates to the level of restricting movement or use of security measures.

Guidelines to follow during an evacuation include the following:

Know evacuation guidelines

- Upon direction of a supervisor, move people in an orderly fashion to a safe, secure area.
- Obtain copies of inmate rosters for identification and counting.
- Give clear and concise commands.
- Close or open windows and doors, if so directed, along evacuation routes if time permits.
- Do not use elevators for evacuation.

- Conduct an inmate count when reaching the evacuation area.
- Account for everyone who was in the facility.

To maintain safety and security and preserve possible evidence do not leave an inmate who may be a victim or perpetrator unsupervised. As conditions escalate, inmates who were not participating may be drawn to the incident and become involved. Therefore, maintain focus on proper procedures and carry out the emergency plan quickly and efficiently.

Each agency's emergency plan includes an evacuation guide for emergencies and other events, such as fires, floods, and hurricanes. Alerting the Incident Command System to the emergency may be part of an agency's emergency plan. The ***Incident Command System (ICS)*** is a systematic approach to command, control, and coordinate emergency response. The ICS conveys emergencies to designated persons or authority and follows an established agency protocol, depending on the nature of the emergency. Emergency plans developed by ICS may require specific training. The ICS will identify levels of responses and specific teams that will respond to different types of emergencies.

RESOLVE THE INCIDENT OR EMERGENCY

Know how to resolve an emergency

Resolving an incident or emergency involves defusing the situation and returning the facility to normal operations. Although supervisors or special response teams are responsible for resolving an emergency, any staff member can play a part in these efforts. In response to an emergency, you may be called upon to:

- transport
- escort and supervise people
- use physical force or control
- provide first aid
- record events
- serve as a witness in investigations
- debrief

Each agency will determine the roles and responsibilities of its staff members and provide an emergency plan. Any emergency presents dangers, and liabilities exist in the actions and choices you make to keep everyone safe and secure. To reduce liability while resolving emergencies, you must observe your surroundings, take note of activities as they occur, respond within the scope of your training, and use reasonable judgment in responding, while practicing officer safety. Review report details and confirm information for further investigation during the deactivation and debriefing process.

LESSON VOCABULARY

Incident Command System (ICS)

Review Items

1. *Who should you notify during an emergency situation?*
2. *List the evacuation guidelines.*
3. *List the actions you may be called upon to resolve an emergency situation.*
4. *Describe the Incident Command System.*

UNIT 1 IDENTIFYING EMERGENCY SITUATIONS

LESSON 2
EMERGENCY PLANS

LESSON GOAL

You will be able to use an emergency plan during an emergency situation.

THINK ABOUT THIS

Officer Collins is the first person to arrive on the scene during an emergency. Since he isn't a supervisor, he decides to call for help and wait for his supervisor to arrive. Is this the correct protocol? Did he misunderstand the meaning of chain of command during an emergency?

CHAIN OF COMMAND

Know the protocols for chain of command during an emergency

Chain of command defines the order of authority and responsibility that joins one level of an organization to another, and that outlines the coordination of resources in an emergency situation. The emergency plan, which can include an ICS, will determine the protocols for chain of command.

An agency's emergency plan identifies the person in charge. As the first person on the scene, however, you begin the chain of command. Until relieved by command staff, you are considered the person in charge and must make decisions. Strive to operate within the chain of command at all times and keep supervisors informed of all activities.

During an emergency, you may need to set up a command post at a strategic point away from the emergency. Some control rooms or central towers may move if there is an emergency. People in the command post may use radio bands or other communication devices designated specifically for them, separate from the non-emergency devices. The person in command on the scene will be responsible for keeping staff members updated about the status of the emergency. The command post staff will receive all communications and make all major decisions during an incident or emergency.

DOCUMENT THE EMERGENCY

Document an emergency

Although you may not be directly involved in an emergency, you must submit a report about what you observed. Reports should be complete and accurate, as they may be needed for reference during an investigation or for other purposes. When documenting an emergency response, you should include details of the date, time, place, people involved, when they arrived and left, what time outside agencies, such as emergency services, were contacted, and the scope, nature, and status of the emergency. Each agency will determine the proper report format, and should include guidelines for writing the report in a clear and concise manner.

Review Items

1. *Describe who begins the chain of command during an emergency.*
2. *Explain how you should document an emergency.*
3. *Explain why it is important to ensure that reports are complete and accurate.*

Unit 2 Determining Level of Response Assistance

Lesson 1

Determining Level of Response Assistance

Lesson Goal

You will be able to determine the level of assistance needed in an emergency situation.

Think About This

Several inmates are fighting in the courtyard. Since Officer Allen is close to the fight, she tries to break up the fight, even though the number of inmates involved keeps increasing. What would you do?

DETERMINING THE LEVEL OF RESPONSE ASSISTANCE

Try to identify the type of emergency, such as medical, fire, hazmat, or criminal act. The severity of an incident determines what type and level of response is needed, such as implementing the Prison Rape Elimination Act (PREA) for a sexual assault. Examine the facts, and practice good situational awareness and officer safety.

Know the type and severity of an emergency to determine the level of assistance needed

Do not engage in unsafe behavior when approaching a dangerous situation. For example, do not investigate a suspicious item by touching or smelling it. If an incident poses a security threat, respond to the threat appropriately and notify a supervisor.

Emergencies can involve more than one type of incident. Inmates can intentionally create emergencies as distractions to accomplish other purposes. For example, inmates could use a fight as a distraction during an escape attempt or as a cover for other illegal acts.

Request assistance if you could be overpowered in the situation. The level of threat determines the level of assistance. You should request assistance if a situation is not successfully being resolved. Follow protocol and chain of command, and document the details of the emergency and any actions taken to resolve it.

Each agency will have specific equipment for different emergency responses, such as different types of communication devices, vehicles, medical equipment, and fire equipment. You should know where needed equipment is located and maintain certifications for using equipment.

Know the location of equipment available for emergency response

REVIEW ITEMS

1. *List four types of emergencies.*
2. *Explain how an emergency can be an intentional distraction.*
3. *List four examples of equipment that is available for emergency response.*

UNIT 3 TYPES OF EMERGENCIES

LESSON 1

INMATE ESCAPES

LESSON GOAL

You will be able to respond to an escape or escape attempt.

THINK ABOUT THIS

Officer Davis monitors the same area each day and at the same time. Each time he conducts a search, he does it during the same timeframe. Several inmates noticed this pattern and planned an escape using the tools they created. How could he have prevented this escape?

Understand the signs of an escape attempt and how to prevent it

One of your responsibilities as an officer is to prevent escapes. Escapes commonly occur during participation in work release programs outside the correctional facility or during transport. An inmate in an unauthorized area is considered a violation but not necessarily an escape. An escape occurs when an inmate breaks free from custody. Indicators of a possible escape include inmates not in their designated area, suspicious behavior, odd phone conversations, maps or civilian clothes, inmate-created tools, or alterations to the facility's structure.

You can directly affect whether escape attempts occur by taking preventive measures. Some measures are conducting constant surveillance, keeping an unpredictable schedule, using mobile or stationary posts, and using regular and irregular searches. Searches should include inmates, their cells, and all general facility areas. Make sure that you identify and count inmates while conducting a search. You need to observe their surroundings and take note of irregular or unusual behavior. You must also monitor areas where inmates can escape, whether through ventilation access routes, doors taken off the hinges, or windows broken with projectiles.

EQUIPMENT

Know the equipment and resources needed when responding to an escape or attempted escape

Necessary equipment used to prevent or resolve an escape or escape attempt may vary by agency.

The following is a list of common equipment and resources used when responding to escape attempts:

- canine teams
- communication equipment
- cameras or video equipment

- vehicles
- face sheets (identification of inmates, for example, pictures, aliases, or tattoos)
- information about known associates
- mechanical restraints
- manual inmate counting and electronic identification devices
- flashlights
- local maps of the area
- weapons

STANDARD PROCEDURES

Follow standard procedures if an escape occurs

When an escape occurs or is in progress, you or a group of officers will need to verify the location of the escape and escape routes. It is important to communicate effectively with supervisors and other staff members. Escaped inmates are considered dangerous; therefore, take extreme caution. Standard procedures in the event of an escape are as follows:

- Secure all inmates as quickly as possible.
- Lock down the facility when appropriate, to aid in searches and investigations. Different actions may be taken, depending upon the agency and location.
- Conduct a master roster count of the inmates to confirm an escape has occurred.
- Tell the control center or supervisors that an escape has occurred as soon as possible, including the number of escaped inmates, their names, clothing, and direction of travel.
- Secure and isolate the surrounding area and remove all inmates and uninvolved personnel from the suspected escape location. Keep the area clear, because it is considered a crime scene.
- After the escaped inmates have been identified, collect articles of their clothing without contaminating them. As discussed in Chapter 3, this is done by using gloves and storing the items properly. Canines will use these articles as scent items. Review mail and phone communications in an effort to determine possible destinations.
- If the escape happens outside the facility, such as during a work squad or transport, secure the remaining inmates and follow standard procedures.

REVIEW ITEMS

1. *List the signs of an escape.*
2. *List seven examples of common equipment or resources used when responding to escape attempts.*
3. *Describe the standard procedures to follow when an escape occurs.*

LESSON 2
MEDICAL EMERGENCIES

LESSON GOAL

You will be able to respond to a medical emergency.

THINK ABOUT THIS

You notice that an inmate is sweating and has shortness of breath. Would you consider this a medical emergency? How would you respond?

Know what a medical emergency is and how to recognize signs and symptoms

A medical emergency is when a person experiences medical or psychological distress, a severe illness, or an injury. Signs and symptoms of a medical emergency may be unusual or excessive bleeding, pain, medical distress (for example, sweating, nausea, shortness of breath, paralysis), or loss of or altered consciousness. If the inmate uses medical devices (for example, intravenous [IV] lines or monitors), this equipment may become dislodged.

EQUIPMENT

Know the medical resources available when responding to a medical emergency

Know the equipment needed when responding to a medical emergency

Each emergency is unique; assess the situation to determine the proper equipment to use. Refer to first-aid or other training to correctly use medical equipment and supplies during a medical emergency. Resources used to address a medical emergency include staff, on-site medical personnel, or outside Emergency Medical Services (EMS). Equipment available during a medical emergency may include PPE (for example, gloves, masks), an automated external defibrillator (AED), and a first-aid kit. Medical equipment must be used according to training and agency policy. Observe universal precautions to avoid contact with a person's body fluids. Treat every person as if they are infected to minimize risk of infection when providing aid.

STANDARD PROCEDURES

Follow standard procedures to resolve a medical emergency

To resolve a medical emergency, follow these standard procedures:

1. Identify the severity of the medical emergency to determine the level of response. If the inmate is conscious, ask, "Are you declaring a medical emergency?"
2. Make sure that the area is secure and safe. Enforce crowd control by removing all inmates and uninvolved personnel from the area.

3. Notify medical staff and supervisors—inform staff of the number of affected persons, their location, and the nature of the emergency.
4. Administer aid using PPE to observe universal precautions. Provide assistance only within the scope of your training.
    a. Administer first aid as appropriate until medical help arrives.
    b. Protect inmates against self-inflicted injury or death; if an inmate has attempted hanging, call for assistance as the situation dictates. Proceed according to agency policies whether the inmate is injured or deceased.
    c. Wait for assistance as necessary.
5. Transport to a medical facility or, if applicable, designate staging areas for outside agencies.

Review Items

1. *List the signs and symptoms of a medical emergency.*
2. *Identify the resources used when responding to a medical emergency.*
3. *Describe the equipment available during a medical emergency.*
4. *List the standard procedures to follow when resolving a medical emergency.*

UNIT 3 TYPES OF EMERGENCIES

LESSON 3

RIOTS

LESSON GOAL

You will be able to respond to a disturbance or a riot.

THINK ABOUT THIS

The number of fights between inmates increased over a three-week period. An inmate approached Officer Jordan and advised him to take the next day off, and he did. Later Officer Jordan found out that a riot caused a lot of damage. Officer Jordan felt somewhat responsible for what happened. Was he responsible? What would you have done if you were in this situation?

Understand the difference between a riot and a disturbance

Any incident that disrupts the normal operations within a facility is a ***disturbance***. A food strike, inmates refusing to return to a work squad, or a fight between two inmates in a dorm could be considered minor. Such disturbances can usually be handled with minimal staff. However, disturbances can escalate into a riot very quickly. A ***riot*** is a disturbance with uncontrolled violence by inmates, usually directed at the administration. An example of a riot could be fights breaking out in several locations at once, significant property damage, or hostage situations. External support, such as local law enforcement, may be needed to contain or control a riot.

Know the conditions that prompt a riot or disturbance

Know the indicators preceding a riot or disturbance

Conditions that may lead to a riot or disturbance can include overcrowding, racial tension, poor living conditions, STG activity, dissatisfaction with food, mail, or medical service, policy changes, loss of privileges, and fights. You should be aware of indicators that precede a riot, such as changes in the behaviors of inmates, food hoarding, weapons manufacturing, unusual groupings of inmates, and an elevation in fights and requests for protective custody. An inmate may also share specific information about an impending riot or disturbance with you, or suggest that you take a day off.

Staff should have a heightened sense of awareness when the normal routine changes and inmates seem tense. Abrupt changes within the correctional facility (for example, it gets too quiet or too loud) may be an indicator that a disturbance or riot is pending.

EQUIPMENT

Know the equipment needed when responding to a riot or disturbance

You need to be aware of post orders and emergency procedures and be prepared to use any equipment necessary to resolve a riot or disturbance.

Equipment will vary according to each agency's resources but can include restraints, chemical agents, electronic control devices (ECDs), firearms, non-lethal and impact weapons, shields, emergency keys, and communication devices.

STANDARD PROCEDURES

Follow standard procedures to respond to a disturbance or riot

Disturbances or riots can be handled in similar ways; the level of response will be reduced for a disturbance. You will need to make quick decisions regarding immediately exiting the area or directing any non-certified staff to safety. Techniques for responding to a disturbance or riot include increasing communications among staff, or freeing up additional personnel and resources to respond simultaneously to the threat with appropriate use of force. Due to the nature of riots, the emergency can move into other areas. Procedures to contain a riot may involve using structures, such as internal gates, roll gates, doors, and cross fences and posting of additional security personnel. During a riot or disturbance, provide the control room with as much information as possible. Include the location, status and scope, approximate number of inmates and bystanders involved, and any weapons involved.

Post-riot procedures may include:

- accounting for all on-duty staff and visitors
- checking security of the facility
- administering first aid to the injured
- separating ringleaders and agitators
- performing a strip search of all involved inmates according to agency policies
- conducting an institutional inmate count
- debriefing staff
- conducting a thorough investigation of the riot
- repairing damage

LESSON VOCABULARY

disturbance

riot

REVIEW ITEMS

1. *Explain the difference between a riot and a disturbance.*
2. *Identify the conditions that prompt a riot or disturbance.*
3. *List the indicators that precede a riot or disturbance.*
4. *What are the procedures used to respond to and contain a disturbance or riot?*

LESSON 4

HOSTAGE INCIDENTS

LESSON GOAL

You will be able to respond to a hostage incident.

THINK ABOUT THIS

Officer Shaw heard a lot of commotion and went to see what was going on. He saw two inmates fighting and immediately tried to stop the fight. Once he opened the cell, the inmates held him hostage. What should he do?

Understand why a hostage situation occurs

A hostage situation can occur with or without warning when one or more persons are held against their will by another person or group with the purpose of achieving a specific goal. Any person can be held hostage, including inmates, civilians, officers, visitors, and staff. Keep in mind that when you respond to an incident or a riot, you may be taken hostage.

EQUIPMENT

Know the equipment needed when responding to a hostage situation

Equipment available for use during a hostage incident may vary according to each agency's resources. It can include restraints, chemical agents, lethal and non-lethal impact weapons, emergency keys, and monitoring equipment such as camcorders, closed-circuit televisions, or cameras. Building blueprints and floor plans could be required. You will use communication devices, such as radios, megaphones, or cell phones. Equipment and technical assistance may vary among agencies and departments and will be based upon the conditions encountered and decisions made during the incident.

STANDARD PROCEDURES

Follow standard procedures to respond to a hostage situation

The goal in any hostage situation is to resolve the conflict without injury or loss of life. In a hostage situation, response varies depending on agency resources, policies, and procedures. Steps taken during a hostage crisis change according to circumstances, status, and severity. Different teams may be involved, such as tactical and negotiation teams.

Standard hostage situation procedures include:

- notifying a supervisor immediately, following the chain of command
- containing the subject(s) in the smallest area possible
- restricting the movement of the subject(s), if possible, and always keeping officer safety in mind
- gathering information, such as taking pictures or recording the situation
- moving non-participants as far from the hostage situation as possible—inmates may be locked down
- providing assistance and support to specialized teams as needed

When initially responding to a hostage incident, contain the situation to prevent more hostages from being taken. Be careful not to agitate the hostage taker; build rapport and actively listen. Gather as much information as possible, including the location, the names and number of hostages, the names and numbers of hostage takers, if known, injuries, weapons involved, and demands of the hostage takers.

A staff member being held hostage is not viewed as having rank or authority in the incident. If you are taken hostage, recognize that you have no authority to make any decisions. Do not interfere with discussions being conducted between response teams and the hostage taker. Do not try to be a hero.

Follow standard procedures if you are taken hostage

Follow these procedures if you are taken hostage:

- cooperate with, but do not enable, the hostage taker
- recognize that staff will respond as soon as possible
- avoid using insults, trigger or hot words (words that may empower the hostage taker), such as prisoner, guns, or police
- avoid being confrontational by keeping a low profile
- if possible, avoid giving up your uniform
- keep your face down or avoid eye contact
- remain calm, rest when possible, and try to eat only food provided by the negotiating team
- cooperate fully with any response team member

Review Items

1. *Define a hostage situation.*
2. *List the equipment needed in order to respond to a hostage situation.*
3. *Recall the procedures to use when responding to a hostage situation.*
4. *List the procedures to follow if you are taken hostage.*

LESSON 5
OUTSIDE THREATS TO A FACILITY

LESSON GOAL

You will be able to identify types of facility assaults and respond to them.

THINK ABOUT THIS

Several vehicles are approaching the facility at a high speed with no sign of slowing down. A few seconds later, gunshots are fired. What would be an appropriate response to ensure that inmates and others are safe?

Know the indicators of a facility assault

A facility assault is a physical attack from outside the facility or any other assault that creates physical damage to the correctional facility. Attackers may be on foot, or the assault may include a speeding vehicle approaching the perimeter and failing to yield, gun shots, or an aircraft flying nearby.

Indicators of a facility assault may include an outside threat on a person's life or someone coordinating an escape attempt. You should be aware of any threats to the security of the facility, including demonstrators, media, or high-profile inmates (such as inmates associated with a drug cartel or death-row inmates). Known associates of high-profile inmates may use technology to see the layout of the prison. Be cautious of unknown individuals around the outside of the facility. Another threat to security is the arrest and transfer of high-profile inmates.

EQUIPMENT

Know the equipment needed when responding to a facility assault

Common equipment used for responding to a facility assault includes barriers, non-lethal and impact weapons, electronic control devices, firearms, shields, vehicles, megaphones, restraints, chemical agents, and communication devices. You may need to use recording devices or cameras. You may also need to call external law enforcement, such as SWAT.

STANDARD PROCEDURES

Know the measures used to prevent and resolve a facility assault

Facility assault incidents are rare. High-quality, effective and visible security measures, alert systems, perimeter controls, or appropriate warning techniques can help prevent facility assaults. Be aware of people who have permission to be on the facility grounds. Notify correctional staff of likely protests, staging areas for protestors or media, or the presence of outside agencies.

To contain an assault, some agencies may approve use of force. Staff assignments may vary according to agencies' resources or policies and procedures. There may also be a show of force (a visible presence of authority). It is your responsibility to maintain order and safety of the inmates within the facility; this may include locking down inmates. Local law enforcement may be contacted to contain incidents outside of the facility. The commander of ICS may deploy specially trained teams, such as CERT (Correctional Emergency Response Team) in an assault. Facility assaults can escalate into emergencies, such as a hostage situation, an escape, or a medical emergency.

In the event of a facility assault, follow these standard procedures:

Follow standard procedures for responding to a facility assault

- Notify the appropriate staff and communicate with the response teams. Communicate the following information:
  - the area of the compound or perimeter affected
  - the nature of the assault
  - the extent of the damage to the perimeter
  - the number of assailants and weapons
  - the direction in which the assailants are traveling
- Follow evacuation protocols according to the agency's emergency plan. Move inmates and staff members to a safe location. Be aware that the assailant may change tactics or methods that result in blocking or damaging planned evacuation routes. Pay attention to radio communications, including updates on the situation.
- Set up barricades.
- Establish perimeter security including surveillance.
- Maintain safety and security procedures, such as moving to cover and relocating to a tactically advantageous position.
- Debrief after the incident. This may involve reviewing report details for further investigation.

Review Items

1. *State the indicators of a facility assault.*
2. *Give examples of the equipment that you will need when responding to a facility assault.*
3. *Explain how you can prevent and resolve a facility assault.*
4. *Explain the procedures to follow when responding to a facility assault.*

LESSON 6
FIRES

LESSON GOAL

You will be able to respond to a fire.

THINK ABOUT THIS

Fire! Fire! Help! As you walk toward the kitchen, you hear someone yelling for help. An inmate was cooking with grease, and a fire started. The inmate responded out of panic and threw water on the grease fire. How would you respond?

Know the major components and indicators of a fire

The potential for fire exists in all areas of the facility. Though rare, fires are dangerous because they can spread quickly and can be difficult to contain. The kitchen is the most common area where fires occur. However, fire also could occur anywhere throughout the facility grounds, such as in a laundry area or dormitory. Staff should always be vigilant and cautious of fire hazards, including cooking grease, dryer lint, improperly stored cleaning agents, and lightning strikes.

Maintaining the safety of staff and inmates is the first priority during a fire. The major components of a fire are heat, fuel, oxygen, and chemical chain reactions. Indicators of a fire include the smell of smoke, alarm notifications, and heat, light, and flame. The type of fire determines which extinguishing agent to use. For example, using water on a flammable liquid will increase the fire. Likewise, using water on an electrical fire can create great danger of electrical shock. There are five classes of fire.

Understand the classes of fire

Fire Classes:

- **Class A:** ordinary combustibles; for example, wood, cloth, paper
- **Class B:** flammable liquids; for example, gasoline and diesel fuels, kerosene, propane, butane, alcohol, motor oil, paint, paint thinners
  - **Class K:** subcategory of Class B (kitchen fires; cooking oils or fats)
- **Class C:** electrical; for example, appliances, panels, switches
- **Class D:** combustible metals; for example, magnesium, titanium, potassium, sodium

EQUIPMENT

Each agency will determine the availability of specialized equipment to use during a fire. Equipment needed to respond to a fire may include:

Know the equipment needed when responding to a fire

- portable extinguishers
- fire alarms
- fire suppression systems (fire extinguishers set into the wall that run into piping when the system is activated, sprinklers, and smoke detectors)
- Self-Contained Breathing Apparatus (SCBA) (used during a fire to help prevent smoke inhalation, with proper training)
- facility map
- emergency keys
- restraint devices
- fire hydrants
- fire hoods
- fire hoses (used by specially trained staff to extinguish fires)

The type of fire will determine which fire extinguisher to use. Types of portable fire extinguishers that are commonly used include:

Understand the types and uses of fire extinguishers

- **ABC** (used for ordinary combustibles, flammable liquids, and electrical)
- **ABCD** (used for metal fires, such as magnesium fires; if a class D extinguisher is not available, you can use sand or dirt to extinguish a class D fire)
- **K** (used for kitchen fires; easier to clean up than other extinguishing agents)
- water-based (used for ordinary combustibles)
- **CO2** (used for class B and C fires, such as flammable liquid and electrical fires; useful to protect electrical equipment, because these extinguishers leave less residue and displace oxygen; after using them, you need to exit the room quickly, especially in confined areas)

The portable fire extinguisher may be all that is necessary to extinguish a small fire. Basic procedures for using a fire extinguisher in a correctional facility include performing a safety check, which should be done during every shift. This involves checking the gauge on the extinguisher to see if the charge is adequate. If it is adequate, the needle will be in the green area. If the charge is not adequate, do not use that extinguisher. Notify the control room immediately if the fire extinguisher fails the safety check. The safety check should also include the hose and nozzle to confirm that they are free of cracks or obstructions.

The basic steps for using a portable fire extinguisher are:

Follow the steps for using a portable fire extinguisher

1. Pull the pin.
2. Aim the nozzle at the base of the fire from a distance, usually about 10 feet.
3. Squeeze the handle.
4. Sweep the base of the flame (from side to side and front to back).

STANDARD PROCEDURES

Follow standard procedures for responding to a fire

If you see fire or smell smoke, assess the situation. Notify the control room immediately with the exact location and size of the fire; activate the agency's emergency plan. Pull the manual fire alarm; there may also be an automatic fire alarm. Attempt to extinguish the fire if it is small enough. Begin evacuation procedures if the fire is out of control. Follow posted evacuation routes.

You will be required to maintain control of inmates during an evacuation. During inmate movement, it may not be possible to group inmates according to their classification and custody levels. Use a sufficient number of officers, especially when moving high-risk inmates or large groups. Conduct and continuously update an inmate count. Account for everyone in the area, including staff and visitors. Make sure the perimeter is intact and secure. Be alert; inmates can also use fire as a distraction during escape attempts and assaults.

You should be thoroughly familiar with the posted evacuation routes. Available routes change according to the location of the fire and the volume of smoke. Ideal evacuation routes are those that allow everyone to get as far away as possible and upwind from the threat. Time permitting, shut doors and windows along the way.

Evacuate all inmates and staff in the vicinity as soon as it is safe to do so. If time allows, conduct a count before the evacuation. If there is a discrepancy with the count, call your supervisor; it will be treated as an escape until further notice. Immediately notify your supervisor if someone is trapped or not accounted for. If the fire is substantial and someone is trapped, rescue will be delegated to the local fire department or staff with proper training.

REVIEW ITEMS

1. *What are the major components and indicators of a fire?*
2. *Explain the classes of fire.*
3. *List the equipment needed when responding to a fire.*
4. *Describe the types and uses of fire extinguishers.*
5. *Explain the steps to follow when using a portable fire extinguisher.*
6. *Describe the procedures to follow when responding to a fire.*

LESSON 7
HAZARDOUS MATERIALS

LESSON GOAL

You will be able to respond to a hazardous materials emergency.

THINK ABOUT THIS

Inmate Scott was on work detail and decided to clean with bleach. Since there was a small amount of bleach left, he combined it with another bottle. Some inmates started coughing, while others had trouble breathing. At this point Inmate Scott realized that he had accidentally mixed bleach and ammonia. Explain your initial actions.

Know how to recognize hazardous materials

Hazardous materials are used throughout a correctional facility or work detail. They include cleaning agents, floor wax, bleach, laundry detergent, fuels, pesticides, or fertilizer. A hazardous materials incident also could occur during a fire. A hazardous material (hazmat) emergency occurs when a substance capable of causing harm to people, the environment, and property is released or is not properly controlled. While inmates are on work details, they could accidentally combine common chemicals, such as bleach and ammonia, creating a hazardous environment.

Inmates could use containers to transport hazardous materials or biohazardous materials, such as urine. Urine or other body fluids, including contaminated blood, could be considered hazardous materials. Be thorough in your searches when inmates return from work assignments. A group of inmates could deliberately work together and separately take items that are hazardous when combined.

People can be contaminated with hazardous materials through inhalation, ingestion, absorption, and injection. Hazardous materials can pose immediate and long-term health hazards, such as asphyxiation, chemical burns, tissue destruction, cancer, or death. They can also cause harm to the environment, such as water, air, and land pollution, as well as death or serious injury to wildlife and domestic animals.

Hazardous materials may have certain smells, but not all hazardous materials have an odor. There may be no warning of a hazmat emergency. Never check a container by smelling or tasting it. You can rotate a closed container to test its weight and consistency; a shampoo bottle filled with bleach will feel and sound different than if filled with shampoo.

Because of their nature, hazmat emergencies:

- are more likely to cause a need for outside assistance

- require multiple agency response
- may be long lasting
- may involve unseen hazards

During a hazmat incident, the Department of Transportation (DOT) ***Emergency Response Guidebook (ERG)*** is a resource used as a guide. A first responder's initial actions include the identification of hazardous materials, areas of personal protection, and initial safety plan. The following is a list of the classes of hazardous materials and the dangers associated with each class, according to the *ERG*, a copy of which will be available to all staff:

Know the classes and dangers of hazardous materials described in the *Emergency Response Guidebook (ERG)*

- Class 1 explosives: exposure to heat, shock, or contamination could result in thermal and mechanical hazards
- Class 2 gases: container may rupture violently under pressure (or as a result of a fire); may become flammable, poisonous, a corrosive, an asphyxiate, and an oxidizer; may cause frostbite
- Class 3 flammable and combustible liquids: container may rupture violently from heat/fire; may be corrosive, toxic, and thermally unstable
- Class 4 flammable solids: some are spontaneously flammable; may be water reactive, toxic, and corrosive; may be extremely difficult to extinguish
- Class 5 oxidizing substances: supports its own combustion through using oxygen; sensitive to heat, shock, friction, and contamination
- Class 6 poisons and infectious substances: toxic by inhalation, ingestion, and skin and eye absorption; may be flammable
- Class 7 radioactive substances: may cause burns and biologic effects; can cause contamination of surroundings
- Class 8 corrosives: causes disintegration of contacted tissues; may be fuming, water reactive, and destructive to metals
- Class 9 Other Regulated Materials (ORM): miscellaneous

Hazardous materials are indicated by placards (diamond-shaped signs), markings, shipping papers, SDSs (Safety Data Sheets), or storage containers. Refer to the *ERG* for exact information. Use extreme caution when using your senses at a hazmat incident, including:

Know the indicators of hazardous materials

- vision—you may use your vision to see indicators of the presence of hazardous materials, smoke, fire, vapor, or gas clouds; when light or visibility is poor, these signs are harder to see

  For example, green smoke is a particularly dangerous sign. Also, watch out for hazardous material placards.

- hearing—important, especially when interacting with witnesses or identifying unusual sounds, such as hissing from a gas leak or a tanker spill, or a bubbling sound from mixing chemicals

- taste, touch, or smell—use of these senses risks exposure to the substance; they should not be used intentionally in an incident

EQUIPMENT

Know the equipment needed when responding to a hazardous materials incident

Each agency will determine the availability of equipment to use during a hazmat incident. Some of the equipment may include PPE to observe universal precautions, such as a face mask, protective gloves, masks and gowns; a hazmat suit; SCBA; a bloodborne pathogens cleanup kit; and barriers. Refer to the *ERG* for a detailed description of, and instructions for, appropriate use of equipment related to hazmat incidents or emergencies. Make sure you have current versions of all reference guides.

Equipment, informational guides, and hazardous materials references may be managed by a supervisor.

STANDARD PROCEDURES

Follow standard procedures for responding to a hazardous materials emergency

Due to the dangers associated with hazmat incidents, be aware of your surroundings and take note of activity, practice officer safety, and follow special precautions at all times.

Each agency's policies, procedures, and emergency plan will dictate the roles and responsibilities of each staff member. You may be the first person on the scene, but the resolution of a hazmat incident is usually the responsibility of supervisory staff and specialized response teams.

As an officer, you should respond only within the scope and level of your training.

When looking for hazards and investigating an incident, stay constantly aware and be prepared to relay information. Even when assisting in cleanup, you must follow officer safety, universal precautions, and the SDS. Avoid tunnel vision and be aware of the variety of complications that might arise, since hazmat situations can be dynamic and evolving. For example, do not immediately run over to assist if you suspect a hazmat incident.

Consider all hazmat incidents a life-or-death situation. Remain calm and focus on a resolution.

Resolving a hazmat situation involves the following:

- Locate and verify the nature of the hazardous materials emergency.
    - Observe from a safe distance.
    - If the spill is minor, respond according to the SDS guidelines. For example, dilute a bleach spill and ventilate the area.

- Refer to the posted SDS for the hazardous materials. Make sure a copy of the SDS is readily available for any emergency personnel.
- Communicate with control room staff and supervisors, who may coordinate response activities. Relay the following information:
    - types of substances or hazards (do not attempt to smell or taste the substance)
    - areas affected
    - any medical emergencies or injuries
    - wind direction (for example, if any vapor or smoke is blowing toward the dining hall)
- Enter the area only when it is safe to do so.
    - Use PPE, such as a face mask, protective gloves, and a gown, immediately. Use disposable equipment as much as possible.
- Provide first aid for the injured.
    - Separate contaminated persons.
- Evacuate areas affected by hazardous materials.
    - Everyone should be evacuated as soon as it is safe to do so.
    - Ideal evacuation routes will take people as far away from the incident as possible and be upwind and uphill from the threat.
    - Follow the posted evacuation diagrams. Evacuation may not be possible in some cases.
- Isolate the situation so that it does not spread to unaffected areas. Shut down air-conditioning units and close doors and windows.
    - Stay as far away as practical (a minimum of 500 feet if possible), and keep others away.
    - Use binoculars or video surveillance if available or approach from upwind.
    - Don't take an ignition source into the affected area (a vehicle can be an ignition source).
- Create a barrier or perimeter around, and restrict access to, the affected area.
    - Use signs, warning tape, and physical barriers, such as a mound of dirt, or officers stationed outside a secured area. Structures such as internal gates, roll gates, doors, and cross fences can greatly aid in accomplishing these efforts.

Observe special precautions when dealing with decontamination efforts.

- Make sure that contaminated victims and equipment are decontaminated before your contact with them.
    - If you become contaminated, make sure that you and your clothing are fully decontaminated as soon as possible.

Restrict or control access to the affected area, until the area is declared safe by emergency personnel.

- Supervisors will issue a direct order for no one except emergency personnel to enter the area.
- Keep a record of the events and complete follow-up documents as directed by the agency. You can get help during a hazmat/waste spill by contacting the Chemical Transportation Emergency Center (CHEMTREC) at **1-800-424-9300.** CHEMTREC has the capability to contact the shipper, manufacturer, or other sources for more detailed assistance and follow-up support. For example, if a spill occurs in the area where the SDS is located, and you are not able to access the information on or identify the substance, you can contact CHEMTREC for immediate help.

Lesson Vocabulary

Emergency Response Guidebook (ERG)

Review Items

1. *Explain how you would recognize hazardous materials.*
2. *What are the classes and dangers of hazardous materials?*
3. *What are the indicators of hazardous materials?*
4. *Identify the equipment needed when responding to a hazmat incident.*
5. *Recall the standard procedures for responding to a hazmat emergency.*

LESSON 8
BOMB THREATS

LESSON GOAL

You will be able to respond to a bomb threat.

THINK ABOUT THIS

During a routine search, Officer Raines discovers a suspicious device that he thinks is a bomb. He immediately calls his supervisor using his cell phone. What could have happened as a result of Officer Raines using his cell phone?

Know the indicators of a bomb threat

A bomb threat is any threat of an explosive device, whether mechanical, incendiary, or chemical. You must take every threat seriously. A supervisor may determine how a threat should be handled. All personnel need to maintain a heightened sense of awareness during a bomb threat. Bomb threats could be used as a distraction for an escape attempt. Indicators of a bomb threat may be the discovery of a suspicious device or package, or a bomb threat delivered by mail, phone, or electronically or in person.

EQUIPMENT

Know the equipment needed when responding to a bomb threat

During routine inspections, searches, or facility checks, you may find a suspicious device. Do not touch, inspect, or remove it. You need to be alert and use good observational skills; look for something out of the ordinary. When responding to a bomb threat, you may use the following equipment: mounted long-range cameras, or non-electrical communication devices, such as landline phones, or pens, pencils, and paper. Contact your supervisor, but do not use cell phones, radios, or any other electronic device that could emit electromagnetic signals, as these may create a spark. Outside agencies may use bomb-detecting canines or explosive ordnance devices (bomb-defusing robots).

STANDARD PROCEDURES

Follow standard procedures when responding to a bomb threat

If you discover a suspected bomb or suspicious package, do not touch or tamper with it in any way whatsoever.

Each agency will determine when to call 911 or when to contact a specialized response team. Correctional facility staff should communicate verbally, in legible writing, or by using a landline phone. Stay calm and communicate clearly so that control room and supervisory staff may coordinate response activities.

Standard procedures for responding to a bomb threat include the following:

- Notify the supervisor or command staff of the exact location of the device and its description or if you receive a bomb threat.
- Supervisors or command staff will give an order to stop using all electronic devices, including microwaves, radios, phones, car alarms, or remote keys for cars.
- If you find a device, establish a secure perimeter around the device.
- If you receive a threat, lock down the inmates and conduct a controlled search of the facility.
- Follow evacuation protocols according to your agency's emergency plan.
- If you receive a bomb threat via phone, you must follow protocol, such as using a checklist while talking, keeping the caller on the line as long as possible, and, if appropriate, using the telephone tracer feature on the phone.

Review Items

1. *What are the indicators of a bomb threat?*
2. *Describe the equipment needed when responding to a bomb threat.*
3. *List the standard procedures for responding to a bomb threat.*

UNIT 3 TYPES OF EMERGENCIES

LESSON 9
DISASTERS

LESSON GOAL

You will be able to respond to disasters.

THINK ABOUT THIS

A tropical storm hit Florida and caused a lot of rain. There was so much rain that it flooded an entire block. How will you handle this? How will you evacuate inmates to another location?

Understand the difference between natural disasters and human-instigated disasters

A ***natural disaster*** is an event or force of nature that has catastrophic consequences, such as a hurricane, earthquake, tornado, flood, lightning, or wildfire. It is unpredictable and unplanned.

A ***human-instigated disaster*** is a consequence of technological or human hazards that brings great damage, loss, or destruction to the facility, such as chemical spills, a water main breaking, a plane crash, a train derailment, or a fire. It may be intentional or accidental.

EQUIPMENT

Know the equipment needed when responding to a disaster

The equipment used to address a disaster will depend upon the type of event and its severity. Each agency may have resources identified for different emergencies. Outside agencies may also be called upon to assist. Properly identifying the disaster and methods of communication plays a vital role in responding to the emergency.

Equipment needed in a disaster includes:

- backup communications equipment
- backup power source
- flashlights with batteries
- emergency food supplies (non-perishable)
- stored water
- medical supplies
- tents or temporary shelters

- additional bedding or linens
- vehicles
- weapons

You must be properly trained and familiar with the equipment you might use during an emergency.

Each agency will determine the focus and level of training for equipment use in emergency situations.

If communications are disrupted, use backup communication systems, such as a temporary or mobile command center. You may also need to use secondary radio systems. You may need to administer first aid to ill or injured staff or inmates. Distribute drinkable water and emergency food supplies. The facility may be operating only off of generators and not at full power. If necessary, erect temporary shelters. If an evacuation is necessary, multiple vehicles will be used.

STANDARD PROCEDURES

The nature and extent of the disaster will determine what procedures to follow. An emergency plan addresses the procedures for enhanced security measures and transportation needs that could arise. Standard procedures to resolve an emergency are:

Follow standard procedures when responding to a disaster

- Verify and communicate the emergency by notifying the control room or a supervisor of the event.
- Conduct an institution inmate count, accounting for all inmates and staff.
- Inspect for structural damage, making sure there is no breach in the perimeter.
- Activate the emergency plan.
- Evacuate everyone to a safe place.
- Provide first aid and medical treatment.
- Document the incident.
- Debrief after the incident.

Lesson Vocabulary

human-instigated disaster

natural disaster

Review Items

1. *Compare and contrast natural and human-instigated disasters.*
2. *Name the equipment used when responding to a disaster.*
3. *List the standard procedures to follow when responding to a disaster.*

UNIT 4 INVESTIGATING CRIMES

LESSON 1

CRIME SCENE CONTROL

LESSON GOAL

You will be able to protect and control a crime scene.

THINK ABOUT THIS

Inmate Cooper stabbed Inmate Williamson in his neck. Blood was gushing out of Inmate Williamson's neck and all over the floor. How will you respond to this? How will you administer first aid without disturbing the evidence?

Some crimes in the facility will be crimes against persons, such as assault or battery. Different crimes require different responses. For example, an inmate stealing another inmate's property might result in an incident report. An inmate stealing keys will result in a facility-wide lockdown and thorough search. A sexual assault will require activation of PREA, and all PREA guidelines must be followed. You need to isolate any sexual assault victim to prevent loss of evidence by putting the victim in a dry cell (a cell where they cannot clean themselves).

Know which staff to notify when a crime has occurred

If a crime has been committed, inform your supervisor and any other personnel needed. If known, include the type of crime, as well as the severity, any injuries, and the location. If necessary, make requests for assistance or backup. Provide the names of the inmates who were in the area. Mention any details, such as blood spatter or weapons.

When a crime occurs, there may or may not be a crime scene. If you determine that a crime scene exists, notify a supervisor, medical staff, and / or control room staff. Inform them of the location of an established crime scene area using a radio, phone, or verbal communication. Be aware that authorities and divisions, such as medical staff, may be informed simultaneously. Outside agencies, such as law enforcement, may be contacted.

Know how to control and isolate a crime scene

Clear a crime scene immediately of aggressors and all other unauthorized people. Take note of all actions taken. Monitor the area; give verbal commands to inmates to return to their cells for a lockdown. Control access and isolate the crime scene by restricting access to unauthorized personnel.

Know when to enter a crime scene to administer first aid, while not disturbing evidence

Determine if the crime scene is safe before entering by visually scanning the area and listening for hazards and using other senses.

If you must enter a crime scene to render aid, do not rearrange or move anything. Be very careful not to disturb evidence, such as bloody prints or objects that might have been used to commit the crime. Once backup arrives and if it is safe to do so, conduct a medical assessment. (You will learn more about conducting medical assessments in First Aid.) Continue administering aid until specialized personnel, such as EMTs, firefighters, or trained medical personnel, arrive.

Once a crime scene has been cleared of any victims, witnesses, or suspects, secure the area and make sure no one enters.

Know how to secure and protect a crime scene

Protect the scene by preserving the area, as well as possible evidence, to minimize contamination.

To secure the crime scene, tape off the area or create a perimeter or barrier. Establish a perimeter with physical barriers, such as fences, barrels, or crash gates (which separate the different parts of an institution that is all under one roof). Personnel who act as a barricade should be stationed far enough away from the crime scene so that other people cannot contaminate the scene.

Each agency may have its own procedures for documenting a crime scene, including photographs, images from cameras, standard forms, and items moved, removed, or altered. The on-scene officer needs to keep a continuous log of the activities happening at the crime scene; this should include which authorized personnel enter and exit the scene, along with the date and time.

Document activities of a crime scene

Review Items

1. *Describe how you will notify staff if you discover a crime scene.*
2. *How do you control and isolate a crime scene?*
3. *Explain how you enter a crime scene, while not disturbing the evidence.*
4. *Explain how to secure and protect a crime scene.*
5. *Identify what activities you should include when documenting a crime scene.*

LESSON 2
MANAGING VICTIMS, WITNESSES, AND SUSPECTS

LESSON GOAL

You will be able to manage victims, witnesses, and suspects involved in an incident.

THINK ABOUT THIS

Recall the incident between Inmate Cooper and Inmate Williamson from the previous lesson. Once Inmate Williamson recovered from the stabbing, he attacked Inmate Cooper while Inmate Cooper was attacking Inmate Downy because he witnessed the stabbing. How will you handle this? How will you decide who is the victim, witness, or suspect?

You may be the first to respond when an inmate commits a crime in your facility; therefore, you should know how to manage victims, witnesses, and suspects until a supervisor or agency investigator arrives.

Isolate and restrain any inmates who look suspicious, are breathing hard as if they've been in a fight, are bleeding, have abrasions, or have torn or missing clothes. Even after being ordered to be quiet, inmates may talk among themselves and reveal information about the crime. However, do not begin questioning inmates. The investigator will conduct a formal interview later.

Understand the importance of identifying and separating victims, witnesses, and suspects during an investigation

Conduct an inmate count as soon as possible. Separate the individuals involved before trying to determine who the victims, witnesses, and suspects are. Potential victims, witnesses, or suspects may be identified through observation and questioning of individuals in the area. Separate each person to preserve evidence and information, and for clarity in dealing with and assessing the situation. Separating individuals will minimize possible threats and collaboration that may confuse the investigation.

Know how to secure victims, witnesses, and suspects during an investigation

Restrain individuals if appropriate and place them in secure areas to provide a safe environment for the interview process. Due to liability issues, do not put victims out of sight and sound; they may need medical or psychological support. Follow the investigator's or supervisor's instructions while dealing with victims. Do not leave the suspect alone—they could remove or purposely contaminate evidence.

Know how to determine the people involved in criminal activity

Determining the roles of people suspected of being involved in criminal activity is done by obtaining statements from others, using interviewing techniques, and making observations based on physical evidence. Physical indications that an inmate may have been involved in a crime include suspicious activity, injuries, labored breathing, possession of weapons, or presence of contraband.

Review Items

1. *Why is it important to identify and separate victims, witnesses, and suspects during an investigation?*
2. *How do you secure victims, witnesses, and suspects during an investigation?*
3. *Explain how you would determine the roles of the people suspected of being involved in criminal activity.*

UNIT 4 INVESTIGATING CRIMES

LESSON 3
INVESTIGATIONS AND REPORTING

LESSON GOAL

You will be able to document a crime using investigative techniques.

THINK ABOUT THIS

Officer Jackson was responsible for investigating and writing a report of the incident between Inmates Cooper, Williamson, and Downy. Officer Jackson wanted to return a favor to Inmate Cooper, so he altered the report so that Inmate Cooper wouldn't receive a severe punishment. What do you think will happen to both Inmate Cooper and Officer Jackson?

Learning the components of an investigation will help you participate in an investigation, follow proper protocol, and avoid contaminating evidence. Participating in or having any type of involvement in an investigation will be directed by a supervisor or lead investigator.

When directed, apply basic investigative techniques during investigations

You may be asked to take statements from victims, witnesses, or suspects, and then give the information to an investigator. If you are tasked with making a report, carefully question the person; you may empathize by verbally comforting the person, but do not touch them (this includes hugs or pats on the back). If you are not directly questioning a person, it is nonetheless appropriate to let them talk on their own if you are in their presence. Document what you hear, but do not encourage the person to interact with you. You may be called upon to testify in court. Investigation techniques may include collecting and preserving evidence, taking statements, taking photographs or video recordings, and working with other agencies or departments to process evidence or investigate facts. Remember the chain of command, and proceed only within the scope of instructions given to you in the investigative process.

Know how to write an incident report for an investigation and the consequences for recording false information

Documenting an incident could involve filling out a template, or writing a standard incident report of the details of an incident for an investigation. Each agency will determine the criteria and methods required for writing a clear and concise report, as well as the timeline for submitting reports. It is important to clarify the details you write in a report, representing details as either approximate—"I went in at approximately 9:00 a.m."—or absolute, such as, "I went in at 9:00 a.m." Always keep copies of reports you submit, and refer to your written report when recalling facts during questioning in an investigation. Your reports will help during legal matters and investigations of incidents. Referring to them will also help you maintain consistency with your own account. If you intentionally give false information during an investigation, you may be terminated.

Review Items

1. *Describe the basic investigative techniques used during an investigation.*
2. *Explain how you should write an incident report for an investigation.*
3. *What will happen if you intentionally give false information?*

LESSON 4

CHAIN OF CUSTODY FOR EVIDENCE

LESSON GOAL

You will be able to establish and maintain the proper chain of custody for evidence.

THINK ABOUT THIS

Officer Peters found a sharp object on the floor with blood on it. He picked it up without using gloves and threw it away. This object should have been collected as evidence. What should Officer Peters do?

Know how to identify and collect evidence for a crime scene

Inmates may try to destroy evidence. To aid future investigations, use caution and tact while securing the scene. Each agency may determine the methods and materials to use for proper evidence gathering. Evidence at a crime scene is any item or fact that may clear a person of guilt or may be considered proof that a crime has been committed, such as clothing, sheets, body fluids, or any other item that could be related to or affected by the crime. Use the techniques determined by your agency to collect and preserve evidence, and be careful not to contaminate the evidence or the crime scene. This involves properly bagging items, taking pictures or videos according to instructions, and initiating proper chain of custody procedures.

Apply proper techniques for handling evidence

To handle evidence properly:

- Use PPE, which must be put on outside of the crime scene.
- Correctly document and secure the item through appropriate chain of custody.
- Correctly identify the type of bag or container to use for the type of evidence being gathered.

Know the necessary information for establishing chain of custody

Know the main components of chain of custody procedures and how to use them

Chain of custody is documentation of how evidence is handled and preserved to ensure the integrity of the evidence. The chain of custody also proves that any evidence submitted in court or at a disciplinary hearing is the same evidence that was collected at the crime scene. Information necessary to establish a chain of custody may include what the evidence consisted of, who handled the evidence, where the evidence was found, when the evidence was discovered, and how it was handled, transferred, and preserved. Your agency may require a detailed account of the chain of custody for evidence in an investigation or incident. This involves tracking and verifying evidence as it is handled using charts, logs, and electronic databases. Some agencies may require that information involved in chain of custody procedures remains confidential.

Know the safeguards to maintain the chain of custody

Following the agency's chain of custody policy or procedure is vital for evidence preservation, as it may be years before evidence is examined. Established safeguards include following specific protocols for handling and storing evidence. Designated personnel will be in charge of evidence storage areas, and specific protocol must be followed for accessing the areas where evidence is stored. Interagency collaboration may involve addressing different procedures for chain of custody protocol to transfer evidence. This activity should be directed by a corrections supervisor. Do not clean up a suspected crime scene, or an area where a disruption may have occurred, until it is ruled out as a crime scene. The lead investigator dictates all action within it and will release the crime scene.

Review Items

1. *Explain how you would identify and collect evidence for a crime scene.*
2. *List the techniques for handling evidence.*
3. *Explain what information is necessary to establish a chain of custody.*
4. *Describe the safeguards that will maintain the chain of custody.*

Glossary

A

acting within the scope of employment: the range of reasonable and foreseeable activities that an officer does while carrying out the agency's business (Introduction to Corrections)

active listening: giving full attention to what is being said and taking time to understand the message without interruption (Communications)

administrative confinement: temporary removal of an inmate from the general population to provide for safety and security until a more permanent inmate management process is in place (Supervising Special Populations)

arrest papers: paperwork generated by an arresting officer that allows for a subject to be arrested and taken to a county detention facility for admission (Intake and Release)

assumption: a notion, statement, or belief about a person, group, or event that may or may not be factual (Introduction to Corrections)

B

Baker Act: provides for emergency services and temporary detention of a person for evaluation and voluntary or involuntary short-term community inpatient treatment; also known as the Florida Mental Health Act (Supervising Special Populations)

bias or prejudice: a strong belief or feeling about a person, group, or subject, whether positive or negative, that is formed without reviewing all available facts or information (Introduction to Corrections)

Bill of Rights: the first 10 amendments to the U.S. Constitution (Introduction to Corrections)

C

categorically: the grouping of recorded information into types of collection sources, such as informants, victims, witnesses, suspects, weapons, rule violations, evidence, and crime elements (Communications)

chain of command: the order of authority within an organization (Introduction to Corrections)

chain of custody: documentation of every person who handled evidence, as well as when, why, and what changes, if any, were made to it (Introduction to Corrections)

chronologically: the grouping of recorded facts by date and timeline, usually from the first event to the last (Communications)

civil liability: responsibility for a wrongful act or the failure to do an act that an officer has a duty to perform, which results in injury to another person or property and most often involves negligence (Introduction to Corrections)

civil rights violation: an unlawful interference with the fundamental rights of another person, such as the right to due process and equal protection under the law (Introduction to Corrections)

classification: a management tool used to assist facilities in defining inmate custody or security levels (Intake and Release)

clinical restraints: measures that keep inmate-patients from injuring themselves in a medical facility (Supervising in a Correctional Facility)

clinical seclusion: isolating inmate-patients from the general population at a medical facility for medical and safety reasons; may include placing them in a padded room for their safety (Supervising in a Correctional Facility)

close custody grade: state custody grade that refers to inmates who must be maintained within an armed perimeter or under direct, armed supervision when outside a secure perimeter (Intake and Release)

color of law: when an officer acts or claims to act in the performance of official duties under any law, ordinance, or regulation (Introduction to Corrections)

command presence: body language that projects confidence, poise, and a professional demeanor (Communications)

commitment papers: documents or orders generated by the court after an offender is found guilty of a crime and that commits the offender to a correctional facility or to a mental hospital (Intake and Release)

community control (house arrest): a form of community supervision that is closely monitored and is more restrictive than probation or parole (Introduction to Corrections)

community custody grade: a state custody grade that refers to inmates who are eligible for placement at a community residential facility (Intake and Release)

contact visits: visits in which both the visitor and the inmate are in the same room without a physical barrier, and can have limited physical contact (Supervising in a Correctional Facility)

content: the significant facts of an incident or occurrence in a report (Communications)

contraband: any unauthorized article or any authorized article in excessive quantities or altered from its intended purpose (Introduction to Corrections)

controlled behavior: the practice of demonstrating confidence and control by avoiding such distracting behaviors as foot tapping, nail biting, and fidgeting (Officer Safety)

correctional officer: any person who is appointed or employed full time by the state, county, or a contracted private entity, whose primary responsibility is the supervision, protection, care, custody, control, or investigation of inmates within a correctional institution; does not include any secretarial, clerical, or professionally trained personnel (Introduction to Corrections)

corrective action: steps that are taken to eliminate the cause of inappropriate or unlawful behavior to prevent recurrence (Supervising in a Correctional Facility)

corrective consultation: usually an agency-specific form that documents an inmate rule violation (Supervising in a Correctional Facility)

counseling: an in-depth explanation of a rule violation, including suggestions for an inmate to correct their behavior (Supervising in a Correctional Facility)

courtesy: behavior that involves showing consideration, respect, and cooperation when interacting with others (Communications)

criminal act: a violation of the law; in Florida, a crime is designated as either a felony or misdemeanor according to s. 775.08(4), F.S. (Introduction to Corrections)

criminal justice: the structures, functions, and decision-making processes of the agencies that deal with the management and control of crime and criminal offenders (Introduction to Corrections)

criminal liability: when an officer is found guilty of committing a crime (Introduction to Corrections)

D

deception: the act of deceiving someone by lying, misleading, tricking, or fooling them (Officer Safety)

disability: a physical or mental impairment that substantially limits one or more of the major life activities of an individual (Supervising Special Populations)

discharge gratuity: money given to qualified inmates discharged from the custody of the Department of Corrections in accordance with 33-601.502, F.A.C. (Intake and Release)

disciplinary confinement: formal punishment in which the officer segregates an inmate for a length of time to an individual cell because a disciplinary committee has found them guilty of committing a violation of agency rules (Supervising Special Populations)

disciplinary report (**DR**): a detailed report of the facts surrounding an inmate's rule violation (Supervising in a Correctional Facility)

discipline: the enforcement of a penalty or consequence for a violation of established rules used to ensure compliance and obedience to established rules (Supervising in a Correctional Facility)

discrimination: the negative behavior toward a person or group that is based on color, race, sex, age, religion, ethnic and national origin, disability, or marital status (Introduction to Corrections)

disturbance: any incident that disrupts the normal operations within a facility (Responding to Incidents and Emergencies)

drug addiction: a chronic, relapsing brain disease where constant drug use changes the structure of the brain and how it works (Supervising Special Populations)

E

editing: the process of ensuring that all pertinent facts have been included in a report in an organized and accurate manner (Communications)

***Emergency Response Guidebook* (*ERG*)**: a resource used to guide a first responder's initial actions to a hazmat incident, including the identification of hazardous materials, areas of personal protection, and initial safety plan (Responding to Incidents and Emergencies)

escort: a correctional officer or staff member accompanying the movement of an inmate from one point to another (Supervising in a Correctional Facility)

ethical behavior: principled, values-based decision-making that is practiced daily (Introduction to Corrections)

ethics: the standards of conduct based on the principles of right and wrong (Introduction to Corrections)

evidence: anything tangible that proves or disproves a fact in a judicial case or disciplinary hearing (Introduction to Corrections)

F

face sheet: a document that has a current picture of an inmate, name, inmate identification number, physical description, incarceration date, date of birth and end of sentence date, and inmate's custody level (Supervising in a Correctional Facility)

felony: any criminal offense punishable under the laws of this state by death or imprisonment in a state facility for a period exceeding one year (Introduction to Corrections)

Florida Administrative Code (**F.A.C.**): the body of law that oversees public regulatory agencies (Introduction to Corrections)

Florida Model Jail Standards (**FMJS**): standards set by the Florida Sheriffs Association and with which all local jails must comply (Introduction to Corrections)

format: the way information is organized and presented in a report (Communications)

friction ridge: a raised portion of the skin on the finger or palm of a hand, consisting of connected ridge units (Intake and Release)

fruits of a crime: anything gained or obtained by committing a crime (Introduction to Corrections)

G

grid search pattern: a variation of the strip / line search pattern; it overlaps a series of lanes in a cross pattern, making the search more methodical and thorough (Officer Safety)

H

hard / hazardous contraband: any item that poses a serious threat to the safety and security of the staff, inmates, and facility (Officer Safety)

hazardous materials: also known as hazmat; substances (solids, liquids, or gases) that, when released, may be capable of causing harm to people, the environment, and property (Facility and Equipment)

homophones: words that are easily confused in use and spelling, sounding the same but with different spellings and meanings (Communications)

human-instigated disaster: a disastrous event caused directly or principally by one or more identifiable deliberate or negligent human actions (Responding to Incidents and Emergencies)

I

Incident Command System (ICS): a systematic approach to command, control, and coordinate emergency response; an advanced emergency response plan (Responding to Incidents and Emergencies)

instrumentalities of a crime: anything used to commit a crime (Introduction to Corrections)

insubordination: a failure to follow lawful orders from supervisors in the chain of command (Introduction to Corrections)

intake: the process in which an inmate is admitted to a county detention facility (Intake and Release)

interpersonal communication: the exchange of thoughts, messages or information between two or more people through speaking, writing, or behavior (Communications)

interview: a conversation between a correctional officer and an interviewee (inmate, visitor) with the goal of obtaining factual information (Communications)

introduction of contraband: any attempt to bring or send contraband into a correctional facility (Introduction to Corrections)

J

jargon: words used by a particular trade or profession that are not commonly understood by the general public; the technical vocabulary of a particular profession that has meaning specific to people who work in that field (Communications)

jurisdiction: the types of cases in which the court can make decisions (Introduction to Corrections)

juvenile adjudication: occurs when the court charges, sentences, adjudicates as delinquent (including *nolo contendere*), and commits a juvenile younger than 18 to the Department of Juvenile Justice (Supervising Special Populations)

juvenile inmate: an inmate who is not legally an adult or adjudicated as an adult; may be assigned to the Department of Juvenile Justice (Supervising Special Populations)

K

kickback or three-way mail: a method used by inmates to try to send unauthorized communications to other inmates within the same facility or other institutions (Supervising in a Correctional Facility)

L

legal mail: a category of mail that includes mail to and from municipal, county, state, and federal courts, and state attorneys, private attorneys, public defenders, legal aid organizations, and agency clerks (Supervising in a Correctional Facility)

M

manipulation: the act of manipulating or trying to influence someone to do something they would not usually do (Officer Safety)

maximum custody grade: a state custody grade that refers to inmates who are sentenced to death (Intake and Release)

maximum security level: county custody or security risk levels for inmates considered high risk: those who have serious or violent felony charges pending or who pose a threat to the safety of staff and security of the facility (Intake and Release)

medium custody grade: state custody grade that refers to inmates who are eligible for placement at a work camp with a secure perimeter but who are not eligible for placement in an outside work assignment without armed supervision (Intake and Release)

medium security level: county custody, or security risk levels for inmates considered moderate risk (those who have adjusted to being incarcerated in the past and have limited violence in their criminal history) (Intake and Release)

mental illness: an impairment of the mental or emotional processes that exercises the conscious control of one's actions; mental illness can impair one's ability to perceive or understand reality (Supervising Special Populations)

minimum custody grade: state custody grade that refers to inmates who are eligible for outside work assignments but not for placement in a community residential center (Intake and Release)

minimum security level: county custody, or security risk levels for inmates considered low risk (those who have adjusted well to being incarcerated, have a minimal criminal history with no violent charges in their history, or are currently charged with a non-violent crime) (Intake and Release)

***Miranda* warning**: a warning given to provide protection by the Fifth Amendment right against self-incrimination when a suspect in custody is interrogated in a criminal investigation (Introduction to Corrections)

misdemeanor: any criminal offense punishable under the laws of this state by a term of imprisonment for one year or less in a county correctional facility (Introduction to Corrections)

N

natural disaster: an event or force of nature that has catastrophic consequences (e.g., hurricane, earthquake, tornado, flood, or wildfire) (Responding to Incidents and Emergencies)

negligence: failure to use due or reasonable care in a situation where an officer has a duty to act, and which results in harm to another (Introduction to Corrections)

nolo contendere: a legal plea in which a person does not accept or deny responsibility for the charges but agrees to accept punishment (Introduction to Corrections)

non-contact visits: visits in which the inmate and visitor are physically separated by some kind of barrier or communicate using electronic equipment (Supervising in a Correctional Facility)

note-taking: writing down brief observations or, if it is an interview, quotes from people involved (Communications)

nuisance contraband: any authorized item found in excessive amounts or altered from its original state that usually does not pose an immediate threat to the safety or security of the staff, inmates, and facility (Officer Safety)

O

observing: staying aware of any occurrence or activity, such as irregular mood changes, emotional outbursts, acting out, threatening behavior, or changes in inmate energy levels, that may signify safety and security problems (Officer Safety)

organization: a group of two or more people who cooperate to accomplish one or more objectives (Introduction to Corrections)

P

parole: the release of an inmate from a correctional institution before the inmate's court-imposed sentence ends (Introduction to Corrections)

perimeter: a secure area that surrounds a facility and is a critical element of security (Facility and Equipment)

positioning: placing yourself in a tactically advantageous location to observe an area (Officer Safety)

posture: holding the body in a manner that shows strength, confidence, interest, and control (Officer Safety)

Prison Rape Elimination Act (**PREA**): a law enacted by Congress to address the problem of sexual abuse of persons in the custody of U.S. federal, state, or local correctional agencies; implemented to create national standards for detecting, preventing, reducing, and punishing prison rape (Introduction to Corrections)

privileged communication: inmate communications that are given special privacy considerations, such as between an inmate and an attorney (Introduction to Corrections)

privileged mail: a mail category that includes mail to and from public officials, governmental agencies, and the news media (Supervising in a Correctional Facility)

probable cause: a fair probability or reasonable grounds to believe that a crime was committed, based on the totality of the circumstances (Introduction to Corrections)

probation: a court-ordered sentence that places a person under the supervision of a probation officer under specified court-ordered terms and conditions (Introduction to Corrections)

professionalism: behavior that demonstrates good character and is marked by pride in self and career (Introduction to Corrections)

proofreading: checking a report to ensure that all words are spelled correctly, punctuation is used accurately, appropriate words are capitalized, and proper grammar is used (Communications)

protective management: a form of confinement where an inmate is placed into segregated housing because of concerns for their safety (Supervising Special Populations)

Q

qualified immunity: a defense that protects the officer from personal liability (Introduction to Corrections)

R

reasonable accommodation: any modification or adjustment that will allow a qualified inmate with a disability to participate in the programs, services, or activities of an institution or facility (Supervising Special Populations)

reasonable force: the type and amount of force that the officer reasonably believes necessary to overcome resistance (Introduction to Corrections)

reception: a multifaceted process in which an inmate is admitted to a state institution (Intake and Release)

release: the process by which an inmate is discharged from a county detention facility or state correctional institution (Intake and Release)

report: a written document prepared by a correctional officer that gives information about an incident, event, situation, or person encountered by the officer (Communications)

riot: a disturbance with uncontrolled violence by inmates, usually directed at the administration; a riot is not necessarily localized (Responding to Incidents and Emergencies)

routine mail: all mail received by inmates, including publications, except legal mail and privileged mail (Supervising in a Correctional Facility)

rule violation or infraction: an activity or behavior that is not permitted in the correctional facility (Supervising in a Correctional Facility)

S

Safety Data Sheet (SDS): required for any hazardous material shipped to and from a correctional facility; it includes the manufacturer's name, the product name, and spill and leak procedures (Facility and Equipment)

sally port: a system of two openings (doors or gates) designed to open only one at a time (Facility and Equipment)

search: governmental intrusion into a place where a person has a reasonable expectation of privacy (Introduction to Corrections)

security equipment: any item or technology used to enhance or maintain protection, and to ensure safety (Facility and Equipment)

security threat group (STG): a criminal enterprise, an organization of a continuing nature that engages repeatedly in acts of crime, and individually or collectively poses a safety or security threat within, as well as outside of a correctional facility (Supervising Special Populations)

seizure: the act of taking possession of evidence or contraband for a violation of rule or law (Introduction to Corrections)

sentence: a group of words that contains a subject (a noun), a verb (action), and usually an object (affected or receives action) and that expresses a complete thought (Communications)

sentence fragment: a group of words that lacks a subject or verb or fails to express a complete thought (Communications)

sexual abuse: sexual abuse of an inmate, detainee, or resident by another inmate, detainee, resident, staff member, contractor, or volunteer where the victim does not consent, is coerced by overt or implied threats of violence, or is unable to consent or refuse. (Supervising Special Populations)

sexual harassment: repeated and unwelcome sexual advances, requests for sexual favors, or verbal comments, gestures, or actions of a derogatory or offensive sexual nature by one inmate, detainee, or resident directed toward another; repeated verbal comments or gestures of a sexual nature to an inmate, detainee, or resident by a staff member, contractor, or volunteer, including demeaning references to gender, sexually suggestive or derogatory comments about body or clothing, or obscene language or gestures (Supervising Special Populations)

situational awareness: the act of paying attention to what is going on around you (Officer Safety)

slang: informal vocabulary composed of invented words, or arbitrarily changed words, that are often used by a specific group, region, trade, or profession (Communications)

sovereign immunity: a list of circumstances and requirements that must be met before the agency or any of its employees can be sued in a state tort action; provides protection for state and county (governmental) correctional agencies and its employees as per s. 768.28, F.S. (Introduction to Corrections)

special populations: classifications of inmates that an officer may encounter in their day-to-day routines that require different interactions or services (Supervising Special Populations)

spiral search pattern: usually used by one person, a search pattern that begins at a central point and moves in increasingly larger circles to the outermost boundary of the search area (Officer Safety)

squelch: a circuit that suppresses the output of a radio receiver if the signal strength falls below a certain level (Communications)

statement: a permanent oral or written record of a person's account of an incident or occurrence that may or may not be made under oath (Communications)

stereotyping: judging a group of people who are different from you based on your own or others' opinions or encounters (Introduction to Corrections)

strip / line search pattern: usually used in a predetermined area by several people; the search area is divided into lanes that are searched by one or more people in both directions until the entire area has been examined (Officer Safety)

substance abuse: a pattern of substance use that leads to significant impairment or distress (Supervising Special Populations)

T

tagging: the marking of a security threat group's territory on a wall, fence, or ground (Supervising Special Populations)

textspeak: language characteristic of text messages and digital communications, typically using abbreviations, acronyms, or initials, and usually not following standard grammar, spelling, or punctuation (Communications)

trailing or chase vehicle: an armed escort vehicle used during transport to follow an inmate transport vehicle and to provide additional security (Supervising in a Correctional Facility)

transfer: movement of an inmate from one housing location to another (Supervising in a Correctional Facility)

transgender: a person whose gender identity differs from the sex they were assigned at birth (Supervising Special Populations)

transport: when an inmate is removed and escorted from the confines of a secure facility to another location (Supervising in a Correctional Facility)

U

unusual occurrence: an incident that is out of the ordinary and disrupts the normal facility operations and routine daily activities (Supervising in a Correctional Facility)

V

values: principles, standards, or qualities considered worthwhile or desirable; core beliefs or desires that guide or motivate a person's attitude and actions (Introduction to Corrections)

verbal command: the authoritative statement used to direct, influence, or give orders to a person or group (Communications)

verbal warning: a statement directed to an inmate that they have committed a rule violation and should stop the behavior immediately (Supervising in a Correctional Facility)

voyeurism: an invasion of privacy of an inmate, detainee, or resident by staff for reasons unrelated to official duties, such as peering at an inmate who is using a toilet in their cell to perform bodily functions, requiring an inmate to expose their buttocks, genitals, or breasts, or taking images of all or part of an inmate's naked body or of an inmate performing bodily functions (Supervising Special Populations)

Y

youthful offender: any offender younger than 24, who has either been sentenced as an adult by the judge or assigned youthful offender status by the Department of Corrections (Supervising Special Populations)

Z

zone / quadrant search pattern: used for searching an area that is large; the area is divided into four sections and searched using a spiral, strip / line, or grid search pattern (Officer Safety)

References

Chapter 1 Introduction to Corrections

American Correctional Association. (1994). *Code of Ethics.* http://www.aca.org/ACA_Prod_IMIS/ACA_Member/About_Us/Code_of_Ethics/ACA_Member/AboutUs/Code_of_Ethics.aspx?hkey=61577ed2-c0c3-4529-bc01-36a248f79eba

Florida Sheriffs Association. (2015). *Florida model jail standards.* https://www.flsheriffs.org/florida-model-jail-standards/fmjs-manual/fmjs-manual

Garner, B. A. (Ed.). (1999). *Black's Law Dictionary* (7th ed.). St. Paul, MN: West.

York, G. (2015). Professional ethics and corrections, a professional responsibility. *Corrections.com.* http://www.corrections.com/news/article/40952-professional-ethics-and-corrections-a-professional-responsibility

Chapter 2 Communications

Connecticut Department of Correction. (2002). *Pre-service correctional training.*

FCC portable radio rules. http://www.ehow.com/list_6831218_fcc-portable-radio-rules.html

Goodman, D. J. (2007). *Report it in writing* (4th ed.). Upper Saddle, NJ: Prentice Hall.

Hunter, R. D., Barker, T. (2011). *Police-community relations and the administration of justice.* (8th ed.). Upper Saddle, NJ: Prentice Hall.

Hurst, C. H. (2005). *Self-talk—keep the arrows up.* Booksurge.

New Jersey Department of Corrections. (2004). *Report writing for corrections.* Basic Course for State Corrections Officers.

Chapter 4 Facility and Equipment

Florida Department of State, Division of Library and Information Services. (2012). *Florida Administrative Code & Florida Administrative Register.* Tallahassee, FL. https://www.flrules.org/gateway/Division.asp?DivID=404

Florida Sheriffs Association. (2015). *Florida model jail standards.* https://www.flsheriffs.org/florida-model-jail-standards/fmjs-manual/fmjs-manual

United States Department of Transportation. (2016). *Emergency response guidebook (ERG).* Washington D.C. https://www.phmsa.dot.gov/sites/phmsa.dot.gov/files/docs/ERG2016.pdf

Chapter 5 Intake and Release

Facial Identification Scientific Working Group (FISWG), *FISWG Capture and Equipment Assessment for Face Recognition Systems.* https://www.fiswg.org/FISWG_CaptureAndEquipmentAssessmentForFRSystems_v1.0_2011_05_05.pdf

Garner, B. A. (Ed.). (1999). *Black's law dictionary* (7th ed.). St. Paul, MN: West.

Scientific Working Group on Friction Ridge Analysis, Study and Technology (SWGFAST). (2013). *Document #19 Standard terminology of friction ridge examination (latent/tenprint).* San Diego. http://www.swgfast.org/documents/terminology/121124_Standard-Terminology_4.0.pdf

Chapter 6 Supervising in a Correctional Facility

York, G. (2016). Why inmate hospital watch is a dangerous shift. *CorrectionsOne.com.* http://www.correctionsone.com/officer-safety/articles/193680187-Why-inmate-hospital-watch-is-a-dangerous-shift/

Chapter 7 Supervising Special Populations

Abuse, N.I. (n.d.). National Institute on Drug Abuse (NIDA). https://www.drugabuse.gov/

Bedard, L. E. (2008). Female vs. male inmates: The rewards and challenges of managing both. https://www.correctionsone.com/women-in-corrections/articles/1843155-Female-vs-male-inmates-The-rewards-and-challenges-of-managing-both/

Justice, N. C. (2014). Juvenile offenders and victims: 2014 national report (report summary). https://www.ojjdp.gov/ojstatbb/nr2014/

United States Census Bureau. https://www.census.gov/

INDEX

D

E

F

G

H

I

J

K

L

M

N

O

P

Q

R

S

T

U

V

W

Y

Z

NOTES

NOTES